Stephen Evans

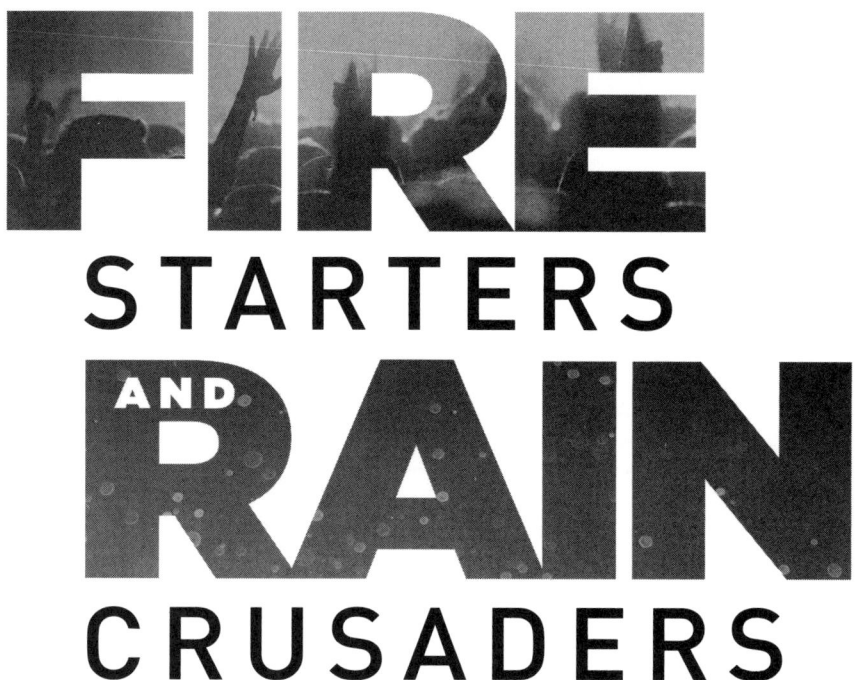

Fire Starters and Rain Crusaders

A Fire Was Started, That No Rain Can Quench

Fire Starters and Rain Crusaders

Copyright © 2015 Stephen Evans
All rights reserved
Printed in the United States of America

Published by Light of Life International
4360 Western Center Blvd / PMB 124
Fort Worth, TX 76137

This book or parts thereof may not be reproduced in any form without
prior written permission of the author.

All Scripture quotations, unless otherwise indicated, are taken from the New King James Version.
Copyright © 1982 by Thomas Nelson, Inc. Used by permission. All rights reserved.

Design: Peter Gloege | LOOK Design Studio

ISBN: 978-0-9961138-0-9

This book is dedicated to my mom and dad,
Des and Mary Evans.
Thanks for the Welsh tea and living room conversations. You are dearly loved!

1 : Legacy and Law School 9

2 : Walking with Giants 19

3 : Seeing the Bigger Picture 37

4 : Transition and Small Beginnings 53

5 : It's Not about Me! 71

6 : Commissions and Confirmations 89

7 : Soccer Accidents and Prophecies 107

8 : Kings and Castles 125

9 : Jungles and Bears 143

10 : Praying and Preaching 163

11 : Fire Starters and Rain Crusaders 179

12 : Treasures in Earthen Vessels 197

13 : Old Disciplines and New Surprises 213

14 : Calling All Souls 231

15 : Shouting in the House 251

16 : Walking into Destiny 267

17 : Before Great Men, Don't Be Great 287

18 : A Historic Gathering 303

19 : More than Another Mountain 317

20 : Nicaragua Prays 337

21 : You Are an Overcomer 353

FOREWORD

Having written 67 books, I find it difficult to endorse manuscripts and maintain my writing schedule. However, I must say that *Fire Starters and Rain Crusaders* by Stephen Evans is a must-read. I've read every word and found it to be inspiring, anointed, and will stretch you to dream bigger dreams than you've ever dreamed. Even more important than the words on the page is the author who wrote it. I've known Stephen all his life. If it were possible for a man to have a second father, I'm sure Stephen would call me that. He is a man of impeccable integrity, consumed with a passion for the lost, filled with faith and determined to change his world. There is no doubt in my mind that Stephen will succeed. It is an honor and a rare privilege to meet a young man who has surrendered all to glorify the Lord and reach the lost. May you be inspired by his story and may your life be transformed by reading this book.

—Dr. Michael D. Evans

CHAPTER 1

LEGACY AND LAW SCHOOL

"**ALL YOU NEED** to do is walk up to him and scream as loudly as you can in his ear," the man urged Dad as they stood in the New Guinea jungle village. The tribal chief and male warriors stood alert, waiting.

Several days prior, news had arrived of an impending conflict in Kiminubus. The tribal community at the top of the hill had been challenged by their rivals at the bottom of the hill. In the 1950s and 1960s, New Guinea had many hostile tribes. And in a culture where revenge dominated, battles between two or more villages were not uncommon occurrences.

The lower community had lost the previous conflict and sent a small image to the tribe at the top of the hill. The object, a small clay head stuck on top of a piece of stick and wrapped around with grass, communicated a clear and insulting message. Those at the bottom of the hill were calling the warriors in the upper village "straw-men." It was a challenge to fight.

Dad and two missionaries were asked to intervene in this hostile environment, with the plan being to use their jeep to reach the base of the hill, then hike the rest of the way up to the village. But when it came time to go on foot, one of the missionaries suddenly felt the need to stay behind and guard the jeep. So it was left to the remaining two to find their way up and meet with the tribal chief.

When Dad reached the summit, the tribal chief was discussing the straw-man and how they should respond to the challenge with his council of elders and warriors. "All you need to do is go stand by the chief and scream in his ear at the top of your voice," urged the missionary next to dad. Of course, Dad had absolutely no desire to do such a thing—especially to an animated chief surrounded by tribal warriors. But his partner insisted: In Kiminubus, noise meant power—and it would get their attention!

Dad went straight to the chief and started hollering every Scripture and prayer he could think of into his ear. On and on he yelled. Finally the other missionary interrupted and announced to the chief and warriors: "This man of power has come to talk to *you*!"

It worked. The tribe received them and for the next couple of hours, Dad and his cousin spoke about real power. Not the kind found in spears or bows or arrows, but the power of Jesus Christ.

That night, for the first time in the upper village, men believed in Jesus as their Lord and Savior. When a similar grace fell on the village at the bottom of the hill, a war was averted and tiny churches were planted.

I WOULD NEVER SEND MY SON TO DIE

I grew up listening to missionary stories like this from my dad. It seemed to my young point of view he lived a life of adventure—not to mention possessed a brave and powerful faith in the Lord Jesus Christ.

He described many of the villages as having deep moats dug around them, with a long plank stretching between the village and the opposite bank. This served not only as the only way in and out but also as a defense mechanism, preventing thirty rival warriors from rushing in all at once. If the enemy was going to attack, they would have to cross over one at a time.

I often imagined what it must have been like to walk across one of those planks, suspended over a river or something else even more treacherous. And that is exactly what you had to do to enter the village to share the Gospel.

If you decided to step on the plank to cross, the danger intensified. No one dared to pass the halfway point on the beam. Instead, there you paused—and waited. Alone, vulnerable, and standing above the moat, you waited for a sign to come from the warrior chief.

Permission or denial to the village was clear and unmistakable. Whatever the chief did with his spear determined your fate. If he lowered it, then you were welcome to cross the rest of the plank and enter the village. But if the chief raised his spear into the air, you were not welcome. The uplifted spear was a warning that you had to leave the beam immediately.

Taking the Gospel to the jungle villages of New Guinea certainly carried risk. But if you were received, it was an opportunity to talk with the head of the tribe. These conversations often dealt with power, because much of their lives revolved around war and revenge. Dad certainly agreed the chief was important and very strong. He would expand the conversation to talk of one bigger and stronger still—someone so powerful His feet rested on the mountains surrounding their villages!

One day Dad read the Scripture: "'For God so loved the world that He gave His only begotten Son, that whoever believes in Him should not perish but have everlasting life'" (John 3:16 NKJV). The chief started shaking his head. He said, "I would not do that. I would never send my son to die." It was absolutely impossible for him to grasp the enormity of such a thing.

He grasped the justice and judgment of God because it made up a large part of the world he lived in. If they raided another tribe and were defeated, it would only be a matter of time before they regrouped and fought again to regain prestige and position. But the idea of humbling yourself—of taking a lower level in order to reach that which was different than you or in opposition to you—was beyond comprehension.

THE LORD JESUS CHRIST AND AMAZING LOVE OF GOD

It is impossible for every one of us to fully grasp the enormity of the love of Jesus and what He did to reveal it. Imagine heaven as your home—a place of perfection and unspeakable beauty. A place made of gold pavements, walls lined with precious jewels, and gates of priceless pearls. Infinitely vast and timeless, a wondrous place brighter than the sun, filled with voices of choirs of angels. At the center of all this splendor and majesty—the Lord Jesus! Can you imagine ever leaving such a place? But Jesus did!

It was more than just leaving His eternal home. Jesus had to humble Himself to fit into time, into our space, into our history, into the womb of a virgin! He reduced Himself over and over again to become one of us.

But it was even more than that, more than Him humbling Himself to fit within His own creation. Jesus submitted Himself to mockery, torture, and excruciating death to be crucified on a Roman cross. Jesus did all of that, humbling Himself over and over again, because He loved us!

This is why Paul penned: "Jesus, who being in the form of God, did not consider it robbery to be equal with God, but made Himself of NO reputation, taking the form of a bondservant, and coming in the likeness of men. And being found in appearance as a man, He humbled Himself and became obedient to the point of death, even the death on the cross" (Philippians 2:6–8, emphasis mine).

What depth of love and compassion! He is not distant or unmoved. He has been touched with our pains, our grief. He has borne our sin and shame, changing places with us! He cast aside His robes of majesty and splendor to become like us—to hang on a wooden beam for us.

They did not humble Jesus when they spat on Him. They did not humble Jesus when they mocked Him. They did not humble Jesus when they hit Him, bruised Him, or killed Him. They could not humble Him, because Jesus had already humbled Himself! This is the amazing Jesus who gave Himself up, because He loved us and had compassion for us. This is the love of God and it is beyond comprehension!

A SMALL PUB AND THE WELSH REVIVAL

My heart burns for missions and evangelism today in large part because I heard stories of Papua New Guinea. Not just from Dad but also his cousin Andrew Evans and others in Australia who made a decision a long time ago they would commit their lives to doing something significant for God.

Dad would point back to a rekindling of the Welsh Revival during the time of his father and Uncle Tom. There in the tiny coal-mining town of Aberaman, Wales, a small pub on the corner was transformed into a Christian chapel at the end of the First World War.

Wales was a nation touched by revival at the turn of the twentieth century. It had once again ignited in the hearts of this small group of families in South Wales. A holy compulsion to go and take the Gospel released a divine mantle to touch nations and generations.

Out of this small mining town, a shaft of revival burst forth into

Africa, India, and a generation later New Guinea, Australia, South Africa, Europe, and North America. My Welsh family—the Evans family—was part of this group.

It is remarkable what the Lord has done nearly a century later. Dad's uncle Tom went to India, then New Guinea. His son Andrew Evans continued in New Guinea and Australia, where God graced him with amazing favor and influence. These two men played significant roles in Dad going to New Guinea. Today my second cousins, Ashley Evans and Russell Evans, follow in the legacy of their dad's footsteps leading large and influential churches in Australia and beyond.

I am blessed to be part of this family line. The heritage of the Welsh Revival is in my blood, along with the divine calling imparted upon those families generations ago in a transformed bar. And like the supernatural surge that moved my dad, granddad, and so many others, a fire burns deep inside my soul. It, too, is the holy compulsion to preach the Gospel of Jesus Christ!

HOLY SPIRIT ENCOUNTER

I was twelve years old, and the moment that would radically set me on fire throughout my teenage years and beyond was fast approaching. I walked into a youth service and sat down at the back, totally unaware that in one hour I would encounter the Holy Spirit like I had never experienced before.

While musicians led us into praise and worship, I noticed a girl to my right. She was older than me, maybe fifteen or sixteen years old, and pretty. She was also totally caught up in singing and ministering to the Lord. It was clear she was hungry for Jesus.

During the ministry that followed, something began to happen to her. She was praying and worshiping the Lord with her whole heart, and some of the leaders had now gathered around her. They were praying with her too. She was crying, and something was happening—something supernatural.

Something was happening in me too. I knew the Lord was touching her in a very special way, and I wanted to experience God like that! The pastor in charge of the service stepped back on the platform. He explained briefly what was going on. He said there was another person in the room the Lord wanted to release this Holy Spirit gift in. I did not know about the others, but that person had to be me. I knew that because my stomach was full of fire!

By the time the pastor reached me, I was sitting down in my chair, doubled over. I knew he was kneeling next to me, but it was the intense presence of the Lord that held my undivided attention.

The pastor encouraged me to respond to Jesus by telling Him how much I loved Him. However, I could hardly breathe, as my stomach felt like an explosion had gone off inside! As I sat in my seat, the fire began to expand upward and soon filled my entire chest as well. I was crying now, not because I was in pain but because something very real was happening inside me.

The fire reached my throat then touched my tongue. What came pouring out of my mouth was not something I recognized or understood. Rather, for the first time, I uttered words birthed by the Holy Spirit. I had received a prayer language!

It was only a couple of words at first, but the pastor urged me to keep repeating them. I did and the two words grew into a small phrase.

But it was more than syllables. I felt like someone had dipped me in molten lava! My whole being was on fire, praying in the Holy Spirit.

As I continued to sit there, tears flowing down my face and fiery words whispered toward heaven, a door to my front left opened. A lady I had never seen before entered the room and rushed to sit down next to me.

She leaned in and whispered three promises over my life. The first one was: "You will be a light to the world." I know it sounds generic—and maybe everyone has received a similar word of encouragement at camp or in a prayer service—but it fell deep into the chasms of my soul. I knew it was more than a prophetic declaration, it would be part of my destiny.

GOD USES THOSE WHOM HE WOUNDS

When I enrolled in law school, a decade later, a dream had come true! I wanted my life to count, and for as long as I could remember, the road to significance meant law school.

I had traveled to Europe, the Middle East, and Asia growing up, and loved it. Being in my twenties, I was eager to launch into something that would enable me to work with the nations in view.

I dreamed of sitting in rooms with political leaders, orchestrating unity and peace, and offering answers to national and international crises. I also imagined giving my time to pastors and missionaries to empower them to preach the Gospel.

This was my dream—not something that had come together at the last minute. It had been rooted deep down in my heart since I was a teenager. My life would make a difference!

Entering law school, I knew the dream was coming true. I had also met a young lady who would soon become my fiancée. Life was very good.

My third semester did not start well, however. Somehow I thought taking on the tax code would help me, but it ate me alive. Usually you can weather one bad class, but I had a couple of other challenging courses as well, making for a stressful semester.

The morning they posted grades is the day my world fell apart. I picked up my report and rushed to find a quiet place to see how things went. I ended up in a stall in the men's bathroom, and that is when my dream died.

All the grades were listed except one class—one that had caused me plenty of headaches. As I quickly processed the information, I realized if my grade in the yet-to-be posted class was not high, then I had probably lost my opportunity to pursue a career in law.

I was a nervous wreck. The grades for my last class would be posted after lunch, and I had a knot the size of Texas in my stomach. When the time came to see the grade, my worst fears were confirmed. It was over.

I will never forget the phone call I made to my parents that afternoon. It was the most devastating conversation I have ever had. Their son who they were so proud of in pursuing his legal dream now had a hard decision to make.

Yes, I could return for a fourth semester and spend a ton of cash, but the grades would need to be higher than anything I had ever made. Everyone was in shock, and everything inside me went numb.

It was a brutal stretch in my life as I faced brokenness both with law school and my engagement. But the hand of the Lord was in it. The heartache and soul-searching turned into a desperate need for the Lord to intervene and have His way in my life, my work, my relationships, everything! It was the beginning of the rest of my life.

Looking back, I learned something: Whatever humbles us also prepares us. It draws our attention to His strength in the midst of our pain and weakness. Put another way: God uses those whom He wounds. It took Him getting the legal ambitions out of me—even if it hurt—to start shaping my heart and character for something far better.

PREPARATION MODE FOR THE REST OF MY LIFE

The years following law school became a training ground in ministry. I had been on numerous mission trips and ministry retreats before, but this was different. I was in preparation mode for the rest of my life.

I went through seminary, joined Dad's pastoral team, grew as a youth and college pastor, met my wife, Alisa, and stayed active in missions. Law school was now a distant memory, and something was brewing—something big.

I was about to step into the office of Evangelist Reinhard Bonnke. It would be a game-changing moment, setting us on an improbable and sometimes impossible path, soaring far beyond what we would ever have scripted for ourselves. We did not choose this path; it chose us.

The journey of the past ten years has changed us, broken us, and left us with one conclusion: There is nothing like life with Jesus. I pray that, as you read, the Holy Spirit will challenge you and that you, too, will discover there is an invisible hand of God. It is what dreams and destinies are made of.

CHAPTER 2

Walking with Giants

"HOW DID YOU get that job!" someone asked me after learning I served with Evangelist Reinhard Bonnke in Africa. It is the first thing people want to know when they hear the stories of traveling with him to the massive Nigerian crusades and meeting people from all over the world.

There was no Facebook posting, no resumes requested to find a person qualified enough to work with Reinhard. If so, I'm sure it would have generated countless entries and I would have missed the opportunity of a lifetime.

Instead, it happened almost by accident. Looking back, though, it was more than chance or good luck. It was destiny.

SUZETTE HATTINGH AND THE INNOCENT ADDITION

I first met Suzette Hattingh at lunch with my dad. It did not take long listening to her stories about Reinhard and Anni Bonnke or her deep passion for prayer to become aware of a hunger growing inside my soul.

No one at the table could doubt the reality she had touched something—or more accurately, Someone had touched her. Suzette was full of contagious faith and fire.

It was my mom who first came across her path at the Brownsville Revival. Suzette was teaching and revealed she was in the middle of a forty-day fast. Among other things, she was believing for a greater anointing to raise the dead. All of this left little doubt in my mind that day: We were sitting at the table with one of God's generals.

She was also the first person I had ever heard talk about the humbling of Jesus—leaving heaven and shrinking Himself to fit into His creation. Her vivid imagery of the love of God stirred my heart and only deepened the longing to do something significant for God.

After speaking at the Friday night missions banquet, Suzette sat down at our table. She asked if the sanctuary could be opened the next morning so she could pray. A moment later she added that people were welcome to join her. That seemingly innocent addition was birthed of the Holy Spirit, because it is what changed the course of my life forever.

I turned up the next morning excited to see how the former head of intercession for Reinhard Bonnke prayed. I'm not sure what I expected but for several minutes I watched her read her Bible, walk around quietly listening and communicating with the Lord Jesus, then sit down to journal some thoughts—all things you would expect from someone committed to Him.

The Holy Spirit started pulling at me. It was time to quit spectating and turn aside and pray myself. I walked down to the front of the sanctuary, knelt down at the altar, and began to pray.

It is amazing what a few minutes alone with God in prayer can do for someone. I know sometimes when people pray, it feels like prayers hit the ceiling and bounce back down. But sometimes it feels as if all of heaven opens up and completely envelopes you in His presence. That morning at the altar I experienced the latter. Acutely aware of the presence of King Jesus, I buried my face in my hands and poured out my heart before Him. Humbled and broken, I worshipped Him with all my soul. And I completely forgot about Suzette Hattingh.

The ironic twist was that while I was at the altar, the Holy Spirit tapped Suzette on the shoulder and drew her attention to me praying. When she observed me, a word from heaven fell into her heart, one laced with destiny.

The next day at lunch with my parents and Alisa, she said, "Stephen, I believe the Lord is calling you into crusade ministry, and I'm supposed to show you how!" She didn't know how that would work exactly. Maybe we could come to Germany for some training then join her in one of her Indonesian crusades. What she did know and hear was the Holy Spirit was calling us into mass evangelism.

I tried not to look stunned as I sat at the table. I was furiously trying to process what I had just heard come out of her mouth. Did she just say that the Lord was calling us into crusade ministry?

It would certainly be a new and unforeseen direction. But as the words began to to sink in, with it came a fiery expectation, an awareness that destiny was being thrust upon us.

INTERVIEW WITH EVANGELIST REINHARD BONNKE

I must have read and reread the email a dozen times before printing it out and walking into Dad's office. I closed the door gently but firmly behind me, an unspoken sign between the senior pastor and his son that we needed to talk immediately.

I had received an email from Suzette indicating something had changed. There would be no trip to Germany or Indonesia. I handed the paper to Dad and watched him read every word. The expression that washed over his face mirrored the emotions I, too, experienced when the email first arrived. Neither of us could believe it—how could this be happening?

Suzette had received a confidential phone call from Reinhard Bonnke. He asked if she knew anyone who could serve as his personal assistant. He needed someone at his side daily to handle contacts, accompany him to meetings, assist behind the scenes at the crusades, and help with anything that came up pertaining to him personally. She told him yes.

The timing of it was nothing less than the invisible hand of God dropping the gift of a lifetime directly into my inbox! Suzette had told Reinhard about me, then sent me the email saying she could not think of a better way to learn crusade ministry than serve one of the giants of the faith and experience personally the African mass crusades. Oh, and I had a personal interview set for Friday.

I flew to Orlando two days later to meet Evangelist Reinhard Bonnke. I remember everything—the drive from the airport, sitting in the reception area, and looking at the big pictures on the wall full of massive crowds and testimonies of the saving and healing power of God. I kept trying to grasp the enormity of what was going on: I was about to interview face-to-face with Reinhard Bonnke!

The speed at which everything was moving had left me breathless. First came the email, then the rush of adrenaline and sense of wonder. Then a flight, the driver picking me up at the airport, and walking through the front doors—everything was happening so fast! Sitting in the reception area, I was scrambling to get my mind around what I was doing there? Was this really happening?

Siegfried, the director over their Full Flame media group, suddenly appeared, and with a start I stood up and shook his hand. He warmly welcomed me to Christ for all Nations. I liked him immediately.

We walked by more jaw-dropping wall portraits of the African crusades, and I was sure my heart was about to explode. It didn't help that the few office staffers I met along the way smiled knowingly. I barely heard any of their names but promised I would learn them if I survived the next forty-five minutes.

Walking into Reinhard's office suite, Peter Van den Berg, the president of CfaN, shook my hand, and the three of us sat down. Peter sat on the couch to my right and Sigi in the chair to my left. Before me was a long rectangular table, followed by an empty seat. I tried to relax and make a good first impression. But just when I felt like I had my breathing under control, Evangelist Reinhard Bonnke came striding into the room, full of energy and purpose. I was overwhelmed!

I called Alisa at the airport three hours later and couldn't hide my disappointment. I had just blown the chance of a lifetime. I had failed to get comfortable in front of such influential men—failed to connect, failed to communicate. I felt sick.

I'm not sure what type of response I was looking for from Alisa, but I definitely did not get it. I could hardly believe my ears when she said, "Stephen, that is exactly what I was praying for!"

It is said that men and women are from different planets, and certainly with that type of response I was thinking we were in completely different galaxies. Did I not just say I had miserably failed at the most inopportune time imaginable?

But Alisa pushed forward. All day she had felt if I walked into that interview and wowed them with my experiences, family, or personality, then we would always face the temptation to take credit for the hire.

But since the interview seemingly blew up in my face, we had to look to Jesus for our future and trust that the Holy Spirit would speak clearly into Reinhard's heart.

It took several long days to learn our fate. But when Siegfried called to welcome us to the CfaN family, a new direction for us was cast, along with the opening to a whole new wonderful world.

ALISA IS MY MVP!

It is one thing to hope for something. It is another thing entirely when it becomes a reality. Alisa was excited when the invitation came for me to join Reinhard in Orlando as his personal assistant. But the reality of what it meant for her quickly sank in: Not only would I be gone a lot during the crusade season, but most of my emails would be about testimonies of blind eyes opening and the deep things God was doing in my heart. This would only make her feel more alone, as she would be missing out on core experiences shaping my life. And while I traveled to Africa, she faced the prospect of selling our first house, packing our belongings, and moving away from her family and friends in order to be by herself much of the time in a new town. Saying yes to Reinhard was a dream come true, but for Alisa it also meant a substantial sacrifice.

Our *big conversation* on whether to say yes or no went something like this: We realized an extraordinary door had sprung open—one that could dramatically impact our lives and future. It would be a lot easier for me to say yes, since I would be reaping most of the benefits, but there was no way I could say yes if Alisa did not sign off on it 100%. The tipping point came in the details. Serving as Reinhard's personal assistant was packaged for one year, and having a set amount of time made the critical difference for Alisa. We could both see the hand of the Lord in it, and she decided that she would make whatever sacrifices were needed on her end to walk through this door. That was the end of the conversation, and I will forever be grateful to her for believing in me and recognizing the destiny hanging over our lives.

It did not take long for Alisa to face her first reality check. I had left for Africa with Reinhard, and Alisa was spending her first week in Orlando getting acclimated to her new surroundings. She had just finished up some grocery shopping, loaded the bags in the back, put the keys in the ignition—and nothing. The car battery was dead.

She looked around, but no one in the parking lot would help. Panic began to set in as she faced the reality of being in a new town and her husband thousands of miles away. She knew one name at the CfaN offices, and even though Alisa had never met the person before, relief swept over her when he came on the line.

We can laugh about the hardships now, but the Lord was always with us. Never once were we alone! Alisa's character and courage in the beginning to believe for what God had in front of us is a major reason for the testimonies that fill this book. On a path full of so many spiritual giants, my wife, Alisa, is my MVP!

THERE'S A MAN OF GOD ON THIS PLANE!

It only takes a few seconds being around Evangelist Reinhard Bonnke to pick up on his gripping passion for Jesus and souls. It is absolutely contagious! And on my first flight to Africa with him, his reputation went before us.

We boarded Lufthansa 564 in Frankfurt, Germany, and took off for Lagos, Nigeria. As is common on that flight, having crossed over the Mediterranean Ocean, we reached the Sahara Desert, where the plane encountered turbulence.

My aisle seat put me next to an elderly African lady by the window.

As we talked, I started sharing part of my testimony. I told her how exciting it was to work for Reinhard Bonnke and about the upcoming crusade in Port Hardcourt, Nigeria.

The lady recalled that nearly fifteen years earlier, Reinhard had visited Guinea, West Africa, her hometown. It had blessed her life and the whole community.

The turbulence continued to intensify as we talked, and it was clear this precious lady was growing increasingly alarmed. To take our minds off it, I simply said, "Since I'm traveling with Reinhard Bonnke, we have friends picking us up."

It was like I had said something sacred. She looked at me with wonder. After a short pause to gather her thoughts, she asked, "Evangelist Reinhard Bonnke is on *this* plane?"

Bumping around in the heavy turbulence, I nodded yes. To which she released a huge sigh and thankfully exclaimed, "We have a man of God on board this flight!"

It did not matter what she thought of me or anyone else on board Lufthansa 564, we were going to make it to Lagos—delivered out of this turbulence—because Reinhard Bonnke was with us.

SOWER AND THE SEED

Yes, we made it safely to Lagos. And a couple of days later we touched down in Port Hardcourt. It was there I heard Reinhard say for the first time, "A silent Gospel is no gospel at all!"

During that first team devotion, he had us all riveted to our seats as he preached on the Sower and the Seed (Matthew 13). Hearing his passion for Jesus and for souls imprinted something deep inside of me. It obviously had the same effect on everyone else in the room, because afterward the team stormed into prayer and intercession for Africa and the world.

I never forgot his teaching on the Sower and the Seed. Later I merged them with my notes from Dad's teaching on the same passage. Here are five appetizers, from two men I hold in the highest esteem, I hope will set your heart ablaze for souls:

There Is No Harvest Without Sowing

How serious is God about the lost? Jesus stepped down from heaven, reduced Himself to fit into what He created, and humbled Himself to be tortured and crucified on a cross. Jesus did all this because He loved us!

In light of His passion, how motivated do you think Jesus is to help us win souls? It is very important to Him. So when you do something to reach the lost, you can have full confidence that all of heaven lines up behind you!

Look at what the Bible says about the first-century disciples: "And they went out and preached everywhere, the Lord working through them and confirming the word through the accompanying signs" (Mark 16:20). God partnered with them! And He will work with you as well to bring in the harvest.

The opposite is also true. There is no harvest unless we act. If we do nothing to win souls, we cannot expect divine help or assistance. We must preach Jesus!

The Word of God Is Always Good Seed

The Good News is Jesus! He alone forgives sins, mends broken hearts, restores our souls, heals our bodies, and gives eternal life.

The Word of God is potent! It only takes one seed to

fall to the ground to change a life. The Bible says the Word is the seed (Luke 8:11). It "is living and powerful, and sharper than any two-edged sword, piercing even to the division of soul and spirit, and of joints and marrow, and is a discerner of the thoughts and intents of the heart (Hebrews 4:12). The Word of God is always good seed!

Sow Everywhere Indiscriminately
Jesus said, "A sower went out to sow!" This is by definition what a sower does—he or she sows. As kingdom agents, we sow and reap because that is who and what we are. It is part of our fiery spiritual DNA.

Jesus also said, "Some fell by the wayside...some fell on rock...some fell among thorns." On the surface, this would appear to be a waste of seed, sowing in such unproductive places. But in the words of Reinhard: "Jesus didn't call us to be soil evaluators, He commissioned us to sow!" We must sow everywhere!

We see this clearly in the life of Jesus. He ate with tax collectors and prostitutes. He showed compassion to widows and Gentiles. He welcomed the leprous and insane. He was sowing everywhere, all the time!

The question is not the supply of seed in our bags. You will never run out of seed, because your bags will always be full! Instead, our challenge is to never stop sowing.

We must always remember that Jesus is with us, working through us. We must operate with His fiery passion for souls, because this is our identity. This is our mission assignment!

There Will Always Be a Harvest
Jesus then said: "Others fell on good ground...and yielded a crop a hundredfold." This is the divine promise! Isaiah described it this way: The Word of God "shall not return to Me void, but it shall accomplish what I please, and it shall prosper in the thing for which I sent it" (Isaiah 55:11). No one is beyond the reach of Jesus! It may take time, but the Word will always bring harvest.

Consider what happened with Jesus and some of the Jewish priests and leaders. For three years He spoke to them, worked wonders in front of them, and all it brought Jesus was scorn and heartbreak. But look what the Bible says happened after the resurrection and ascension of Jesus: "Then the word of God spread, and the number of the disciples multiplied greatly in Jerusalem, and *a great many of the priests* were obedient to the faith" (Acts 6:7, emphasis mine).

Some of the same priests who rejected Jesus and cried out for His death ultimately became part of the wonderful harvest. This should encourage us, because there will always be a harvest.

The Harvest Is in the Hands of the Lord, Not Ours
Sowing is not about manufacturing results; it is about teaming up with the Holy Spirit to reach souls! Once we acknowledge that we cannot save or heal anyone, it totally takes the pressure off. Jesus is the Savior. Jesus is the Healer. But hear this amazing promise: If we will plant and water, God will give the increase (I Corinthians 3:7).

I remember Reinhard talking that day about how

God honors every decision born out of a passion for souls. Having won millions of people to faith in Jesus Christ, he said this: "I will not receive credit for the number of souls saved—but for the number of seeds sown!"

What a huge revelation. Our heavenly success is not determined by our wins, but by our faithfulness and obedience!

The harvest is in His hands. Our job is to go forth and sow. Or as Jesus put it: "The harvest truly is plentiful, but the laborers are few. Therefore pray the Lord of the harvest to send out laborers into His harvest" (Matthew 9:37–38).

PRAYING WITH REINHARD BONNKE

The night of that first crusade with Evangelist Reinhard Bonnke was a busy one. I had touched up his suit and shirt, prepared hot tea with honey to sip before he took the microphone, along with other last-minute odds and ends. It was just about time to leave the hotel.

As the people of Port Hardcourt readied themselves for a supernatural invasion of Gospel power, Reinhard invited me to join him and Peter Van den Berg in his room to pray. I was blessed to be asked! I understood my role as personal assistant: be ready at any moment, for any reason. But to receive an invitation to pray privately over that night's crusade with Reinhard and Peter before they walked out the door went beyond my job description. I said yes immediately!

It is said that prayer is better caught than taught. That is exactly what happened to me that day. I don't know what I expected to hear behind closed doors, but the most remarkable thing was listening to Reinhard pray. As he quietly paced the room, I heard him whispering

"I love you, Jesus, I love you, Jesus. Thank you, Jesus, thank you." It was so intimate, so real, so powerful.

Those thirteen words of prayer repeated over and over by Reinhard changed the way I prayed, especially in the moment leading up to our future ministry assignments. To enter His rest, to breathe above a whisper how much you love Him, and to offer Him your sincere appreciation—wow, Jesus really is the prize!

That day, like most of our private times of prayer, ended with Reinhard, Peter, and me clasping hands in a small circle. Reinhard called upon God for souls in the evening crusade. I can only tell you every time he said amen, I left the room with no doubt that hell was about to get pummeled and the population of heaven expanded!

PORT HARDCOURT, NIGERIA CRUSADE

We walked down to the hotel lobby together and slid into a waiting vehicle. As usual, I sat up front, with Reinhard and Peter in the back. This was a very large crusade and I could feel the anticipation. The loud police escort skillfully meandered us through traffic, oftentimes charging us down the wrong side of the road, before they deposited us directly behind the stage.

I will never forget my first impression in Port Hardcourt. Reinhard climbed up the steps at the back of the stage and I followed. There in front of me was an almost incomprehensible scene, as hundreds of thousands of people stood ready to hear the Gospel.

It was a sea of black faces: believers and nonbelievers, some from Muslim backgrounds, some with Satanic intent, others hungry to experience the power of God. I thought, *Where else could you find such a gathering of people?*

None of it fazed Reinhard. He sat quietly in his seat among the dignitaries on the stage, drinking his tea, preparing to speak.

When the moment came, Evangelist Reinhard Bonnke stood, strode purposefully to take the microphone, raised his other arm straight up in the air, and let out a shout of "Ha-lle-lu-jah!" His German-accented declaration boomed forth full of Gospel power and authority. The Africans loved it, roaring back at him and waving their white hankies in the air. He loved them and they loved him back—a powerful connection obvious to all.

My only responsibilities that Wednesday night were to grab his suit jacket when he took it off and make sure he had plenty of liquids. It sounds simple enough but with my heart pounding from everything I was seeing and hearing, it was a mighty challenge to remain focused.

There were so many amazing things about that first night: the electricity of the crowd, the beautiful and colorful dress of the African people, dramatic miracles, and certainly the authoritative preaching of Evangelist Reinhard Bonnke. But one thing I will never forget: the overpowering roar of the African people.

Nothing could prepare me for it. It was so powerful, so loud. When over a quarter of a million voices cried out "HALLELUJAH" in response to Reinhard, it sent fiery shock waves pulsating down my spine!

As the Africans continued shouting out praise, it hit me that the roar sounded like many rushing and powerful waters. I thought about the energy and penetrating sound described by John when the nations gathered to praise God before His throne: "I heard, as it were, the voice of a great multitude, as the sound of many waters and as the sound of mighty thunderings, saying, 'Alleluia! For the Lord God Omnipotent reigns!" (Revelation 19:6).

Indeed our God does reign! Surrounded by multitudes, I lifted up my hands and voice to join in the surging chorus. "Hallelujah!! Bless the mighty name of Jesus!"

CAST THE FIRST STONE

Reinhard was born to preach in Africa. The people love his powerful declarations and colorful stories. Of the many fiery sermons, my favorite was his retelling of John 8—the woman caught in adultery. Listening to him paint the picture of the religious leaders trying to trap Jesus, then expressing the majesty of our Savior always stirred fire inside my heart.

It impacted me so much that John 8:12 later helped shape the name and identity of our own evangelistic ministry: Light of Life International. This Gospel verse reads: "I am the light of the world. He who follows Me shall not walk in darkness, but have the light of life."

I love this story and have to share it with you. Drawing again from the notes of two of my heroes—Reinhard and my dad—here is a devotional on a famous New Testament passage.

The Trap

The religious leaders came to Jesus saying: "Teacher, this woman was caught in adultery, in the very act. Now Moses, in the law, commanded us that such should be stoned. But what do You say?" (John 8:4–5).

It was a question designed to trap Him. They asked Jesus this question to find something to accuse Him of. The emphasis here is on *something*, because up until this point they had *nothing* of which to accuse Him. Jesus was perfect!

The leaders had no comprehension of God's plan: that Jesus would come in the flesh to purchase their salvation. If they had understood this, they would never have tried to trap Him or cause Him to stumble.

They persisted: "But what do You say?" It was a clever way to set a trap! They knew He often launched His teachings by saying, "You have heard it said, but I tell you ..." So the religious leaders summarized Moses and put Jesus on the spot to answer a hard question.

NO meant disregarding the laws of Moses, which would discredit Him with the Jews. *YES* meant disregarding the laws of Rome, as only the Romans had the power to sentence someone to die. Both answers would trap Jesus.

The Tragic Decision

To spring the trap, the leaders dragged and shamed a daughter of Israel through the streets. But where was the adulterous man? He was not there, since their objective had little to do with the sin of adultery—only trapping Jesus.

So what did Jesus do? He ignored them, started writing in the sand, and said, "He who is without sin among you, let him throw a stone at her first."

The Bible says: "Those who heard it, being convicted by their conscience, went out one by one, beginning with the oldest even to the last" (v. 9). These men were convicted, which was good because a few feet away was Jesus, the One who had come to offer forgiveness and eternal life. But they all made a tragic decision: they turned and walked away.

These leaders turned the wrong way. Instead of acknowledging their pride and envy, and turning to God, they said NO to the prompting in their hearts and turned away from the Light of life.

The Bible has a lot to say about turning. Acts 26:18 says the desire of God is to open our eyes, in order to turn us *away* from darkness to light, from the power of Satan to God, that we might receive forgiveness of sins and an eternal inheritance.

Later on, some of these religious leaders did repent and turn toward Jesus. But others remained in their sins and in darkness, and that is the most tragic decision of all.

The Reprieve

The woman was having a bad day. It started with her decision to enter into an adulterous relationship and resulted in public humiliation—and almost death by stoning! It has been said before: Sin takes you farther than you wanted to go, keeps you longer than you intended to stay, and costs you more than you expected to pay. And that was definitely her present experience!

Alone with the woman, Jesus stops writing and asks: "Where are those accusers of yours? Has no one condemned you?" The men had departed without throwing any rocks at her, but what about Jesus? He said only someone without sin could throw the first stone. He met that requirement!

Maybe it was how He spoke to her, or how He dealt with her accusers, or what He had written on the ground. But Jesus was different from anyone she had ever met. She must have barely been able to get the words out: "No one, Lord."

She did not use the impersonal title of *Teacher* to respond to Jesus like the men had earlier. She personalized it, saying "Sir" or "Lord." She had been forcefully humbled by the others, but now her humility came willingly as Jesus looked at her and replied, "Neither do I condemn you; go and sin no more."

This is Jesus—loving, merciful, and bold. Instead of rocks tearing her face, He would receive the crown of thorns. Instead of her blood flowing in the streets, He would accept the death sentence—one that would tear His back and pierce His hands and feet. His words *Neither do I condemn you* cost Jesus His life, as He exchanged His sinless life for the death sentence hanging over this adulteress.

The Promise

The great exchange was made on our behalf as well! Paul described it this way: "There is therefore now no condemnation to those who are in Christ Jesus" (Romans 8:1).

This is the provision of Jesus. He saves us from the condemnation of our sin and empowers us to walk above the entrapment of it. All of which brings us to the end of the story and the promise found in verse 12: "I am the light of the world. He who follows me shall not walk in darkness, but have the light of life" (John 8:12).

A GOSPEL FOR INDIVIDUALS AND NATIONS

I returned to Orlando with Reinhard Bonnke several days later. The week in Port Hardcourt, Nigeria, served as a crash course in power evangelism. Thousands received salvation, healing, and the fire of the Holy Spirit.

I had a lot to share with Alisa, along with an expanded perspective. The Gospel held the authority to change a person's life—and it does. But I had also seen with my own eyes how its radiating power can transform cities, nations, and even a continent.

CHAPTER 3

Seeing the Bigger Picture

LIFE WITH REINHARD was never dull. One moment I would be sitting in a staff devotion listening to his passion for souls. The next, grabbing his stuff and racing to the airport.

One day we flew to California for TV interviews on two different networks then went to an evening birthday party for the son of another famous evangelist. On another day, we drove to a privately held gathering of evangelical leaders at a magazine publishers office. Another day we had our pictures taken with a movie star. It was busy and often tiring, but what made serving him remarkable were the times we had alone.

Whether it was a sidewalk cafe in Frankfurt or sitting in his private prayer study at home, those moments alone were priceless. He would often share stories or reflections on his life and ministry. I was blessed to listen to such beautiful words, share meals with him and his wife, Anni, and watch Reinhard delight in his grandchildren.

ROOMING WITH REINHARD BONNKE

We soon returned to Nigeria. Being in the smaller city of Ijebu-Ode, housing was more difficult. I was grateful to be part of Reinhard's inner team because no matter how challenging our accommodations, it would always be best-case scenario. Of course, we were in Africa, so when the venues were remote, the "best case" usually was not that promising.

This place was not too bad. Reinhard had two bedrooms with a small living area in between. If you looked past the torn-up bathroom tiles, lights that did not work, punched-through drawers, and air-conditioning that operated part time, you could make it work.

But when a local university rented the pool next door, just outside his window, and cranked up the music, I went to check on him immediately. It was classic Reinhard. He smiled and said, "The Nigerians like it loud and I'm a loud speaker—so we get along fine!"

By the next day, I had located the person who had packed the best snacks, sent an email by satellite signal, grown accustomed to the motel blackouts, and moved in with Reinhard. It was for security purposes, and since there were three doors into our space, we barred the one into his room and the living area. So for the rest of the week, the only way in or out was through my room.

MEETING THE GOVERNOR

Things move at a different speed in Africa. The agenda called for a formal lunch with the governor of the Ogun State and his entire cabinet. Since Nigeria is a collection of federated states, having the head of one invite you to a banquet is a big deal. It also means lots of protocol and press coverage.

At noon Reinhard and I were dressed and ready to go. Ten minutes passed. No phone call, no dignitaries anywhere to be seen. I made the appropriate calls to find out what was going on. No one answered and no one called back. For ninety minutes we waited in our small living room. Nothing happened.

At 1:30 p.m., we gave up. Reinhard retired to his bed so he could rest for the fifth and final crusade service of the week. Just as he closed his door, my phone rang.

The African crusade director relayed the urgent message: His Excellency had not only arrived, he was on his way up to our room! I raced into Reinhard's room, woke him up, and straightened up the room just in time to hear a knock on the door. I steeled myself to welcome His Excellency and opened the door.

A circus of media and cameras and lights, along with many important-looking people dressed in suits, awaited me on the other side. I was totally outnumbered. They shared one purpose: to push their way past me into the tiny living room for the meeting between Reinhard and His Excellency.

Once inside, thankfully, the atmosphere calmed after greetings were exchanged. In what reminded me of a scene out of a medieval painting, Reinhard laid his hands on the head of the governor, kneeling in front of him, and prayed for him.

The circus returned with full force once the governor stood. Lots of pictures and chatter and, finally, out the door, carrying us with them to the dining hall to join the rest of the Ogun governmental officials. It was a far cry from what the agenda had read, but this was Africa, and Reinhard looked right at home.

FIRE AND MICROPHONES

The night before, nearly one hundred thousand people had gathered in a field to hear Reinhard Bonnke speak on the fire of the Holy Spirit. At the end, he called for the fire of God to fall on the people, and it was a supernatural exchange. As the multitude cried out to the Lord Jesus, the glory of God washed across the field.

The presence of the Lord touched us on the platform too. I cried out to Jesus as the roar of the multitude crescendoed and intensified. Heaven was touching earth, and I could feel the fire burning inside my soul!

Then, without warning, Reinhard spun around. He motioned me to step forward. I did not know what he wanted but it was my job to respond. I reached him, and he put the microphone in my hand.

I was dumbfounded. He was not asking me to change its battery, and the service was far from over. For a moment I just stood there looking at the microphone. I did not know what to do. But Reinhard's little nudge toward the front of the platform confirmed what I sensed rising inside.

I stepped forward to join the crusade director in crying out before the Lord Jesus. I started praying in tongues and urging the people to receive the fire of God. The cries for fire, the prophetic declarations, praying in the Holy Spirit just poured out of me as if I had been created for such a moment.

After a while, I turned and gave the microphone back to Reinhard. I sat down and buried my face in my hands to pray. The first thought that raced across my brain was, *Oh my, Stephen, you just ministered to nearly 100,000 people!* But instantaneously my soul and my heart screamed out, *NO! You just ministered before the Lord!* Overwhelmed by the beautiful and fiery presence of the Holy Spirit, I wept freely.

SAKI FIRE CONFERENCE

A similar scene unfolded less than three weeks later at a fire conference in Saki, Nigeria. People had started lining up outside the stadium at 5 a.m.! Despite the absence of light, the people were singing and dancing, hungry for more of God.

Due to the intense heat of the African sun, conferences were intentionally held in the morning. But time did not matter. Reinhard could have held it at 2 a.m. in darkness or at 3 p.m. in suffocating heat, and the people would still have come. Such was their expectation and faith.

We arrived at 7:30 a.m. to 25,000 people crammed into a soccer facility. Reinhard preached from Acts 2. When he finished, he told the people to stand. He called for the fire of the Holy Spirit to fall on them—and the cry was answered with enormous power. The place was absolutely electric!

Reinhard turned and gave his microphone to his crusade director, then took the microphone from the interpreter and passed it to me. Even though I was alert to such a possibility this time, it still flooded me with awestruck wonder. Who was I to stand and proclaim blessing and fire? And that is when it happened.

As I cried out in tongues, I stretched my left hand toward the people. Suddenly, my hand felt like it was ablaze! It started burning, and instinctively I pulled my hand back down to my side. The Holy Spirit corrected me, so I stretched out my left hand again. I could feel the power of God flowing from the platform into the crowd. I started shouting with boldness, "Receive the Holy Spirit, receive the fire of God! Receive the Holy Spirit, receive the fire of God!"

The people were alive, shouting praise to God! Reinhard strode purposefully off the stage and into the multitude. Laying hands and praying over the people as he went, many crumpled straight down to the ground. It was amazing to watch the power of God move freely across the stadium, and it only intensified the passion for Jesus inside me.

I finally stopped looking at the people. The presence of the Lord Jesus was thick and palpable. I lifted my head toward the sky, thanking Him for the marvelous works and His amazing love.

As we headed back to the hotel, I would never be the same again. There was so much to process, pray over, and communicate with Alisa.

I also thought about something Reinhard had recently said while looking out on a crowd and again driving back afterward: *"Stephen, can you see your destiny in God?"* At the time I did not have an answer. I wanted to say yes—but did he mean a destiny in Africa, crusade evangelism, continuing on as his personal assistant, or something else entirely? Now as I prayed alone in my tiny room, the question ran over and over again in my mind.

I knew the Holy Spirit was working on me. I did not know if I was an evangelist, I just wanted my life to count for Jesus. Receiving the microphone to pray and prophesy before the people left me wondering what was going on and had me crying through the night for direction.

A SHEPHERD BOY SEEING PAST THE WALL

The mind-blowing thing about all of it was only a few months earlier I had been serving on Dad's team overseeing student ministries. Then sovereignly I was selected to walk alongside Reinhard Bonnke, and now I was wrestling with the calling of doing crusade ministry with Alisa!

I felt like the shepherd boy David, minding his own business while taking care of his dad's sheep. There were tons of youth pastors around the world, many with bigger student ministries and doing a better job than I could ever dream. Any one of them may have been a better choice. But the Lord remembered me and my prayers and anointed me for a radical change of direction.

I had been warned. A year earlier, a friend from college had passed through and invited me to lunch. We talked while eating fajitas—how I felt like change was in the air, that our years in student ministry were coming to a close.

Jim looked across the booth at me and said, "Stephen, it's because you're not a youth pastor!" I did not know how to take that, but before I could protest he pressed on.

He touched the wall that framed our booth. He said my life was moving parallel to this wall. On this side the Holy Spirit was preparing me. On the other side was His destiny for my life. Holes in the wall had provided brief glimpses of what would one day be revealed—like a mission trip or special camp service. But they were only glimpses and left me desiring more.

Jim intensified his look and said, "Stephen, at some point this wall is going to end, and when you walk out past it you will see your destiny in God." Those words were like fire in my soul that day.

Now, here in Africa, there was no denying the wall had ended. I was staring my future square in the face.

IRONING AS UNTO THE LORD

In Africa, the highs were amazing. Mighty manifestations of God's glory and power left me breathless, broken and hungry for more of His presence.

But on the road, behind the scenes, there were a few things that irked me—none more than ironing Reinhard's shirts and pants. My frustration had nothing to do with Reinhard, simply the reality that I never had a good relationship with an iron. Throw in some jet lag, a hectic schedule, and less than ideal living conditions—trying to iron out wrinkles using a bed, a wall, or a towel on the floor was a recipe for disaster. It was so stressful—what I would have done for a dry cleaner!

Stressed out over how poorly I was doing with Reinhard's clothes, I finally picked up my laptop and sent Alisa an email: *Today, I almost threw the iron out the window because after 2 hours the suit was more wrinkled than when I started! I really don't have a clue how to iron on a board, let alone on the bed or table—with a machine that either gives off too much water/steam or turns itself off for no apparent reason. I was so embarrassed tonight at the meeting when Reinhard started to preach. You would have thought he just stepped off the plane from Orlando. I believe the results will improve over time, but the Lord keeps dealing with the issues of my heart.*

Well, the results didn't improve. Only when Annie Bonnke joined us did Reinhard really look sharp. Frustrated and totally defeated, I cried out one afternoon to the Lord about how much I loathed ironing. And in that hot room in Nigeria, I heard Him whisper to me, *If you will iron as unto Me, then you will share in Reinhard's reward.*

The whisper hit me like a ton of bricks and I broke before the Lord. I repented for my pride, for believing that somehow ironing was beneath me, that I needed to be doing more important things with my time. I also repented for letting the task of ironing clothes steal my joy, and not recognizing the Lord truly was my reward.

This little interjection by the Holy Spirit did wonders for me! Not only did it remind me of the privilege to serve such a mighty man of God, it affirmed me. My labor (even if invisible) had value!

Ironing is certainly not the most critical part of crusade ministry, but from then on it became my opportunity to pray for Reinhard. So as I prayed over his clothes (with or without holes), I began to realize the Lord was ironing out some wrinkles in my life and character as well.

SIDEWALK CAFE AND 100 EUROS

We left Saki and made the long drive back to Lagos. I had no idea at the time that this would be my last trip to Nigeria serving as Reinhard's personal assistant. We still had several other adventures in front of us, but the winds of change were starting to blow again.

The itinerary called for Lagos to Frankfurt, across the Atlantic to Chicago, then onward to Orlando. But one look at Reinhard after the first flight and it was evident we were not going anywhere for a while. Exhausted and sick, he needed rest and medicine immediately.

The Arabella Sheraton, located in the heart of the shopping district of Frankfurt, Germany, turned out to be our R&R destination for the next couple of days. After some solid sleep Reinhard seemed to be on the mend the next evening. By the following day he was out of bed, working on his laptop and generally feeling better. Then something special happened: Reinhard asked if I wanted to take a walk.

We strolled along Zeil Boulevard, lined with trees in the center and shops and cafés on each side. After stopping for fish and chips, we lingered in a sidewalk café for cake and tea. It was so enjoyable!

I learned one of the large Lutheran churches denied his son the chance to wed in its chapel because Reinhard wanted to preside over the ceremony. It launched an openhearted conversation about rejection, persecution, and painful experiences at the hands of his fellow countrymen. Still, Reinhard held no bitterness in his heart, just a prayer for Jesus to bless the German people. I knew this was true because I had often heard him tell the Africans that one of them would take the Gospel to Germany and set it ablaze for Jesus.

When we returned to the hotel, he asked me to locate his wallet and pull out 100 euros. I brought the money to him, but he refused it. Instead, Reinhard asked me to apologize to Alisa for the additional delay returning home and buy her something nice.

I was speechless. It was such a generous and heartfelt act. It was also classic Reinhard—a real gentleman.

THE EGYPT EXPERIMENT

For four months I traveled with Evangelist Reinhard Bonnke. I heard him preach, watched him pray over people in airports and hotel lobbies, even attended an exclusive showing of *The Passion of the Christ* with him and Mel Gibson in Orlando. We traveled across three continents and celebrated birthdays on the road. It had been remarkable in every way.

But change was coming. I sensed something growing in my heart, and Reinhard did too. Instead of twelve months, our time together would be cut by two-thirds. Looking back, the invisible hand of God was at work for our good. It had been a crash course in faith, power evangelism, and character development—and it had brought Alisa and me to the edge of stepping into uncharted territory.

My last trip with Reinhard as his personal assistant was to Cairo, Egypt. About ten years earlier, he had been blacklisted after the fire conference at the World Pentecostal Meeting in Cairo and forbidden to return. But times had improved and he wanted to find out if his name had cleared. It involved some risk on our part, but if things went well we would spend a couple days enjoying Egypt.

Alma, an Egyptian contact, greeted us warmly inside the gate. His hand-held sign saying *Bonnke and Evans* struck me as hilarious, because the moment we arrived, he recognized Reinhard and rushed forward to welcome us. He led us toward the immigration desk, where he suggested I stand a couple of people behind Reinhard just in case he encountered any difficulties.

Initially, everything seemed routine. The officer took Reinhard's passport, smiled, and handed it to a man sitting behind him at a computer station. He stroked some keys, mumbled something in Arabic, and gave it back to the officer. A moment later, a second officer appeared, looked at the passport, and asked Reinhard to step aside and wait for a few minutes. I left the line to join Reinhard standing by the wall and noticed Alma was on his cell phone, talking very fast.

The officer returned and ushered Reinhard into a side room for some questions. By this time another plane had landed, and with it a new wave of passengers filled the immigration hall. As the lines dwindled, Reinhard remained incarcerated, and Alma was anxious because no more inbound flights were scheduled for several hours. Soon the customs officers would leave and we would all be stuck. He urged me to proceed, then ask for readmittance into the customs hall. It worked. The man at the desk stamped my passport and allowed me to rejoin Reinhard.

Ninety minutes passed. The only developments were meeting a couple of other detainees in the immigration hall, none of whom knew what was going on. A young man from South Africa had arrived via Dubai without a visa. Drunk and unable to operate his cell phone, he was oblivious to why anyone would want to detain him. It was comical watching him fluctuate between protests and pouting. Eventually, they just let him in.

Alone and tired, the officer walked up to us and shook his head: "I'm sorry!" It was 9 p.m., three hours after landing. Reinhard Bonnke had been denied entrance into Egypt and would not be released until arrangements were made to deport him.

The final decision apparently was not made by an airport official but by someone in the government. Reinhard was still blacklisted—barred from entering the country under any circumstance. As I had already cleared immigration, I was asked to leave the hall. A guard took a glance at my passport, and a customs official inspected my bag. When I looked back, Reinhard had disappeared.

The next nine and a half hours were the most difficult, especially for Reinhard, as he had to sit in detainment with a cast of colorful characters all night long. It was Saturday night and our return tickets on Lufthansa were for Monday—a day and a half away. No way we were waiting around for that flight!

Stephen Mutua, a member of the CfaN family, met me in the airport and we went straight to the Lufthansa desk. Closed. We tried other airlines—all closed. The airport was vacant.

We tracked down an airport security guard who told us Lufthansa would open for a brief time at 1:30 a.m. for its early morning flight out on Sunday. I sent Reinhard a SMS. He had been searched but was okay for the moment.

At 11:57, Reinhard texted me: *They say I will go to the transit lounge in 5 minutes.* It sounded hopeful, as perhaps his airline status had opened a seat on the next flight out of the country. Nothing happened.

At 1 a.m., Stephen Mutua and I were sitting in the empty terminal outside an office that was reportedly about to open in thirty minutes and would help us get Reinhard on a plane. That is when I noticed the two heavily armed Egyptian soldiers coming our way. A few feet from us they stopped and for some minutes joined us in watching the cleaning crew mop the floors with soap and water. It was dull and heart-pounding all at the same time! One of the soldiers motioned to me, which I interpreted as: *Do you have a cigarette?* I shook my head sideways to say no, but it either did not register or he must have thought I did not understand. He motioned again and this time I shrugged my shoulders as if to say "I'm sorry," but that did not work either. The last thing I wanted to do was irritate a soldier in an empty airport after midnight, so I was relieved when they decided to move on.

At 1:30 a.m. the tiny Lufthansa office opened. The results were not encouraging. The first flight out was packed but given the unusual circumstances, she would check. The lady grabbed my Monday return ticket and walked out the door.

At 2:18 a.m. I texted Reinhard: *Still waiting to get ticket . . . it was overbooked . . . they said wait. So I'm in a holding pattern.* He replied someone told him he was flying out at 11 a.m., but it was all confused. That is when the airline agent returned with my ticket and said what I expected: The first flight out would not include Reinhard or me.

It was time to call in reinforcements. If we could not do it properly, we had to find someone who could push through the back door. At 3:30 a.m., I called Germany and woke up our travel agent.

The text messages from Reinhard during this time only underscored how difficult this whole ordeal was on him personally. People who had been deported from France on drug charges were now sharing space with him. At 4:11 a.m. he wrote: *We will take any airline to Europe—the first and next. I feel like Joseph in jail.*

That is when the first signs of hope appeared. Air France had a flight leaving for Paris at 6:20 a.m. Ninety minutes until takeoff! There was one person in front of us at the Air France office, then we could print the tickets and go. It took forever.

5:21 a.m. Reinhard texted: *I am out at the check-in counter of Air France. Where are you?* 5:23 a.m. I replied: *In the Air France office and she is printing the tickets.* Reinhard four minutes later: *Come quickly.* My response one minute later: *Trying—this lady is really slow.*

We had to get Reinhard on that plane! As I watched the representative process the information very methodically, I knew the window of opportunity was quickly closing. Suddenly, a flight attendant burst into the office and said to come with her. The tickets were still not printed but I had to go—now!

I left Stephen Mutua in the office, caught a glimpse of Reinhard in the distance, and pushed toward security. That was as far as I got. The guards would not let me go through without a ticket. In the chaos, the lady representative from the office came over—not to hand me our printed tickets, but to declare the flight full and gate closed. It sent the flight attendant scurrying off to the plane, Reinhard back to his holding pen, and me miffed at the representative.

Reinhard then texted: *Wow, what is next?* I called our travel agent, then went to each open airline counter to ask if they had any seats for any flight to Europe. Same answer every time: "We are overbooked!" As a final measure, we went over to Terminal One and talked with the management of Egypt Air about getting on board any flight, to anywhere.

At 6:48 a.m. the word from our travel agent was not good. Not one flight was open. We did have our Monday tickets, but I felt sick that he would have to spend another day and night in a holding room because he had preached the Gospel here.

Finally at 7:19 a.m.: *Good news! You are confirmed on LH583 departing at 15:30 p.m.* Stephen, the travel agent, and I had worked straight through the night trying desperately to secure a release for Reinhard. I was on the verge of collapse, as I had flown in from Orlando with zero sleep then walked straight into this ordeal. As best as I could figure, it had been forty-nine hours since I had gotten up on Friday morning in Florida and said good-bye to Alisa. We went to the hotel and from 8 a.m. to 11 a.m. things were quiet and still.

Back at the airport, I received confirmation for both Reinhard and me on the flight to Frankfurt. I sent him a text at 2:03 p.m.: *Are you still in quarantine, or have you passed through passport control and on to lounge?* He replied six minutes later: *I'm back in the old hole! This is very humiliating. I only watched this procedure in Frankfurt when Nigerians were deported. But I'm walking very tall: it's for the Gospel's sake.* At 2:13 p.m. I texted: *I am proud of you for being so strong.* He noted: *They do no favors and they think I'll never want that again.* I could only say: *Bless you, Pastor Bonnke . . . I will meet you at the gate—where we will board rejoicing!*

They held his passport until he was seated on the plane and requested the flight attendant not release it until they had cleared Egyptian airspace. The attendant noticed we had boarded together and asked me what had he done. I told her, "That is Reinhard Bonnke and his crime is preaching the Gospel of Jesus Christ!"

She gave him the passport immediately. We were on our way to Frankfurt. The next day Reinhard celebrated his sixty-fourth birthday.

GOOD-BYE IN BIRMINGHAM

With the Egypt affair behind us and a couple days of rest in Frankfurt with family, we made an overnight stop in Birmingham, England, before flying home. My time serving Reinhard was winding down and my heart was flush with mixed emotions.

I knew this was it—the final stop as Reinhard's personal assistant. I walked down the hall toward his room. I would miss these talks—the two of us—but I wasn't going for nostalgia's sake. I needed clarity and courage.

I trusted God about the timing of my departure. I blessed Him coming in and now I would bless Him going out! Indeed, the Lord had supernaturally opened the door to be here, then spent the time in Africa working on my character, broadening my vision, and deepening my faith. I believed wholeheartedly He had done all of this to launch Alisa and me into mass evangelism.

But now what? As I sat on the side of his bed while he busied himself around the room, I asked him, "How do you actually do crusade ministry?" If Reinhard could see me standing on a platform, preaching the Gospel, then I wanted to know how in the world I would ever do such a thing.

His response was classic Reinhard—quick, direct, and full of unflinching faith. He boomed out, "Stephen, pick your city, choose the largest venue available, advertise signs and wonders, then step out in faith and let the Lord do the rest!"

I remember thinking in large letters: *IS THAT ALL?!* Cities, huge venues, faith for impossible miracles, and believing God for the logistics, finances, people, and details. If it wasn't for the fact that I knew Reinhard was telling me the truth from his heart, I may have actually laughed out loud. It seemed so absurd and utterly unattainable for people like Alisa and me. But looking back now, that is exactly how you do it.

The final thing Reinhard told me that night was: "Remember what God calls for He pays for." And then with a smile: "Just make sure you know that He called for it!"

Well, that was the million-dollar question. Was it true He had called us into this? Because if not, we were headed for disaster.

CHAPTER 4

Transition and Small Beginnings

IT STARTED WITH the hard decision to return home—to go back to what we had left. The Lord had brought us to Orlando supernaturally, so it felt strange loading up to return. I was nervous it would quench the fire in our hearts for crusade evangelism because of the comforts, familiarity, and other options available at home. We promised ourselves we would not lose sight of what had been started inside of us.

PRAYING IN ANCHORAGE, ALASKA

I will always be indebted to my dad for his wisdom and understanding in those initial days. He had never hired a missions pastor before—until now! Creating such a position provided for my family and offered us freedom and accountability to grow our calling. It also meant seeing and interacting with one of my heroes on a daily basis for the next few years, something I will forever cherish.

Still, going home we had lots of questions and really no idea where to start. We did not have an organization set up or a plan on how to build such a ministry. So with no clue what to do next, we did what most Texans do in those situations: We went on a cruise! Mom and Dad sensed we needed to clear our heads, so the four of us flew up to Alaska for a few days of rest before cruising back down to Vancouver.

Now, I know you are supposed to relax on vacation, but I was restless. Alone in my Anchorage hotel room, looking out the window, I started crying out to God. *Where do we go?* I knew the Lord had opened the door to serve and learn from Reinhard, and I also believed He had opened the door for us to step out so we could do likewise. But at the moment we did not even have a place to live, let alone an organization or sense of direction.

I lay our options before the Lord, starting with family connections in Europe and Australia. I felt nothing. I moved on to Africa. After all, that was where the dream of nation-shaking evangelism had come alive. Again nothing. Last, I lifted Latin America up in prayer. And something began to awaken inside.

Of course, this direction made absolutely no sense in the natural. I did not speak Spanish and had very few contacts in that part of the world. There had to be at least a million people more qualified than us to operate in Latin America!

But as I continued to pray in that hotel room, something like fire started to ignite in my heart. We now had a direction, and the doors that began to open led south.

MACEDONIAN CALL

The New Testament has a lot to say about open doors, evangelism, and trusting the Holy Spirit. One of the most famous stories involves Paul in Acts 16—often referred to as the Macedonian Call.

Paul and his companions were in the middle of what would later become known as his second missionary journey. They had visited several areas already and planned to continue on into Asia and Bithynia. The problem was the Holy Spirit said no—twice! So they ended up on the Aegean Sea coast in the city of Troas.

I would love to know if they were asking the question: Where do we go now, Lord? They knew the answer was NO to the east and northeast. What about Ephesus to the south or even sailing home to Antioch or Jerusalem? What we do know is having laid down their plans and submitting to the leadership of the Holy Spirit, Paul and company were in the right place for God to open a supernatural door of historic proportion.

The direction came via a vision, where a man was pleading with Paul to come to Macedonia with the Gospel (vv. 9–10). It was bold and a completely unforeseen direction than what these kingdom agents had initially planned. The gateway to Europe lay over one hundred miles away to the west and included a great deal of risk, such as hazardous travel. No less than three times in the life of the apostle Paul did he suffer shipwreck, including one episode that left him adrift for a full night and day (2 Corinthians 11:25). But Paul, Silas, Luke, Timothy, and the others knew this was an open door and moved forward to preach the Gospel.

This decision radically pushed them beyond their original plans. The consensus among scholars is the Roman colony of Philippi lacked a synagogue. This meant Paul and company could not use their normal strategy of going into the local synagogue and interacting with the Jews. The result was something new: preaching directly to Gentiles, outside along riverbanks, mainly to women. This was much more than a one-hundred-mile redirect; it was a daring leap of faith to win souls and pioneer churches!

None of it happens, though, without the personal involvement of the Holy Spirit. This is a biblical principle. Revelation 3:7 says it is God who opens doors that cannot be shut, and it is God who shuts doors that no one can open. In the Macedonian Call, the Holy Spirit refused to let them go in one direction because He wanted to open wide a doorway to Europe!

And look what happened on the other side of that door: Philippi, Thyatira, Thessalonica, Berea, Athens, Corinth, and more received the Good News. A businesswoman, a jailer, a synagogue ruler, plus many Jews and Greeks experienced the transforming power of the Gospel of Jesus Christ. And if that was not enough, at least five New Testament books were later written to those groups of people—letters that still speak to our lives hundreds of years later!

I wonder if any of them had any inclination of the massive scope of influence and longevity the Holy Spirit was working in them when He said NO to their original plans? Proverbs 16:9 tells us, "A man's heart plans his way, but the Lord directs his steps." Paul wrote: "Now to Him who is able to do exceedingly abundantly above all that we ask or think, according to the power that works in us, to Him be glory" (Ephesians 3:20-21).

What started with Paul and Silas deciding to preach the Gospel ultimately led to a divine invitation that opened the world to them. I think for us it starts with small steps, too, and listening to the voice of the Holy Spirit. As our navigator and compass, we can trust the Holy Spirit to lead us to the right doors in order to win souls for Jesus.

HOTEL CASA BLANCA

Three months after returning from Birmingham, England, I was on board a plane with a medical and construction mission team heading for Honduras. I initially said no but when pressed to preach a couple of small outdoor services, I yielded. We flew into San Pedro Sula, cleared customs, and met our missions contact for the week—JC Yoon. A short drive to Progresso and we checked into the Hotel Casa Blanca.

I was sharing a room with three guys, two of whom I had spent over a week in the Amazon Basin of Peru sleeping on the ground in tents and helping build a church during the day. That had been a difficult trip not just because of the conditions, but one of the men on our team had suffered an injury. My two roommates—Fons and Leland—had remained on site to continue working while I joined the party climbing into a canoe to get our friend home somehow. It was a week none of us would ever forget.

As Fons, Leland, and I unpacked in our room, JC dropped by with a message for me. He had located a potential translator and set up a meeting with him later that day. I was relieved JC had found someone and was getting more and more excited about the two services.

Both Fons and Leland knew my heart to build on what I had seen in Africa. I saw this as a first step in that direction. Leland strengthened my spirit by pulling me aside to say Alisa and I were doing the right thing. Instead of launching out on our own without a covering or accountability, we had returned home and submitted ourselves to our pastor (my dad) and local church. In turn, they had created a position to serve locally with the flexibility and blessing to explore the calling that resonated in our hearts. Even though we had worried it would cost us momentum, Leland affirmed the decision to submit to authority. He said God would bless it.

Two hours later, I would meet our future crusade director. Dennis Aplicano would be one of two men sent by the Lord to form the heart and soul of our Latin America work.

MEETING DENNIS APLICANO

There is absolutely no other way to explain how this meeting came about except to acknowledge the invisible hand of God. Because I did not speak Spanish, JC set out to find a quality translator but found no one. This created a big problem, because holding an outdoor rally in Honduras is impossible if the speaker can't speak the native language. And the rally can't be canceled if the invitations have already been sent out and the guest speaker is in the country!

Staring at the possibility of having to translate himself (difficult, since Spanish is his third best language behind Korean and English), he called his lawyer for help. The attorney recommended someone who had translated in the largest church in San Pedro Sula.

The problem was time. Our team was flying in soon, and the translator was also hosting a group. The busy schedules for both men made the possibility of meeting slim. As a last resort, one suggested a gas station. They could meet while filling up their cars with gas.

The meeting went well and JC asked if he had just a couple minutes to swing by the motel after our team arrived to meet me. "Impossible," said the translator, because he had to go to the hotel where his team was staying. But this was the miracle: Both teams were booked at the same motel! And that is how I ultimately came to meet our crusade director, Dennis Aplicano.

I liked him immediately. He had a passion for crusades and Latin America, knew a lot about Reinhard, and had a fantastic sense of humor. In fact, that balance of talking fervently about souls and revival, then a minute later making me smile with his wit and warmheartedness, bonded us from the outset.

I asked him how he met his wife, Tammy. He launched into an over-the-top story I've now heard a million times. But hearing it for the first time and trying to gauge if he was being serious or not, I was left on the edge of my seat waiting for the punchline. An invitation to preach at a women's conference . . . Tammy responding to his strong preaching . . . Dennis learning of her interested in someone else . . . a prophetic word emerging . . . Dennis boldly declaring: "Leave that ugly Philistine you are interested in; the man of your dreams is standing right before you!"

(Of course, most of it is made up or grossly exaggerated. But the way he delivers it registers a huge roar of laughter and puts everyone at ease. And he is quick to admit he married way over his head!)

After thirty minutes, the meeting ended. Dennis agreed to help in the service, and I walked away with Fons and Leland excited. It seemed like a good fit. I had no idea!

SMALL BEGINNINGS IN HONDURAS

I'm not sure if the community of El Castano is listed on any map you can buy or view of Honduras. But if you drive out of Progresso on the road to Tela, you will pass a Christian mission on the left-hand side that includes a hospital, school, and chapel. It is there that Dennis and I stood together to preach the Gospel for the first time, unaware of the scope of what the Holy Spirit was initiating.

Forty-five pastors showed up Tuesday night. The turnout disappointed JC, as he had arranged to feed 150 pastors before the service. It did not bother me because this was my first pastors' conference since launching from Reinhard!

I preached on the fire of the Holy Spirit. The fire of God fell mightily, with several pastors receiving their prayer language for the first time and others catching fresh vision for soul winning. With pastors on their knees weeping softly before the Lord or walking around the perimeter with hands raised in worship, the service transitioned into a time of prayer. We stepped off the platform to seek the Lord ourselves, and each person found his or her own moment to wrap up and quietly slip out.

Two hundred adults turned up the next night for the evangelistic outdoor rally and swelled to almost four hundred the last night. It was classified "outdoor" mainly because the roof and chapel walls remained unfinished—the perfect conditions for humidity and mosquitos! None of it fazed Dennis as he matched me word for word without a trace of difficulty, facing the audience and presenting the message as if it were his own. It flowed naturally, as if we had been doing this for years.

Anyone who has ever had the experience of speaking with an interpreter knows the challenge of finding a comfort level. Utter a word or expression he or she does not recognize and the result is immediate awkwardness, or worse, mistranslation. But the best interpreters not only catch and echo your words, they match your tone and emotion and cause you to forget that you are actually pausing at all. Dennis displayed this skill and his pastor's heart those two nights.

The bigger deal was the connection and like-heartedness between us. We both dreamed about the nations and preaching the Gospel to the masses! Our first crusade was still a year away, but the Holy Spirit had initiated something bigger than anything we could ever have imagined that night. The next several months He would continue to fashion us together in heart, mind, and soul.

FIRST-CLASS AFFIRMATION

On the plane out of Honduras, Fons and I had upgraded to first class, which was fabulous, with the mixed nuts, warm towels, extra room, and onboard meal. Wow, I could get used to sitting up there! But what made it special was Fons and I had privacy to talk about life and ministry.

I felt strongly deep down inside that something had been set in motion, no matter how small or unlikely it seemed. I told Fons I had treated the pastors conference and two evangelistic services as if I were stepping in for Reinhard in Africa. I had prayed, rested, filled my mind with Scriptures, worshipped, and spent time listening for His voice in readying myself to preach the Gospel in El Castano. It was baby steps for sure, but all I could convey to Fons was my heart burned hotter than ever to do crusade evangelism in Latin America.

I will never forget what happened next. Sitting there in the first row, Fons looked at me and said, "Stephen, I believe you are going see it—it's going to happen!" I have no idea why his response meant so much, but I received it as Godly affirmation that these tiny first steps had great consequences attached to them. We were moving forward!

OPEN DOORS AND OPPORTUNITIES

I sat down in the living room at my parents' house one afternoon to talk about all that had happened. As they had served as missionaries and pastors around the world longer than I had lived, I wanted to get their take on the subject of open doors.

Mom spoke out in her Welsh accent, "Stephen, there are doors that open to let us out, and there are doors that open to lead us in." That was it—one sentence! Somehow in a simple and succinct kind of way, Mom had delivered the wisdom of the ages. I only had to look back on my life to see the invisible hand of God at work: out of law school and in to seminary, out of youth ministry and in to CfaN, and now out of Africa and in to Latin America. The result of the Holy Spirit leading me in and out of those doors was character development, opportunities to share the Gospel, and the unveiling of destiny for my life.

Dad said he had three things to add, all coupled with biblical chapter and verse! Here they are in the order he delivered them:

Focus on Every Opportunity

"I will tarry in Ephesus until Pentecost. For a great and effective door has opened to me, and there are many adversaries" (1 Corinthians 16:8–9).

Paul was not simply announcing his travel plans for the spring, he was letting the Corinthians know the Holy Spirit had opened a powerful door for ministry in Ephesus. It was a great and effective door and Paul was excited about it, which shows his focus of faith was on the opportunity.

Paul was certainly aware of the challenges, but his plans and passion centered on the open door. This is what a door of opportunity means: not focusing on the problem or the enemy, but focusing on the person and power of the Lord Jesus Christ!

Seek Out Every Opportunity

Look at the size of Paul's dream in reaching to the Romans: "Whenever I journey to Spain, I shall come to you. For I hope to see you on my journey, and to be helped on my way there by you, if first I may enjoy your company for a while" (Romans 15:24).

Paul not only believed a door would open for him to go to Rome with the Gospel, he envisioned the Roman believers helping send him to the farthest point in the known Western world!

This same plea and passion to share the Gospel is recorded in Colossians 4:3-4, "that God would open to us a door for the word, to speak the mystery of Christ, for which I am also in chains, that I may make it manifest, as I ought to speak." What is so amazing about this letter is it was written while Paul was in prison!

What is the size of your vision for the Gospel? What is the depth of your passion for the advancement of the Gospel. For Paul there were no boundaries to his calling, and even in prison he was seeking out every opportunity!

Take Advantage of Every Opportunity

"I came to Troas to preach Christ's gospel, and a door was opened to me by the Lord, I had no rest in my spirit, because I did not find Titus my brother; but taking my leave of them, I departed for Macedonia" (2 Corinthians 2:12–13).

Due to the turmoil at Corinth, Paul sent Titus there on his behalf. The plan was to reunite in Troas. But when Titus delayed in arriving at Troas, Paul's concern for the situation in Corinth pushed him past the open door and onward into Macedonia. It is one of the few times we see Paul passing on a chance to preach the Gospel.

Much later we see the faithfulness of the Lord as Paul, Timothy, Luke, Tychicus, Gaius, Aristarchus, and others came to Troas. This time they spent a week exhorting believers (Acts 20:3–12), providing Paul an opportunity to finish what he had left behind earlier.

The Gospel is so precious. Regardless if it is one person or many people, take advantage of every opportunity to share the testimony of Jesus Christ that dwells within you. Do you have any examples in your own life of missed opportunities that you could return to and share Jesus?

AME OFFERING

In the fall and winter months that followed the El Castano trip, a couple important things happened. One, Alisa and I registered the name *Light of Life International* as our nonprofit 501(c)3 ministry designation. Two, we made a return trip to Orlando. It was a wonderful excuse to spend a couple days with friends, but it was also our first ministry invitation anywhere outside of our home church.

Malcolm and I had met at a Benny Hinn event in Orlando. Because I was serving Reinhard at the time, I had unexpectedly ended up on the platform for the night meeting. Three rows of chairs were filled with pastors and VIPs. Malcolm and I occupied the last two seats of the back row in the corner of the stage. We were squeezed in and I had to be careful standing up and sitting down, because the last thing I wanted to do was fall off the platform in the middle of a miracle crusade!

Malcolm had accompanied his senior pastor, who sat one row in front of us. At a break in the service, Malcolm introduced me to his pastor. I wanted to return the favor and introduce him to Reinhard, but with Reinhard sitting on the front row (a couple seats down from Benny) and us pinned in the back, there was no way. But out of that contact came our first post-Africa invitation to speak in a church.

I had never spoken at an AME (African Methodist Episcopal) church before, and evidently it was the first time a Caucasian preacher had ever stepped foot through the front door of their small chapel. But we could not have asked for a warmer welcome as David, Allison, Alisa and I were hugged, kissed, pinched, and made to feel like long-lost family! I shared several stories from the mass crusades in Africa—the people, the miracles, and the impact it had on me. Maybe it was because of the freshness of the experiences, or perhaps something really had been deposited within me, or maybe it was the African–American culture of cheering and affirming the speaker throughout a message, but I spoke boldly and from my heart. I thanked the pastor for the kind invitation to be a part of their Sunday morning service, and sat down.

The pastor stepped down from the elevated pulpit, stood in front of the first row of pews, and asked me to join him. He wrapped his arm around my shoulder and told his congregation this was a special moment. He did not know many people who received a direct call into crusade ministry, but believed we had and that all I had seen, heard, and even cried out for in Africa was in preparation for where the Holy Spirit intended to take us.

He found a basket and told me to hold it with both hands. Then he instructed the people to stand up and come forward with their very best gift and put it in the bucket to honor the call of God upon our lives. I cannot describe to you how overwhelmed I was for the next several minutes as one person after another walked up, smiled and wished me well, and dropped money in the bucket. This was the first time people were sowing into the call and vision God had put in our hearts, and it was coming from one of the poorest communities in Orlando!

I stood next to the pastor holding this bucket filled with dollar bills, and I started to cry. I looked at Alisa and saw the tears in her eyes, too, both of us profoundly aware that something had just happened. In this precious AME church, we had been affirmed in our calling, and for the first time people were sowing financially into Light of Life International!

It was perhaps the next-to-last lady who overwhelmed me the most. She told me she did not have very much to give, but having put all the cash she had in the basket (maybe a couple of dollars), she turned her purse upside down and shook it vigorously to empty out any remaining coins. As we stood there together, two or three pennies fell into the bucket. The second I heard the quiet thud of the coins, I thought of the woman who gave two mites at the Temple. Jesus had not only noticed her gift that day, He made a point to praise her generosity. I was certain He felt the same way about this precious lady too.

I WILL BE YOUR CEO AND CFO

After the AME service, Alisa and I returned with David and Allison to their home. I excused myself to the guest room and closed the door. I sat down on the floor beside the bed and poured the cash out to count it. It held invaluable significance, because it represented the first offering into Light of Life International. It was about $200 in bills and change.

It was not the amount of money that stirred my soul; it was what it meant. I got on my knees and poured out my heart before the Lord Jesus. I thanked Him for the open doors that had brought us here and reiterated the hope and dreams in our hearts for our lives to make a difference for the kingdom.

As I quietly told Him thank you for all His kindness and faithfulness, I heard Him whisper something in my heart. It was a promise. He said: *Stephen, I will be your Chief Executive Officer (CEO) and I will be your Chief Financial Officer (CFO).*

What a promise! From the very beginning, the Holy Spirit drew my attention not to where I would speak next or whom would be the next financial partner—but to Him! If I would walk humbly before Him and set my heart after His presence, He would take care of our calendar and finances. And the testimony to this day is He has indeed remained faithful and true to His promise!

It also brought to mind something that Reinhard said often in regard to crusade ministry: *"What God calls for He pays for!"* The key is making sure Jesus—not me—is the One calling for it. He is the insightful CEO and resourceful CFO. He is the One who offers wisdom and favor, and opens and closes doors! And you can be sure if He is the One initiating the evangelistic crusade, or television program, or book, or any kingdom-minded project, then He will watch over it.

LITTLE BY LITTLE—HAVING THE STRENGTH TO STAND

I remember asking the Lord at the outset of launching Light of Life International for something concrete—a word, a verse, a passage of Scripture that would ground us in soul winning and build our faith for impacting cities and nations. I trusted He would open the pages of the Bible and lead us to something relevant and dynamic, something we could always point back to as foundational, motivational, even prophetic. He did, but it was to an obscure passage that I would never have thought about in terms of building a ministry. As it turned out, it could not have been more on target.

The passage is Exodus 23:29–30. It reads: "I will not drive them out from before you in one year, lest the land become desolate and the beasts of the field become too numerous for you. Little by little I will drive them out from before you, until you have increased, and you inherit the land."

This verse hit me hard and has proven true over the years. The context involves the Lord's strategy for the Israelites in stepping into the Promised Land. Yes, they would inherit their promise, but not all at once. Instead, God would go with them into the Land and drive out their enemies before them piece by piece. Why? So the Israelites could settle and grow—and not allow any part of the Land to become desolate or overrun by wild beasts.

What the Lord was essentially telling them was they were not big enough or ready yet to walk in the entire promise. This was not a rebuke or a disparaging commentary about them; it was the fact that the promise was bigger than what they could presently contain! It did not mean He would withhold it from them either. He pledged Himself to go with them to drive out the enemies. And through the process make them stronger and allow them to grow into and secure the Promised Land.

The more I thought about this verse, the more the Holy Spirit burned it into my heart as His strategy for Light of Life International. Instead of dropping it all into our lap at once, He pledged to parcel out our destiny piece by piece—so that we would not get overwhelmed or overrun. As I considered this, I found confirmation in Deuteronomy 7.

The passage is Deuteronomy 7:22. It reads: "And the Lord your God will drive out those nations before you little by little; you will be unable to destroy them at once, lest the beasts of the field become too numerous for you."

I knew the Lord was speaking something foundational to me through these two verses, so I kept asking Him to reveal more and more of it. While praying about these two verses, I sat in on a service to hear a French pastor-friend of mine speak on the life and dreams of Joseph.

He was speaking without a translator in English and said something like this: "Everyone sees themselves in the fulfilled promises to Joseph—the person who rose to the second most powerful position in the known world at that time. They identify themselves as the prince! But fewer people stop to consider: if that was true, would they be able to stand underneath the weight of it all?"

When I heard Pastor Daniel say having the strength to "stand underneath the weight of it all," it was like fire exploded inside me. Deuteronomy 7 and Exodus 23 started pulsating through my mind and the Holy Spirit said, *Stephen, little by little I want to bring you into the place of promise and purpose.* The reason was twofold: 1) so we could not say we did it or attained it—but it would be evident that this was the hand of God; 2) that we would have the strength of character to stand underneath the weight of all of it—and excel!

It occurred to me that in our fast-moving, in-the-moment culture,

God still cares a great deal about the process, and that wisdom cries out not to despise small beginnings. How many people have arrived at their place of destiny, influence, or financial blessing, but due to a lack of character or unseasoned fortitude, they crumbled into moral failure, spiritual disillusionment, or financial corruption?

The painful reality is such a collapse is all too familiar, and not only ruins their lives but impacts negatively those who prayed for or believed in them. And in some cases the impact is so painful, it would have been better if that person had never succeeded at all. This is not the plan of God for any of our lives.

The Holy Spirit is not in a hurry! He wants to bring us along at a pace that builds strength and character, coupled by a heart of gratitude and humility, so our success can be long-lasting and without a trace of reproach.

Small beginnings may sound old-fashioned, but if the promises of God for your life are big, then is it not worth letting Him fashion and forge in us faith, determination, and a hunger fueled by an eternal perspective? Yes it is! We need more than the strength to reach the promise; we also need the strength to stand under the weight of it and shine for the glory of God!

CHAPTER 5

IT'S NOT ABOUT ME!

IT HAD TAKEN twelve months. But now we had a crusade director, had registered Light of Life International, and had the support of our family and home church. Just one hurdle remained: Where do we go first?

As simple and harmless as that may seem, it would test the character between Dennis and me, and threatened to unravel everything we had started.

CHARACTER TEST WITH DENNIS

The phone rang. It was Dennis calling from Honduras. Our relationship was still brand-new, not yet eight months old. Besides a couple of services, some meals, and a lot of phone calls, we were still relatively unknown to each other.

Still, it had been enough to move forward and believe together to do something in Honduras. The question was where?

It made sense to start in Honduras. He lived there and we had met there. But I did not know the landscape of Honduras, let alone the costs, logistics, or time needed to organize such a large event. It left me unsettled.

The problem was I did not know if I could share that with Dennis. The last thing I wanted was to create tension, doubt, or sound like I lacked faith or resolve. So when he asked me where we should start, I did what most Texans would do: I chose the biggest city available!

I hung up the phone and something inside immediately began to ache. It was not physical in nature, just a deep-down sense that screamed *Uh-oh!*

I shared the conversation with Alisa and how wrong everything felt. I had just put us on the hook for an event in a city way too big for us. It was beyond our experience or budget, and even more alarming beyond what the Lord had called for.

Alisa handed me the phone. I needed to make things right immediately. I also repented before the Lord for pretending to know what I was doing and evaluating myself higher than anything couched in reality.

I remember walking into my bedroom and slowly closing the door behind me so I could make the call to Dennis. I knew the Lord had forgiven my pride and ignorance, but how would Dennis respond? I took a deep breath and dialed the number.

Even while the phone rang on the other end, the Holy Spirit was strongly urging me to humble myself and be fully transparent. Dennis answered and I leveled with him: The city was too big and the budget scared me. In fact, I knew nothing except that I had a burning desire inside my heart to serve Jesus in the nations.

What happened over those next thirty minutes was remarkable. The Holy Spirit enriched our friendship and sharpened our ministry focus. Instead of starting off with a bang in a big city, we would go to a smaller town on the northern coast of Honduras.

This time when I hung up the phone, everything felt different! We had passed a potentially crippling test of character and now sensed the release and blessing of the Lord to move ahead for Tela, Honduras.

NADAB AND ABIHU

From the very beginning, the Lord spoke strongly to me and Alisa about the foundation we were to build upon—reminders that ministry is not about us; it is all about Him. One of the most vivid lessons came out of the story of Nadab and Abihu (Leviticus 10:1–3).

It is a famous account because of how the Lord responded when they brought profane fire before Him. Sons of Aaron, these men were prominent before the people and served as priests before the Lord—until they were devoured by holy fire! So what happened and how does it help us today?

"Moses said to Aaron, 'This is what the Lord spoke, saying: "By those who come near Me I must be regarded as holy; and before all the people I must be glorified"'" (Leviticus 10:3). From the answer given by Moses, Nadab and Abihu died before the Lord because of two MAJOR miscalculations.

They Underestimated the Holiness of God

The beginning of verse 3 says: "By those who come near Me I must be regarded as holy." You would think this would not be an issue after their supernatural encounters with God. Walking across the Red Sea on dry land, the cloud by day and the fire by night, provision of manna for food, and sandals that did not wear out—they were living in the favor and blessing of the Lord.

They also were part of the leadership that responded to the divine invitation to come up on the holy mountain (Exodus 24). Nadab and Abihu joined Moses, Aaron, and seventy elders of Israel in meeting with God!

Yet despite the covenant meal on the holy mountain, the signs and wonders in the desert, not to mention the fire that fell from heaven during their priestly consecration—Nadab and Abihu failed to appreciate the nature and character of God. And they paid for underestimating the holiness of God with their lives.

They Overestimated Themselves Before the People

The end of verse 3 says that "before all the people I must be glorified." Put another way, God was saying: "This is not about you!" It did not matter if Israel gathered before them to worship or hear words of instruction—the reason for the gathering was the Lord! He alone was the One to receive the people's affection and esteem. Tragically, Nadab and Abihu forgot that the Lord shares His glory with no one. And it cost them their lives.

We have an open invitation to boldly draw near God, and we should! But I am reminded here that the character and essence of God is holy and an all-consuming fire. It is a powerful motivator to humble ourselves before Him and give Him honor.

We also have the privilege to communicate the Gospel to the world. And I am reminded that my character must reflect the same humility before the masses as it does before the Master!

It is a powerful motivator that whether we stand before one or one million, it is not about us! We are kingdom agents only, and our mission is to exalt the name of Jesus.

HELLO, RILEY!

We were getting closer to Tela, but two months before the crusade launch we had an even bigger first: the birth of our first daughter! Alisa had made it through the Texas summer heat and was ready to deliver Riley into the world.

We went in for Alisa's final check on a Thursday. Alisa had been told she would be induced the next day. She was certain she was having contractions. She told one of the ladies at the clinic, but no one took her seriously. One even said, "That's nice, honey!" As if to remind us that we were first-time parents and did not know what we were talking about. And honestly, besides the back pain she mentioned occasionally, Alisa was doing remarkably well.

But around four in the afternoon, Alisa's doctor entered the room, asked a few questions, and did a quick exam. I gathered my wallet and keys to pay and take Alisa home, and the doctor reminded us she would be on call tomorrow. We said okay and started to leave, when she suddenly said, "I want you guys to go straight to the hospital and check in. We will induce you in the morning!"

We were totally unprepared for her directive. Not only did we not have an overnight bag with us, we were not yet mentally or emotionally ready to check in for one of the biggest moments of our lives. Alisa was not looking forward to being induced, so we prayed—strength for the delivery, health for the baby, and the blessing of the Lord over our expanding family.

The first issue was dinner. We had not eaten since noon, as the original plan was to eat after our visit to the prenatal clinic. Over dinner we would talk about the next day and speculate how our lives would change. But it had not worked out that way. Instead, we were fasting dinner in a hospital room! The staff at first recommended Alisa not eat, but she was starving. And everyone knows not to mess with a hungry pregnant woman! So thanks to a kind nurse, Alisa feasted on half a sandwich from the hospital cafeteria.

Around 11 p.m. the nurses sent me home. Alisa said she was having contractions, but the chart said her induction was not scheduled until later the next day. So they sent me home, since it was going to be a big day tomorrow and Alisa needed me to be at full strength.

Alone at the hospital, an hour away from home (and me), Alisa was sure she was having contractions, despite what everyone else said. She called her mom. While her mom made the drive, Alisa's water broke! Sure enough, she was in labor.

I had just walked in the door at home when the phone rang. Her mom was on the line speaking very fast. The message was crystal clear: Get back up there! When I returned, Alisa had just received an epidural—not because she was sure she needed it, but because we had prepaid for it! In the middle of all the excitement, Alisa fell asleep.

At 5 a.m., the room included Alisa, me, and two midwives. Everything was moving very fast now. It was obvious there would be no inducement. The doctor on call would not make it either. I like to tell people I helped deliver Riley that morning, as I was much more involved in the process than I expected.

I had no idea babies are generally born with their faces looking down. But when Riley pushed through, she turned her head and we made eye contact! She may not have recognized me immediately, but we definitely connected. That first glimpse of her profile was one of the most beautiful things I had ever seen. She was born at 5:20 a.m., amazingly the date of our wedding anniversary and just over twelve hours after we left the prenatal clinic!

STEVE, NITA, AND COLOMBIA

One month after Riley's birth and one month before the Tela crusade, I headed to Medellin, Colombia, as a guest evangelist for Andrew McMillan. He was hosting a One Hope team—one that included a group from our church. That team included Steve and Nita New, two people the Lord would use mightily in growing and defining Light of Life International.

A huge heart for ministry, they had pastored young couples and college students, led evangelistic outreaches, and loved to pray! Smart, full of warmth, and passionate for Jesus, Steve and Nita walked into our lives at a divinely appointed time.

The week was filled with amazing times together, including a dinner that went four hours long! They told me more about where they came from, and I shared the word Suzette Hattingh had recently shared with me: not to settle as a professional pastor but to plow and pioneer!

One afternoon they came to my room to pray for an hour. The Holy Spirit moved powerfully in that place! I saw my roommate facedown between the two beds weeping, Nita lost in the presence of Jesus, and Steve pacing the room in declarative prayer. That one hour solidified what had been growing in my heart: Steve and Nita walked with the Lord, and He had assigned them to serve with us in Honduras and beyond.

ARROWS OF DELIVERANCE

On Sunday morning, Andrew and Kathy McMillan asked me to speak. Their church has a fiery passion for revival and evangelism, and by the thousands who attend the weekend services it was obvious the Holy Spirit was using them mightily in Medellin, Colombia.

The plan had Andrew translating first for Steve and Nita (greet the people), then I would deliver the message. That was until Steve shared a prophetic word from 2 Kings 13—that the arrow of deliverance had gone forth from there.

In the text, Elisha tells the king of Israel to take a bow and some arrows. He then places his hand on the king and tells him to shoot an arrow out the window. The king obeys and that arrow, Elisha tells the king, is the arrow of deliverance from Syria. He then orders the king to strike the ground with the remaining arrows. The king does it three times but then stops. Elisha angrily declares that because he did not strike five or six times, Syria would not be totally defeated.

Steve's prophetic word was this: They were already seeing the arrow of the Lord's deliverance go forth from their church, and now was the time to strike the ground and call upon the name of the Lord for Medellin. With an open heaven here and revival breaking out, Steve urged everyone not to grow comfortable with what they had experienced, because God had much, much more!

It was powerful. When I got to the podium to preach, I told the congregation the message from heaven had just been delivered! My job was to make sure we acted on it.

Andrew and I both fell to our knees and pressed our heads to the floor. Pounding the ground over and over again as a prophetic act of obedience, we cried to the Lord for our lives, the church, Medellin, and the nation of Colombia. People streamed to the altar, kneeling and praying. It was intense for many minutes, and then suddenly it exploded into celebration! It was as if the Lord poured out His pleasure in response to their cries. The warehouse that served as the church sanctuary flooded with rejoicing, dancing, and shouting. I love revival, and I love Jesus!

KING UZZIAH AND A DE-PRIDED HEART!

Another foundational passage for me and Alisa as we moved forward in crusade ministry was the story of King Uzziah in 2 Chronicles 26. The summary goes like this: He was a humble king who initially sought the Lord. The Lord prospered and helped him. Surrounded by talented people, he became established, his fame grew, and his kingdom grew strong. Then something went terribly wrong!

Verse 16 says when he became strong, his heart was lifted up to his destruction, for he transgressed against God by entering the temple of the Lord to burn incense on the altar.

Uzziah made the same mistake as Nadab and Abihu in underestimating the Lord and overestimating himself. Not satisfied with just being a powerful king, he arrogantly and wrongly determined he could enter the priesthood.

The Bible says the Lord struck him with leprosy, and he spent the rest of his life in an isolated house cut off from the throne and the house of God (vv. 20–21). What a tragic end to someone who had known the blessing of the Lord and walked in His favor. From watching the invisible hand of God work effectively in him to impact nations, to making blind and dangerous assumptions of his own position before the Lord. Ultimately, the same pride that seized the heart of Satan captured the heart of Uzziah, and he, too, was cast down!

The Bible reminds us that "God resists the proud, but gives grace to the humble" (1 Peter 5:5). If we are going to walk in the favor and blessing of the Lord, our hearts must be de-prided!

The word *humble* here means "trustful dependence" on God. Or said another way: "He gives grace to those who are trustfully dependent upon Him!" I learned this with the Tela crusade. In presenting my heart and hopes to Him, He worked character in my life *and* took care of every detail for the crusade!

The word *humble* here also means "to know the truth about yourself." An amazing thing happens when I get real with God—it is often the first time I'm real with myself. So in quieting ourselves before the Lord and allowing the Holy Spirit to search the depths of our heart, the result is often revelation. And discovering the truth about ourselves brings freedom and humility.

This is one of the reasons I love meeting with God in secret, because He heals me, restores me, forgives me, protects me, encourages me, sings over me—all because He loves me! This intimacy demands truthful dependency and humility, but it preserves us from pride because our delight is in Him and not ourselves.

God has a mighty plan for our lives. But remember: He does not share His glory with anyone. He is the One who raises men and women to prominence and power, but He is also the One who lowers and takes it away. The key is to live de-prided before the Lord and everyone else.

TELA CHOIR PRACTICE

A year and a half after we had left CfaN, ten people, including Steve and Nita, boarded an American Airlines flight with me routed for Honduras. Full of anticipation, we arrived in San Pedro Sula and rode with Dennis to the coastal town of Tela. What had been a dream in our hearts was now fully alive!

Our first night in Tela, we enjoyed a short meet and greet with several of the local pastors. Steve introduced the team and I thanked them for their partnership in declaring the Gospel. At the end they had a special treat: a performance from part of our crusade choir. We walked outside and under the pavilion one hundred voices cranked out a full-blown worship service! They sang their hearts out, and it electrified my soul as I thought about the coming weekend.

It came as no surprise to hear the testimony from a week earlier with an English lady. She had come to Tela to party (not a surprising revelation, as people often flooded this beach destination) and to get away from her Christian family.

One night she heard music and voices. Even though it was in Spanish, some of it seemed familiar. Curious, she made her way down the street to the pavilion where the choir was practicing outside.

It was more than a group of people preparing for some kind of performance; this choir sang with heartfelt devotion. The Holy Spirit fell on her right there, and she broke into tears. No one had said anything to her! The song of the redeemed had triggered repentance in her heart.

As I heard this testimony, it hit me: We had not even arrived and the Holy Spirit was already drawing people to Jesus!

TELA TELEVISION

One thing I had not factored in to my preparation for the crusade week was going on local television and doing interviews. l had absolutely no experience in front of a TV camera—only sitting in a studio and watching Reinhard. But that had been in the United States, not in Honduras. Dennis seemed totally unfazed by the invitation, so I breathed in and asked myself what would Reinhard do?

I made it to the top floor of the building where the television station was located. I would be doing two interviews: a Christian broadcast, then live on the 6-o'clock local news. The first interview would last twenty-five minutes.

I recognized the problem immediately: I was sitting on the couch next to the host! I would not have thought about it except I made the mistake of looking at the television monitor that showed real-time broadcast. The host was tanned, maybe 5' 3" and looked fabulous on the screen. But at 6' 3" and 200-plus pounds, I looked like a gorilla sitting by him.

After the first interview, the set transformed. The host and couches disappeared and the anchor and news desk rolled in. The anchor explained to Dennis that because it was a live interview on the local news, it would go quickly. And because of the staging, there would not be enough room for both of us on camera. So the solution was for him to stand off camera translating my responses.

The entire interview probably lasted less than five minutes. But in the middle of the Q & A, Dennis's mobile phone went off. I must have been the only one taken back by it as Dennis relayed my answer off screen and the anchor continued with his next question. Instead of turning it off or putting it on vibrate, Dennis let it ring until he finished translating my answer, then answered the phone.

I'm sure that is not the way Reinhard or a studio in the United States would have done it, but we survived the first Honduras interviews. It was a lot of fun and we laughed about it on the way back to our villas.

MEETING PASTOR MISAEL ARGEÑAL

Dennis and I could see the dark clouds looming ominously in front of us as we drove the seventy-five minutes from San Pedro Sula back to Tela. It had my attention, because we were just several hours removed from our inaugural crusade service.

I was also reflecting on my lunch with Pastor Misael Argeñal. One of the leading voices and fathers to the nation of Honduras, it had been a huge honor to meet him. I recognized the authority and humility he carried the moment he walked in, and listened as he shared how revival had hit his church fifteen years earlier, and La Cosecha exploded from 200 people to 20,000!

He also shared his passion for crusade evangelism. Every year he held a large event in San Pedro Sula, the second largest city in the country, which attracted tens of thousands of people. But he also held multiple crusades in smaller venues around the country, always reaching for lost souls and crying out for Hondurans to turn to Jesus.

It had been a remarkable lunch. I left encouraged and grateful for his prayerful support. What a joy to meet with one of God's generals and have such an open and intimate time together! I had no idea then, but Pastor Misael would become a fatherly advisor and wonderful friend for us. The pieces to the puzzle were starting to be fitted together by the invisible hand of God.

Dennis drove us right into the middle of the rain. The road was not well lit or wide, for that matter, making it one of the more dangerous drives in Honduras. It only added to the unspoken anxiety in the car. *Surely we are not going to be rained out tonight?*

REBUKING THE RAIN

On the other side of the storm the LOLI team was at the house, watching it crouch closer. People were responding differently. A brand-new ministry on the verge of its first big evangelistic effort, there was a sense of excitement and expectancy. It had been building all week but now it had come under siege.

Some looked on with dismay. Others found a private place to pray. But Howard, a soft-spoken friend and counselor, reacted boldly. Filled with the spirit of prophecy, he walked to the balcony door, opened it, and moved outside. Striding by a pastor reading his Bible on the upstairs porch, he went to the outdoor railing. And in a moment of faith, he stretched out his hands and rebuked the storm. He shouted, "Stop! I command you to stop and turn away in the name of Jesus!"

Immediately he turned and, without looking, went back toward the door. Before the screen door closed behind him, the rain had completely stopped!

Dennis and I broke through the rain and arrived in Tela. We had a glowing report: The crusade was a go!

HOW MUCH VALUE DO YOU PLACE IN ONE SOUL?

Nearly a year and a half after serving Evangelist Reinhard Bonnke, the moment had arrived. At an old abandoned factory site, people were gathering to hear the Good News. The choir stood on two trailer beds, one on each side of the platform. I had no doubt they would sing their hearts out in leading those gathered into the presence of the Lord.

Dennis drove and I rode in the passenger seat. As we turned off the main road, I glimpsed the stage and my heart skipped. As we started driving alongside the crowd of people gathering, my mind began to flash back to Africa. I had often wondered about the people who came to the crusades in Nigeria. What was their story? What were they hoping for? Did they know Jesus? Now I wondered the same about the Hondurans.

We parked on the other side of the building, put on our suit jackets, and walked around to the back of the stage. The music was loud and the choir hopping! We made our way to the VIP seating area beside the stage and received enthusiastic greetings from pastors and team members. So much excitement! My senses seemed to be exploding at once. The dream was officially alive, and this was the first step into the rest of our lives.

I had a lot to learn. As much as I thought I was ready, when the microphone was pushed into my hand I felt somewhat overwhelmed. Standing before nearly 8,000 faces—the majority of them passionate to encounter the presence and power of God—I had to breathe under my breath: *Help me, God.*

I even had a heckler to welcome me! Situated to my left, a man screamed at me in Spanish during much of my message. Finally a pastor or usher led him aside, where a group of ministers prayed with him.

The moment came to cast the net for souls. The ushers had created a massive space for people to respond. They obviously had faith for half the city to come forward! I now felt pressure to fill the space. Suddenly the crowd seemed a mile away from the platform and completely detached from me. I wish I could tell you that thousands came to the altar that night to put their faith in Jesus Christ, that we ran out of space because of the massive response—but that is not what happened.

Instead, fifty-two people walked forward that Friday night. Panic rose inside my heart. Where was the big harvest of souls? In such a cavernous space, fifty-two individuals barely made a dent. I kept calling for people to come forward, but that was the final number for Friday night. It was less than what I had expected. I felt crushed and defeated.

Back at the house, the team encouraged me. There had been so much joy and celebration, but it felt like a flop. All that work and effort to reach this opportunity, not to mention the hope and expectations of the local pastors and our team, and the best we could do was fifty-two people? I took some comfort that we had a second crack at it the next night, and people offered hope by saying nice things like we were tilling up the ground for breakthrough, etc. I just hoped they were right.

I preached as hard as I could on Saturday night, even borrowing from one of the texts often used by Reinhard in Africa. Somehow the crowd had increased by a couple of thousand, and the time approached for me to cast the net for souls. Again there was a sizable space prepared by the ushers for the waves of souls that would be swept into the kingdom. I felt a knot of apprehension tighten in my stomach. This was what I wanted to be doing, right—calling people to Jesus?

No one moved when I made the invitation for salvation. I kept calling, and barely a trickle. I asked people to raise their hands who needed Jesus, and I was sure more people than were represented at the altar had at least done that. I did not know what to do, so I asked everyone in the crowd to pray with us. The crowd cheered when we said amen, and the worship team took off in a festive celebration. Several pastors shook my hand and thanked us for coming, but I wanted to disappear. I felt like I had failed as an evangelist. After all, how could you get excited over only sixteen people responding? Sixteen! It was impossible to explain away. Over 15,000 people for the two-night event, and fewer than seventy had asked Jesus into their heart. The numbers just seemed to mock me.

Alone in my room that night, having unloaded all my emotions and frustrations at the Lord, He responded by asking me a question. *How much value do you place in* one *soul?* Immediately everything came clear, and I broke under the convicting reality of the answer to His question.

One soul made His death worth it. One soul triggered rejoicing in heaven. One soul meant hell's loss and heaven's gain. One soul for Friday and Saturday *combined* meant the mission had been wildly successful and pleasing in His eyes.

I wept before the Lord, because His question about the value of one soul stood in stark contrast to the value I had applied to the weekend. I had seen the sixty-eight souls from a place of disappointment and underperformance. The Jesus perspective was different; it had nothing to do with me!

I had an assignment to preach the Gospel; the results were the work of the Holy Spirit. Instead of evaluating myself based on the number of people who came forward, I was free to rejoice and cheer for every person saying yes to Jesus. The answer behind the question had been clearly delivered: It was not about me—it was all about Him!

I will always be grateful for the lesson the Lord taught me that weekend. It is so easy to fall under the temptation of elevating ourselves because of the size of the crowd, or grade ourselves on the measure of success we see. But as kingdom agents, it is not about us. Our place is to walk humbly before God and others, and regardless of the response or outcome, the glory belongs to Him alone.

HUMAN-MADE THINGS IN HEAVEN

It is an awesome thing to consider the fingerprints of God. We see His handiwork on display everywhere—in creation, in human history, and in our personal testimonies. But what if you reversed it? What kind of human influence or design will we see in heaven?

Here human ingenuity is seen in things like spiraling skyscrapers, works of art, or military weaponry. These, and many more, are remarkable human achievements. All of them, though, pale exponentially to the glories revealed in heaven.

It is hard to imagine any human fingerprints being seen in heaven. But without a doubt there is already one thing on full display: the nail scars and piercings on the feet and hands of the Lord Jesus Christ!

These human-inflicted wounds led to His death. It is the blood that flowed freely from these piercings that paid the price for our sins so that we might receive everlasting life! It is these scars that Jesus showed His disciples after His resurrection, and we, too, will see them when we behold Him.

The wounds of Jesus stand forever as a testimony of His amazing love for us. The Bible says: "God demonstrates His own love toward us, in that while we were still sinners, Christ died for us" (Romans 5:8). Amazingly, our human contribution to heaven is a vivid reminder of our depravity and the price He paid to freely offer us eternal life.

HURRICANE GAMMA

The team had spent the week sorting through boxes of food, clothes, diapers, and toys from a forty-foot container shipped to Honduras. The mission team and local pastors had divided into three groups, loaded up the four-wheel-drive trucks, and headed out.

On the last day of distribution, we ran into a problem: We had not given out all the food, clothes, and blankets. In fact, we had a large surplus—to the point no one could explain how we had so much left over. The team took inventory of the remaining items, organized them in a storage area, and gave the key to the local pastors association.

A week later Hurricane Gamma slammed into the coast of Honduras, leaving much of Tela underwater. But here is the amazing grace of God: Because the team had not given out all the contents brought in for distribution, the pastors had food, water, and other supplies on hand. They essentially became the first responders to an area in crisis. Some of the pastors even delivered supplies by canoe!

We learned from that initial distribution effort how to move supplies so that nothing gets wasted. I still wonder if the Lord in His providence didn't multiply the resources somehow so that the people could be cared for.

CHAPTER 6

COMMISSIONS AND CONFIRMATIONS

AS WE PRAYED about the second year, the challenge to believe for two crusades came alive in our hearts. It had taken nearly nine months to raise the funds, build a team, and finalize the logistics for Tela. So to do it again in about half the time—not just once but twice in a calendar year—held some risk.

But the more we prayed, the more our hearts burned to preach the Gospel. That led us to an area in the mountains of Honduras called Santa Cruz. There we would see and experience something remarkable and unprecedented.

TWO MEN AT A BUSINESS LUNCH

It had only been a few weeks into the New Year when a businessman offered to host a business lunch for Light of Life International. The building that housed his office also boasted a nice conference room and adjoining area where lunch could be served. He reached out to a couple of his contacts, and I invited the people who had supported us so far.

Forty-five minutes included a deli sandwich, a name tag, and a presentation from me. I had never spoken in a business lunch setting before, and the idea of pitching the next crusade like it was a product or investment option really made me uncomfortable. I stood in front of maybe a dozen men and shared my heart for evangelism, missions, and Jesus.

Despite one negative review, most of the guys shook my hand and encouraged me. I had survived my first business lunch! As the room cleared, a man in his thirties approached. We had never met but I liked him immediately.

He told me what connected us was a passion for Jesus. Then he said, "Stephen, I want to invest in the Santa Cruz crusade." His check was the largest donation to Light of Life International we had received to date. It meant so much for so many reasons. I threw aside the business formalities and hugged him, fighting back the tears!

Four of us remained in the room—the businessman who organized it, a friend of his, the Santa Cruz investor, and me. As I gathered my things to go, our host mentioned to his friend what had happened and casually suggested he should match it. It led to a few minutes of light-hearted banter back and forth between them, then it turned serious. He said, "Stephen, if you will meet me for lunch next week, I will match the donation!"

In an instant, the Lord had provided the funds to pay for the crusade. More than just a payment, it dramatically confirmed the calling on our lives. Santa Cruz was still a couple of months away, but the divine surprises had only just begun!

MIGHTY MAN OF VALOR

As the Lord was talking to me about great commissions and divine confirmation, I found myself reading the story of Gideon. It starts with God recruiting Gideon, revealing His plan, then releasing him to rescue the people from the Midianites (Judges 6). What a commission!

We first encounter Gideon hiding and fearful of his captors. Suddenly an angel appears and declares: "The Lord is with you, you mighty man of valor!" (v. 12) I am not sure if Gideon viewed himself as a fierce combatant, or as someone who had ambitions to do something great for God. But based on his reaction to the angel, he definitely didn't see himself as a candidate to rescue the nation!

He argues the Lord has forsaken them, delivering them into the hands of the Midianites. How different from the stories he had heard growing up about miracles, the Exodus, and his people inheriting the Promised Land. But where were these things now? The reply of the angel is direct and powerful: the Lord will be with you—and (essentially) you will be the miracle, you will do the miraculous, and you will rescue the people from their tormentors!

Gideon argues he is not the person for the commission. Surely the angel knows that his family is the least of all the families of the tribe of Manasseh, and that he himself is the lowest of his own household! By Gideon's estimation, he clearly was unqualified and certainly incapable of being considered for such an assignment. He was the least of the least! But the angel had a different perspective: The Lord is with you, Gideon, and you will have great success!

Does this sound anything like a conversation you have had with the Lord over the assignment for your life? Is God recruiting you to be part of His rescue plans, but it all seems too big and overwhelming? It may be fear, a low appreciation of ourselves, or a blurred vision of what we could actually accomplish, but the result is we quickly dismiss ourselves as qualified candidates and want nothing to do with it at all.

But just as the angel declared to Gideon that the Lord was with him and that He saw Gideon as a champion, we, too, have the promise of

Jesus: that He will never leave us or forsake us. No matter how we view ourselves or the assignment, the Lord sees you us valiant and important to the advancement of His kingdom!

The amazing thing is: Our commission (like the summons received by Gideon) is urgent in the heart of God. But it is left up to us to determine if we will take action. The Lord committed Himself to Gideon, but it still required action from Gideon. With all the promises and purposes of God hanging over his head, he still could have walked away from the commission—and missed out on destiny. But the instant Gideon acted and cut down the pagan altar, God released a destiny in him that not only brought salvation to the nation, but peace in the Land for forty years.

Yes, it can seem outlandish that God would want to recruit us to impact lives—even nations. But just as He nudged Gideon toward his destiny, the Lord wants to move you and me into the Great Commission and a potent destiny.

The Lord has committed Himself to us. As you step out to share the Good News, all of heaven lines up behind it with supernatural power! He goes before you and walks beside you to show Himself strong.

Jesus is the miracle worker, and you can be His miraculous testimony today. You can walk in His miraculous power because, like Gideon, the Lord is with you, mighty man and woman of God! So take courage: You have a life to live, a destiny to discover, and a message to proclaim.

PRONOUNCED "LOWLY"

With the finances in place for Santa Cruz, we set our hearts to fervently pray over this assignment: for souls, miracles, and an outpouring of the Spirit of God. The more we gathered to pray, the more our hearts united and the hungrier we became for Jesus to reveal His character and nature within us.

Something supernatural was stirring in our gatherings. And that was when the word came that defined everything about us moving forward—down to the absolute core and identity of Light of Life International.

From the very beginning, people started shortening Light of Life International to LOLI. The acronym sounded closer to the flat, rounded candy at the end of a stick (as in *lollipop*) than an international evangelistic ministry. We had not chosen or arranged the letters of the acronym, so we just smiled at the lollipop references and passed it off as if we were really very sweet.

One month before Santa Cruz, our team met at Steve and Nita's house to pray. As we were quietly waiting on the Lord, a team member prayed out these words: "Lord, have mercy on LOLI!" Such a plea would always be appropriate in a prayer meeting, but what made it exceptional was how he said it. Instead of pronouncing LOLI like a piece of candy, he said "LOWLY."

The moment I heard Joe say, "Lord, have mercy on lowly," it was as if a lightning bolt struck me. Immediately I heard the Lord say, *Stephen, that is exactly what I have called you and Light of Life International to be! You must be broken before Me, humble, hungry for my presence—you are called lowly.*

It burned in my soul! The call to live *lowly* was more than just a prophetic word, it became the identification of what He wanted us to be and how He wanted us to handle our assignments.

That night the Lord changed our name from suckers to servants. It is a daily call to character and a reminder that there are no superstars in the kingdom of God—except our Savior. To walk lowly invites His favor, blessing, and protection! The Holy Spirit was working on us and in us, which only fueled our anticipation for what lay ahead in Santa Cruz.

SLAVE OF MAN TO SERVANT OF GOD

The Lord wants to work His character and nature in us so we will be effective and powerful in the commission resting on our lives. The transformation of Onesimus in the book of Philemon is confirmation that we can trust the work of the Holy Spirit.

It started off badly for Onesimus. A discontent slave, he resorted to stealing from his master, then fled for his life. It was a dicey situation because of the consequences if caught. But then something wonderful happened: Onesimus encountered Jesus! No one could ever have imagined how the Holy Spirit would work it all out, but this was the first step toward dramatically turning his life around.

After encountering Jesus, the Holy Spirit crosses his path with the apostle Paul. What are the odds of that happening? Of all the people in the Roman world at that time, Onesimus bumps into Paul! Except with the Holy Spirit there are no coincidences, only endless possibilities. Nothing is impossible! Paul himself confirmed this in one of his letters: "He who has begun a good work in you will complete it" (Philippians 1:6).

Onesimus had encountered Jesus and been embraced by Paul, but his biggest test was still in front of him. Until he got honest with his past, his destiny was on hold. To break the haunting darkness, mature his walk in the Lord, and trigger the promises and purposes of God, Onesimus had to face Philemon—his lawful master.

What a tough decision, even with all the benefits! It was nice that Paul wrote a letter on his behalf and meaningful that Tychicus returned with him, but he was the one who had to make things right. How many times on the return trip did Onesimus face the temptation to do what he had done before—run? His decision and determination to follow through tested his character, humility, and trust in the leadership of the Holy Spirit!

We see similar tests in other biblical leaders, like Moses. Moses encountered the burning bush, then was sent back to Egypt to face his fears and failures. He did it and it triggered destiny and forged leadership. The same thing happened with Onesimus.

According to church history, Philemon forgave Onesimus. And if the Onesimus referenced by Ignatius (a second-century church leader) is the same man sent back by Paul (and that is certainly possible), then he became the bishop of Ephesus and the churches in that entire region. Wow, from thieving slave to trustworthy servant of God! This is the powerful leadership of the Holy Spirit. He is committed to healing your past, forging your character, and commissioning you into a powerful Gospel destiny.

ALLIGATORS AND DUCKS

Our team grew to thirteen people for the second Honduras crusade. Our hotel sat on the shoreline of Lake Yojoa, with the beautiful mountains sitting on the other side. The breaking news the first couple of days concerned an alligator and some ducks.

The momma had spotted the alligator sneaking up on the babies, and made a lot of noise to warn the ducklings. But when one of the babies tried to get away under the water, the alligator went after it. Not only did the baby fail to return to the surface, but when the momma went in after the alligator, she did not come back up either.

I probably heard that story a dozen times during the Santa Cruz week. I laughed when I found out one of the pastors planned to use it in an upcoming message.

SANTA CRUZ TELEVISION

While the team concerned themselves with ducks and alligators, Dennis, Steve, and I returned to San Pedro Sula to have lunch with Pastor Misael Argeñal. He invited us to join him the next morning to promote the crusade on his national TV program.

On the program, I talked about Africa and answered a few questions about how we arrived in Santa Cruz. His endorsement of our ministry and encouraging everyone in the area to attend the weekend crusade blessed us tremendously.

The following day, we received an invitation from a local TV station to come for an interview. It was a far cry from what we had experienced the day before with Pastor Misael.

Dennis, Steve, and I arrived at a tiny country house that had a satellite dish in the backyard. I was pretty sure we had the wrong place, but the person at the door told us the station was in the shed, behind the house, next to the dish. I knew right then things might not go as smoothly or be as polished as the day before.

The shed-station was literally a concrete shell. We walked across the backyard and reached the one door in and out. It was padlocked! So while the man scampered off to find a key, we stood in a stranger's backyard. Several minutes passed, and a new man appeared to let us in.

Inside revealed two narrow rooms. The man went to the right, where the gear and electronics were set up. The room in front of us had a bright light overhead, one glass table, two chairs, one camera—and no host.

The obvious answer at that point was to shake hands with the guy who let us in, and flee. But apparently this guy carried director-type status. He told us to set up and do our own program.

I laughed. I could count on one hand the number of times Steve and

I combined had been on television. The idea of us pulling anything off that looked professional was impossible.

Steve and I set the two chairs behind the table at the end of the narrow room. With a blank wall behind us, it was a tight fit to get us both situated behind the small table. Dennis stood to the side of the camera to ask questions in Spanish, then translate our answers.

It was a comedy of errors. Trying to move subtly in a cramped space, we almost knocked the table over in front of us. But the awkward part came waiting for Dennis to finish translating the answers or formulate a question. With nothing to say or do, we just sat as still as possible, under the blinding light, and smiled awkwardly at the camera and each other.

SANTA CRUZ DISTRIBUTION MIRACLE

During the week, we kept hearing beautiful testimonies from the compassion teams. My favorite was from a couple of team members who climbed a hill to see if anyone was home in a tiny shack.

They encountered a man overwhelmed by stress and despair. With his wife in a hospital, his kids hungry, and him unable to find food, he had been behind his home, in the backyard, pleading with God for mercy.

So when two of the short-term missionaries arrived with bags of groceries, it was a dramatic moment. The man crumbled to the ground at their feet absolutely overcome by emotion. For them to be standing in front of him with food—at the exact time he was begging God for help—was a miracle!

It was also a strong reminder that God did care for him and his family. Of course, sensing this was the invisible hand of God at work, the two team members headed back down the hill to the truck and returned with enough supplies to last his family a couple of weeks.

THE DEMONIAC TRANSFORMATION

One of my favorite stories of personal transformation, and the unquenchable fire that was lit in the heart of the most unlikely of candidates, is found in Luke 8:26-39. It is the story of a wild man and his radical encounter with Jesus.

Named Legion because of the hordes of demons controlling him, they drove him to the wilderness and into tombs, naked and alone. Seized and bound in chains and shackles by fearful citizens of the area, their attempts to control him failed as he would break out and terrorize the people. In darkness, he often cried out in pain, mutilating his own body trying to destroy the power that was within him.

What a vivid picture of the plan of Satan for our lives. The Bible says he comes to steal, kill, and destroy (John 10:10), and that certainly was true with Legion. But his life was about to improve dramatically with the arrival of Jesus. This demonized man, certainly against the will of the demons inside him, runs down the hill to Jesus. (Indeed, God has put within the heart of every person a desire to know Jesus, a desire to be free from the pain, torment, and bondage. This is one of the reasons the Gospel is so very powerful—Jesus attracts people!)

In the presence of Jesus, the demons were terrified! These Satanic agents who despised and abused this wild man knew the purpose and power of Jesus—and they immediately submitted to His authority. This is always the case with the demonic. There is only one Lord, one King, one Master—the Lord Jesus Christ! The Bible declares: "At the name of Jesus every knee should bow . . . every tongue should confess that Jesus Christ is Lord" (Philippians 2:10, 11).

Jesus is magnificent in this story. Everyone else saw a troubled man running down the hill toward them—everyone except Jesus. While some were probably ready to get in their boats and leave immediately, Jesus saw and welcomed a transformed life, an overcomer, and one who would shake cities through the power of his testimony!

This is exactly what happened. The power of Satan broken, Jesus immediately speaks purpose and direction into his life: "Return to your own house, and tell what great things God has done for you" (Luke 8:39). He did that! He took the commission and not only returned home, but traveled through the ten cities on the eastern side of the Sea of Galilee proclaiming the tremendous things Jesus had done for him (Mark 5:20). And the Bible notes that those who heard his testimony marveled.

This is the essence of Christianity: Jesus changes lives! Who would ever have imagined a man so wild and demented would become such a powerful voice for the love and compassion of God? Jesus did!

The same is true for us: He sees things in all of us that no one would ever see or believe. He holds the power and authority to touch and transform us, to commission and empower us. The confirmation is: Those who see or hear the report of what He is doing will marvel.

AS IF ANGELS WERE STANDING ON THE SOCCER WALLS

If the prayer times we had experienced throughout the week had any bearing on Friday and Saturday night, then we were in for something supernatural. His presence and power had continually washed over us as a team, leaving us in awe of Jesus and a hunger to see it poured out upon the people of Santa Cruz.

We arrived to a walled soccer field, jam-packed with people. Venders lined up outside the walls selling food and drinks, while inside families sat on the grass eating and laughing. On a much smaller scale, it reminded me of Africa. People came from all over, including those who had to walk down mountains, find a bus stop, and catch a ride to Santa Cruz. People were filled with anticipation. It was a festive atmosphere.

We were dropped off on the opposite side of the platform. So we looped behind and encountered about a dozen intercessors crying out to God in a wide circle. Some were praying intensely for the service, some singing and worshiping quietly, others on their faces in the grass seeking the Lord. The moment my feet stepped inside that area, fire raced up and down my spine. It was so intense, it actually stopped me for a couple of seconds, sharpened my focus and awareness of Jesus, then released me onward. It was an instant reminder that the Lord was here. This was holy ground!

I listened as the chorus "Let It Rain" rang out in Spanish, and worship deepened. Steve invited the team on the platform. On our knees, we asked the people to pray for us, for the messages, the weekend, for Santa Cruz. Something was brewing.

I spoke on the familiar passage of Elijah and Mount Carmel (1 Kings 18). The key word in the text that night was *"all* the people drew near to [Elijah]." The call went out for everyone to kneel in corporate recognition of the lordship of Jesus. The field was full of people on their knees! The crowd repeated my prayer of repentance, and we presented Santa Cruz and the surrounding mountain areas to Him.

The people started singing "Hallelujah," and the glory and holiness of His presence fell. People in witchcraft and darkness started reacting, but Jesus brought deliverance and salvation!

The presence of the Lord was so powerful on the stage that I urged the crowd to keep singing, because it was as if the angels were standing on the soccer walls and the mountains beyond that crying out with us in worship. Heaven was touching earth!

I had intended on preaching a second short message on the fire of God, but it was so intense and holy. So I called for the pastors and team to line up in the front of the stage and released them to move among the people, laying hands on them in the name of Jesus as they went.

The power of God fell with such intensity! Then joy flooded the stadium, and the people started to celebrate. The choir of nearly four hundred voices started jumping and dancing, then took off on a victory lap around the stadium. Can you imagine thousands of people shouting, singing, dancing, rejoicing, and celebrating—all in wonder of the Lord Jesus Christ? Amazing, yes, wonderful absolutely, and it was only the first night! But what would happen the next night—Saturday night—would dramatically impact my life and our ministry forever.

CALL FOR INTERCESSION

On Saturday night, we arrived to the outer walls lined with vendors selling drinks and food. People were everywhere. Worship drew the people inside the walls, and the energy and anticipation of the crowd continued to build.

I walked around behind the platform and my heart stirred for the men and women praying. Each of them had sacrificed the festivities happening on the other side of the platform to pray for the people and their communities.

As soon as I received the microphone, I asked for the intercessors to join me on the platform. It was not part of the schedule but I wanted to do something to say thank you. They lined up behind me as best they could. I asked the people in the crowd to stretch out their hands and pray for the intercessors. Not just with casual effort, but with urgency and purpose.

As the crowd stretched their hands toward the stage and began praying *for them*, the power of God fell. Steve, Nita, and other LOLI team members only touched them on the head or shoulder and all of them collapsed to the ground at once. The entire stage was littered with bodies as the intercessors lay on the stage, out under the presence of the Lord!

Something supernatural was happening. As I looked out over the crowd, I cried: "Who will take up the call for intercession?" Hundreds started hurrying to the front of the platform and fell on their knees and faces. People started calling on the name of the Lord at the altar, from the platform, everywhere! The crusade had suddenly turned into a gigantic prayer meeting!

Steve took the microphone and started crying out verses of Scripture for victory and breakthrough over sickness and darkness. Meanwhile, on my knees at the edge of the platform, I heard the Holy Spirit whisper, *Call for the miracles!*

I had never called for miracles before. But this was not a suggestion—it was an executive order! My job was to call for miracles. So I stood up and did exactly that: "If the Lord Jesus has touched you supernaturally, come to the side of the stage." People started coming immediately.

THE GOD OF AFRICA IS THE GOD OF LATIN AMERICA

One of those who came forward was a young girl carrying crutches. Hit by a bus, the driver had not stopped, leaving her hurt on the side of the road. In pain and in need of crutches to move around, she could never have imagined how the Lord was going to turn such evil into praise.

She explained that during the service, something like fire had rushed through her body, and the pain left instantly. Aware that something had happened, she tried to stand up—then started walking! When the call for miracles rang out, she was one of the first to respond.

They brought her on the platform to share her testimony. I picked up one of the crutches and moved to the far side of the stage. I asked if she could walk pain free, and she quickly closed the distance between us. She reached me and, overwhelmed, buried her head into my left shoulder and chest. It was a God moment!

I had this picture hanging in my office for years afterward: my left arm wrapped around her, and my right hand stretched straight out from my body, lifting up the crutch she no longer needed. I would tell people who asked about it that two supernatural things happened at that moment: one for her and one for me.

One, it was a miracle. The Lord had restored her and she could walk, run, and jump pain free. We could rejoice together, as it was also one of the earliest miracles we had seen in LOLI. But what made it unforgettable was that at the exact moment she hugged me, the Lord dropped a radical word into my heart. He said, *Stephen, the God of Africa is also the God of Latin America!*

What a loaded statement! How many times had I seen the invisible hand of God move miraculously and supernaturally in Africa? But that was with Reinhard—one of the generals of our generation in front of hundreds of thousands of people. Here in the hills of Santa Cruz, it was a different nation, certainly a much less seasoned evangelist, and a smaller crowd. But I was where God had called me, doing what God had pushed me to do, and all I knew was since Tela, my heart had been screaming to see His Spirit poured out in our gatherings. It did not matter if anyone heard about us or remembered us after we were gone. I just wanted the people of Santa Cruz, Honduras, to know they had encountered the presence and power of the Lord Jesus Christ!

To hear the Holy Spirit say, in the middle of a supernatural testimony, that the God of Africa is also the God of Latin America impacted me profoundly. More than just affirmation, it was His personal promise: that what I had seen in Africa would be seen in Latin America too. He was telling me plainly: *My power isn't geographically challenged!*

AN ASSASSIN'S BACK

Another who came to testify was a professional assassin. He hurt his back several months earlier and had since drained his resources visiting doctors and taking all kinds of medicines. None of it had helped. Unable to work and without any money, he had come to the crusade Saturday night as an act of desperation. He was hoping for a miracle.

I had seen the Lord heal nonbelievers in Africa. A Muslim with a withered hand suddenly could stretch it out pain free and fully operational. Testifying, I would listen to an unbeliever say, "If Jesus can touch my body, then what about my heart—what about my soul?

That is exactly what happened to this hit man. The Lord had suddenly healed his back in the middle of the service. But instead of escaping with the miracle he hoped for, he did not want to leave. That is when the second miracle happened: He asked God to forgive him and for Jesus to take the reins of his life.

ANNA'S ROPES

When it was time to leave, two things happened. One, I noticed that a lady who suffered torment because of the occult had been set free. Everyone on the team knew her, because on Friday night she arrived with her hands bound by ropes, escorted very closely by her father on one side and brother on the other. Her name was Anna.

The reason for the ropes was that she often became uncontrollably violent, to the point she had literally torn their house apart. No father wants to put ropes around the hands of his daughter, but as a last resort, he had done it for her protection as well as the rest of the household.

I cannot think of a more graphic depiction of the Satanic plan for our lives—to be dominated by torment and darkness. The Bible says he comes to steal, kill, and destroy, but Jesus has come that we might have life—and life more abundantly!

The breakthrough came that Saturday night. Members of the team had made it a point to fast and pray that morning and afternoon for Anna, and to see her transformed bolstered their faith.

THE HONDURAN SOLDIER

By the time I had taken note of the celebration with Anna and the people around her, I was off the stage and on my way toward the vehicle. I had almost reached it, when a man with a gun strapped around his neck and shoulders stepped in front of me.

There were two of them, actually—Honduran soldiers hired for event security. He looked at me and said, "I have never seen anything like this before!" This is the power of the miraculous—it points people to Jesus.

This soldier had listened to the testimonies and watched the power of God sweep over the soccer field. Something had started burning deep inside of him. He asked if I could pray for him to receive Jesus into his life. In front of the other soldier and with his hand resting on his weapon, the young man said yes to the Lord Jesus Christ.

As we drove away, we were overwhelmed with what the Lord had done. From the very beginning we had sensed a divine commission to go to Santa Cruz, and had seen the Holy Spirit confirm it over and over again. It was only the second crusade but it was becoming clear the Lord was leading us somewhere. It was as if He was telling us: *I am going into Honduras and Central America and you are invited to come.*

We could never have grasped what that meant at the time. But we did know this: We were hungry for more and would follow Him anywhere!

CHAPTER 7

SOCCER ACCIDENTS AND PROPHECIES

WE CLOSED OUT THE YEAR with another Honduras crusade. Alisa and I could hardly believe we had grown from one crusade to two in a calendar year. Yet as we prayed, we sensed the Holy Spirit stretching us to reach for more: from two to three crusades in the coming year!

We soon discovered this third year would be more than expanding our reach and vision. It would be a prophetic and deeply personal revelation of who He had called us to be.

THE BAY ISLAND BOMBSHELL

It started with a scouting trip. Steve, Dennis, and I returned to Santa Cruz to see the pastors again and learn what had happened in the aftermath. As we finished eating, one of them asked, "What about next year?" We had no idea, but that was why we were in Honduras—to set aside a couple of days to pray and follow up on a contact in the Bay Islands.

If everything went smoothly, we envisioned doing our fourth campaign in Roatan. The pastor replied immediately, "You should pray about doing a crusade in Tocoa!" I had never heard of the place. Besides, our thoughts were already moving toward the Bay Islands.

The next day, Dennis, Steve, and I drove the three hours from San Pedro Sula to La Ceiba. There we boarded the ferry from mainland Honduras across to Roatan. Things were going even better than we had hoped! We had spent time in the hotel pool dreaming about the future, Steve had filled his plate with lobster tails over dinner, and a drive around the island confirmed what we already thought: The Bay Islands was where we needed to be next year!

The next morning we met with a highly successful businessman. He also served as an influential pastor. His approval would be the green light for next year.

He warmly welcomed us into his home. He spoke of the spiritual and personal needs of the islanders. But about coming to Roatan, he said NO. Nothing personal or meanspirited, just no.

How could the answer be no? We had come here because we knew the answer would be YES! I was shocked, confused, reeling—all in the same moment. And that is when he dropped the biggest bombshell of all. The pastor looked at us and said, "Where you really need to go is Tocoa!"

Tocoa? I felt like someone had just thrown cold water in my face. Could it be we had come out to the island for a divine redirect? Two pastors who had never met each other had urged us to consider a place we had never heard of. Surely this was the invisible hand of God directing us.

It was lunchtime, and the challenge for Steve and me was simple: We were flying home tomorrow! Yet we had just received a supernatural commission to go to Tocoa. I started trying to connect the dots.

Option one: We were on an island, sitting in a pastor's home, one hour from the mainland. From there it would be three hours by car to get back to San Pedro Sula and fly home tomorrow. That made for a full day ahead of us. However, what if we opted not to head back immediately? What if after disembarking from the ferry, we made for Tocoa instead?

Option two: Driving two hours in the opposite direction of San Pedro Sula. It meant getting off the boat, driving to a place without any advance preparations or contacts, seeing what happens, then driving five hours home in the dark.

And if you know anything about the roads in Honduras outside the big cities, then you know the last thing you want to be doing after the sun goes down is driving! There are no lights, no shoulders, and it is not uncommon for horses or other animals to get hit after wandering onto the roads. Unmarked potholes and rocks slides, all in the middle of nowhere, only makes driving more risky.

It was impossible—except everything inside all three of us screamed, *Go! Go! Go!* So coming into agreement that this was the nudge of the Holy Spirit, we headed for the ferry to cross back over to the Honduras mainland.

TOCOA DRIVE OF FAITH

We raced off the boat, jumped in the SUV and started toward Tocoa. Steve and I drove while Dennis started making phone calls. With no contacts or meetings, it was a drive of faith and obedience.

Two hours later, all we had was the name of the church pastored by the president of the local evangelical association. It was late Saturday afternoon and we were a long way from home. Dennis had left multiple messages on the one number we had, and we arrived as strangers in Tocoa.

Steve pulled the car to the curb of one of the side streets running away from the main road that cuts through the center of town. Out our front windshield stood the main gas station in Tocoa, seemingly our next stop to refuel before we turned around to drive the five hours back to San Pedro Sula.

Surely we had not come all this way by mistake. So sitting in the car, we started to pray for divine breakthrough. God help us!

I'm not sure who saw it first, but while we were praying a school bus pulled into the gas station for fuel. The sight of a bus in Honduras is not an uncommon thing, as it is one of their primary forms of transportation. But this was no ordinary bus, because painted boldly on its side was the name of the church we had been trying to reach!

What are the odds that while we sat stranded by the curb, praying for direction, a bus from our one contact would pull into the gas station directly in front of us? We didn't wait to figure it out.

The bus driver liked our story. He provided directions to the church and a name to ask for when we arrived. We pulled in to the church several minutes later wondering what would happen next.

The church contact listened and agreed it was worth calling the pastor—even on a late Saturday afternoon. Dennis went inside to talk to the pastor on the phone, while Steve and I prayed in the vehicle. He returned smiling. The senior pastor was on his way to personally welcome us to Tocoa, Honduras.

A few months later, we saw why the hand of God had nudged us to Tocoa. It was an appointed time of miracles, healing, deliverance, and salvation. Pastors united across denominational lines, and their example prompted a neighboring town to create its own gathering of pastors to pray.

It would be a week full of joy and celebration. None of it would have materialized unless two men had pointed us to Tocoa, a bus driver needed gas, and a pastor hungry for revival had left his house on Saturday afternoon to meet with three complete strangers. The invisible hand of God had orchestrated a miracle.

It should come as no surprise that before we left to return to San Pedro Sula, the Holy Spirit had something else for us. Or, more precisely, for me. And this surprise was deeply personal.

TRINITY UNIVERSITY SOCCER ACCIDENT

To understand the significance of what happened next you have to go back many years to when I played soccer on an intramural squad at Trinity University. Soccer was one of my passions growing up. Being tall, I was a natural target for teammates to kick the ball toward. In front of the goal, I could use my head to redirect the ball toward the open net.

I was a freshman in college, second semester, nineteen years old, and loved to compete. The team I played for had qualified for the playoffs and we faced a tough first-round matchup. It was against a group of guys whose fraternity was not recognized by the University, as their brotherhood projected an unsavory image of rebellious, rugged and crude behavior.

I remember the exact spot my roommate and I paused on the way to the soccer field to pray. We normally did not pray before team competitions, but we did that day. Specifically, we prayed for protection because of the thuggish reputation our of opponents, and we wanted to win.

The game was scoreless as we neared the end of the first half. Then one of the players on our team got behind the defense on the right sideline. I ran down the middle of the field, a step ahead of the nearest defender. As I approached the penalty box, my teammate sent a high cross from the right sideline in my direction.

I know this may seem unbelievable, but in the couple of seconds it took the ball to travel from my teammate's foot to where I was in the center of the field, I had processed a number of possibilities of how I should attack. Option one: Bring the ball to my feet. I immediately dismissed it on the grounds the goaltender could smother it or the defender tracking me downfield could clear the ball out of danger. Option two: Play the ball in the air by striking it with my head. This would eliminate the defender behind me from interfering and leave me one on one with the goaltender. If things went well I might get the ball past him clean, or with a bit of luck deflect it off his hands and into the net. So I chose option two.

As the ball neared, I turned my shoulders and neck to punch the ball as hard as I could with my head. Everything would be perfect, as long as the goaltender led with his hands. He didn't.

The good news: I hit the ball first. The bad news: I smashed the side of my face into the forehead of the goalie. It was a violent collision. He had arrived a fraction of a second too late, launching himself headfirst to clear the ball. So when my head came through the ball and continued its downward arch, he connected cleanly—not with the ball, but with my left cheekbone.

The collision knocked me flat on my back. It was no consolation I had actually scored—something was very wrong. Confirmation came a moment later when one of my jubilant teammates came over to help me up. He recoiled and started screaming for help. My face had imploded on the left side and blood was oozing from several places.

One of the people there made the executive decision that we did not have time to wait for an ambulance, and someone from the sideline rushed me to the ER.

There is a lot that could be said about that evening: ICU, bleeding on the brain, trauma to head, face collapsed, multiple bone fractures, concern over potential loss of memory, motor skills, etc. Nurses worried about concussions and coma, so sleeping seemed limited or closely monitored.

The doctors told my parents the first twenty-four hours were the most critical because of the bleeding on the brain. Who knew the brain could actually swell to the point it could kill you?!

Perhaps the first of many miracles was how little pain I felt from the moment the collision occurred. Evidently, the nerve endings in my face had been crushed so badly I did not feel anything, only a terrible sense of confusion and fog.

The first person to visit me at the San Antonio hospital was my senior pastor. He called my parents in Fort Worth, held my hand, and declared life over me. I was scared, but he comforted me.

HOSPITAL ROOM ENCOUNTER

I will never forget that night. I didn't want to die. I didn't want to be deformed. I didn't want to live with scarring on my face. I didn't know what they meant by phrases such as "loss of memory" and "slurred speech," but I didn't want that either.

If I made it through the night, how many surgeries would it take to fix me? Would it hurt? How many semesters would I miss? Could I ever play sports again? At nineteen years old, all by myself in a hospital room, I was unsure of what the future held. I was totally overwhelmed.

That is when something amazing happened. The sweet presence of Jesus filled up the room in a real and intimate way. It was not that He had not been there all along—He had certainly. But my awareness of His presence suddenly heightened dramatically. It was like He walked into my room, closed the door, and sat down on the edge of my bed. He wanted to talk!

That night, I had one of the most profound experiences of my life. I knew He was sitting on the edge of the bed looking at me, comforting me. No, I could not see Him, but every bit of me was keenly aware that I was not alone. I knew He loved me.

Suddenly everything would be okay—physically, emotionally, spiritually. It was as if He said, *Ask Me whatever you want*. I unloaded my fears and questions. The more I asked, the more I became aware of His closeness. His presence was my answer!

Nothing had changed on the outside, but everything had transformed inside. My perspective, my outlook—I had peace and a hopeful confidence! From that point, things quickly (even miraculously) began to improve.

BONES POPPING BACK IN PLACE

A couple days later, Mom and Dad drove me home. For the next few weeks, I lay in bed gathering strength and readying myself for reconstructive surgery. I had made it past the critical life-and-death phase, but half my face was still imploded. I had no idea at the time, but my parents were spending countless hours pacing the hallway outside my bedroom while I slept, crying out to God for grace and mercy on their son. Thank God for the relentless prayers of the righteous!

The day of surgery finally arrived. The plan was for the doctor and his medical team to "pop" my face out, then insert metal plates to support the orbital ridge beneath my eye. Somehow the metal, bone, and everything else in there would all fuse together and in time become stronger than before the accident.

The doctor was more than happy with how the several hours of surgery went. He told my parents it had been a medical success, but as a Christian, he had something else he needed them to know. In all his years of practice, he had never seen a surgery like this one. In the middle of it, the tiniest of bone fragments started popping back into place. He described it as the hand of God working with them to restore the smallest of breaks.

Despite cutting through my mouth, my eyebrow, and below the eye for surgery to pull out my face, the bones had reset and there had been zero damage to my left eye! Back at home, the recovery only accelerated. The scarring disappeared. And no, the plates did not set off the security alarms whenever I passed through the airport metal detectors.

In less than three months everything had returned to normal. Now it was a challenge to guess which side of my face had experienced trauma. It was a miracle! The Lord had preserved my life, revealed His compassion, and healed my body.

A LETTER AND MEETING IN THE GYM

The Gospel is so powerful, all we have to do is get it out there and the Holy Spirit does the rest. That first night in the hospital I felt driven to write a letter to the guys in the underground fraternity. To tell them that no matter what happened to me tonight or in the days and weeks to come, I held no ill will in my heart toward them. I think it was as much a divine directive to keep me from letting a root of bitterness set in as it was to let them know (especially the goaltender) that they would be in my thoughts and prayers.

My roommate, who had prayed with me before the match, took the letter back to campus. He called on friends to gather to pray for me in our dorm and sent word to the underground fraternity that I had written them a letter.

The curious thing was the letter, coupled with my roommate's boldness, resulted in open doors for the Gospel, as some of the roughest and wildest guys on our campus turned up for a prayer meeting!

When it had finished, their representatives took the letter and left. The stage was now set for an even more dramatic encounter a few months later.

I was so happy to be back on campus that fall. Despite the prognostications that I would miss a year of school, my life had returned to normal. I was once again just one of many students getting up early, walking to class, grabbing lunch, and heading off to the library to study.

One afternoon I decided to go work out at the gym. I walked into the weight room and it was almost completely empty. Except for one other guy finishing out his reps, no one else was in the room. I was ready to get started, when the guy turned around. The nanosecond I saw his face, I recognized him immediately and emotion rushed over me. It was the goaltender who had put me in the hospital.

I started walking straight at him. I knew he recognized me. With just two of us in the room, I'm sure he was thinking I intended to punch him. But I was not angry. Instead, as I closed the distance, I blurted out, "I have been praying for you all summer!"

And it was true. I had relived the scene on the soccer field a zillion times. But it had resulted in a letter that expressed forgiveness, a prayer meeting that drew believers and nonbelievers, given me a focused prayer list, and now the opportunity to share my testimony.

There in the gym, I told him how the Lord had watched over me from the field to the hospital through surgery and recovery. He knew what I looked like on the field and he could certainly see the evidence that my words were true. The Lord Jesus had indeed watched over me!

THE TOCOA PROPHECY

That accident had happened seventeen years ago. Now shaking hands with the Tocoa pastor, I was wondering if we had enough daylight to check out a potential venue.

It was a nearby soccer field, enclosed by stands for fans to watch the local team. I walked to the middle of the field while Steve and Dennis fanned out to pray. Just a few hours ago we were on an island wondering why the door had been slammed closed, and now we had clarity of direction and a rising anticipation in our hearts.

I drifted toward the stands and sat down. Looking over the field I could see both guys prayer walking, taking mental inventory of what had happened, and dreaming over our upcoming fourth crusade.

It was almost time to leave. Steve came over and sat down to my left as the last streaks of light started to fade. I asked him what he was hearing, expecting something similar to what I was processing in my own heart. It was much more than that.

Yes, the Lord had been talking to Steve, but not about the venue or town. Instead, he had something to share with me—something deeply personal and potentially defining for LOLI as we moved forward.

He had my complete attention. Alone in the bleachers, looking at the mountains beyond the walls, I waited to hear what had dropped into his heart. I knew Steve heard the voice of the Lord, and I trusted that. I also knew he didn't say something unless he honestly believed it himself.

He paused, then unloaded: "Stephen, the enemy tried to take your life on a soccer field several years ago but failed. And now the Lord is going to use you on soccer fields all over Honduras and Latin America to declare salvation to the lost, hurting, and dying!"

I breathed out. The words had fire in them and brought a rush of emotion. I had never made a connection between what happened so many years ago to what we were doing now.

The accident had almost totally disappeared off my radar! But both the accident and two of our first three soul-winning campaigns had been on soccer fields. It reminded me of how gracious Jesus had been to me then and the amazing grace He was showering on us now.

To sense the Lord's purpose and pleasure while sitting there in the stands was humbling. I had no idea then just how amazing the journey would become or the pinpoint accuracy of the words shared by Steve. What I did know was this: I wanted only to say YES to Jesus and share His testimony wherever He led.

HICCUPS TO PERSONAL REVIVAL AND BREAKTHROUGHS

The Holy Spirit has come to fill our daily lives with power, divine presence, and a zeal for today! This life-fueling relationship draws our gaze upon Jesus and floods our soul with fiery passion and motivation to live for Him. This is who we are as believers: alive, transformed, full of purpose, and armed for impact!

The Enemy of our soul not only knows this about us, he fears it. To have on-fire and engaged followers of Jesus is a terrifying threat to his demonic purposes. To dilute this focus and fire, he lays out subtle detours and distractions.

I have characterized them as hiccups to revival and breakthrough. Let's ask the Holy Spirit to examine and protect us so we do not lose our appetite for the Gospel.

Busy Followers

"I know your works, your labor, your patience, and that you cannot bear those who are evil. . . . you have persevered and have patience, and have labored for My name's sake and have not become weary. Nevertheless I have this against you, that you have left your first love. Remember therefore from where you have fallen; repent and do the first works" (Revelation 2:2–5).

Believers in Ephesus had received much: the gift of the Holy Spirit, exhortation from spiritual giants (like Paul, Apollos, and John), and outbreaks of the miraculous. To the point the citizens were in awe of the greatness of God: burning their idols and magic books publicly, while the testimony of the Lord Jesus grew in strength (Acts 19:17+).

But despite this, something cooled off in the church at Ephesus. Thus, the heart cry of Jesus in Revelation 2. It was not a call for them to work harder, but to recognize their diluting passion for Him. It was a personal plea from the Lord's heart to repent and return to their earlier zeal.

The same is true now. The call is not to work harder on behalf of the kingdom, but to give attention to and stir up the Holy Spirit fire that burns inside our souls.

Bewitched Followers

"O foolish Galatians! Who has bewitched you that you should not obey the truth, before whose eyes Jesus Christ was clearly portrayed among you as crucified? ... Are you so foolish? Having begun in the Spirit, are you now being made perfect by the flesh?" (Galatians 3:1, 3).

The Galatians also started strong in their Spirit-filled life. But somewhere along the way, they lost traction and reverted back to former ways. Paul asks: Why return to your old traditions and habits instead of persevering and overcoming in the resurrection power of Jesus Christ?

Such a challenge confronts believers today. We get fired up for Jesus and have right intentions of moving forward boldly in Him. But a few weeks after a summer youth camp, mission trip, or spiritual emphasis week, people revert back to their old ways and mind-sets.

But we have resurrection power flowing in our veins! It must be our priority to diligently strengthen our spiritual muscles under the training of the Holy Spirit. The end result is more than momentary breakthrough and personal revival; it is the joyful discovery that there is nothing like life with Jesus!

Satisfied Followers

"Because you say, 'I am rich, have become wealthy, and have need of nothing'—and do not know that you are wretched, miserable, poor, blind, and naked—I counsel you to buy from Me gold refined in the fire, that you may be rich; and white garments, that you may be clothed, that the shame of your nakedness may not be revealed; and anoint your eyes with eye salve, that you may see. As many as I love, I rebuke and chasten. Therefore be zealous and repent" (Revelation 3:17–19).

The Laodiceans were blessed on the outside. But a lackluster passion for God and His Gospel had left them spiritually bankrupt. The Lord urged them to repent, catch fire, and invest themselves in things that have eternal value.

In many parts of the world this is not an option due to harsh persecution and the personal cost of even being recognized as a follower of Jesus. But in some places, it is a stern challenge from the Holy Spirit not to settle. Either way, sufferings and comforts of this world are temporary. The real prize is Jesus!

Now is the time to press in to His presence. He loves you and welcomes you as a VIP! If you have hiccups today, drink in the reviving and refreshing water offered you freely by our Lord and Savior. He will cure you of your hiccups and ignite you on fire for Him and His Gospel. This is the key to experiencing lasting personal breakthrough: Get in the presence of Jesus!

THE TOCOA ENERGY FIELD

Like the team devotions in Santa Cruz, the week in Tocoa ushered in an intense presence of the Lord as we gathered to call on His name. With all that had happened to get us here, I should have known something else was around the corner.

We were praying, when suddenly the power factor cranked up exponentially. It was like we had just stepped into an energy field. Everything came to a halt, and a rapt attention on Jesus drew us closer. It was a holy moment!

Like many of the others, I was on my knees facedown. I was crying before the Lord, my senses heightened by His glorious presence. I heard a couple people around me quietly start singing in the Holy Spirit. It quickened in me to do the same. Another and then another joined in, and suddenly it crescendoed into everyone singing loudly in the Holy Spirit. It just poured out—on and on, so beautiful, so intimate, so united. It was a unique moment and something I'll never forget.

Holy Spirit, you are welcome here! We desperately need divine encounters with You—to be surprised by Your presence, shaped to Your nature, and humbled before the supernatural power and glory of our Savior, Jesus Christ. The Holy Spirit is awesome in our midst!

WE ARE VERSE 20 BELIEVERS

What a blessing to partner with the Holy Spirit in the Gospel. This hope contains the power to transform people's lives, including our own. So why the reluctance to share it near and far? Mark 16 provides two classic examples to sharing the Good News.

Group one appears in verse 8, heading to the tomb of Jesus. But when they get there, the tomb is open and waiting for them is an angel. The angel announces: "He is risen! He is not here." This is the power of the Gospel: Jesus has risen from the dead and He is alive!

Having declared the Good News, the angel gives them a mandate: "Go, tell His disciples." But the Bible says: "They said nothing to anyone, for they were afraid" (v. 8).

They said nothing—not even to their friends! Because they were afraid. Afraid of the angel, the mandate, the response they would receive from their friends? Whatever it was that made them fearful, it caused them to say nothing.

Fear is a powerful tool often employed by the Enemy of our soul to pin us down and hinder us from advancing. But the Bible declares: "God has not given us a spirit of fear, but of power and of love and of a sound mind" (2 Timothy 1:7). It is vital we reproduce our faith and share our testimony. Not just for the benefit of others, but for us as well. The blessing, fiery hunger, and supernatural power that follows the messengers of the Gospel is a huge reason to engage in the Great Commission.

Group two appears in verse 20. This time Jesus appears and issues the same assignment: Go and tell! The results are encouraging, as the Bible says: "They went out and preached everywhere." And look what happened: The Lord was with them and confirmed His word through signs and wonders!

What a difference—silent and fearful versus bold and powerful. Given the choice I want to be a verse 20 believer! They impacted the known world, Jew and Gentile, and left a legacy of living out the Great Commission. What a destiny, what a legacy, what an opportunity!

The message we carry is just as potent, and the Lord continues to confirm His Word. Who wants to live the ordinary, safe, silent life? We were born again into a life and destiny full of supernatural power and Gospel opportunities. Indeed, we are verse 20 believers! Go and tell everyone, everywhere that Jesus is alive and *His* passion for souls will ignite a flame inside of you that never goes out.

HEALING OF BACK AND STOMACH PAIN

The Friday and Saturday night crusade services were historic for us, because it marked the first time we had ever seen *lines* of people waiting to testify about what God had done for them. So many people had something to say about the glory and power of God. Even when the final service was over and we were loading up to drive back to the hotel, people kept coming forward to tell the pastors and leaders what had happened to them.

One lady testified that six months earlier her back had locked up and she could not bend over. It was humiliating because she could not even wash her clothes and had to rely on others. But Friday night fire flooded her body and she was suddenly pain free. She could almost touch her toes!

Another woman with pain in her stomach for twenty-six years received a dramatic touch from our Savior. However, it took our two altar workers awhile to understand, because she was sobbing heavily for such a long time. They thought she was in agony or pain, until one of the translators explained she was not hurting. She was just overwhelmed by the mercy of the Lord!

RADIO PERSONALITY

The crusade week also attracted local radio coverage from Christian and secular stations. We first encountered the white van belonging to the secular station during the parade on Thursday night. Believers from various churches united to prayer-walk the community in celebration of their faith and as a promotion for the weekend evangelistic event.

The guys in the white van interviewed several of the local pastors and people in the parade. In a small town like Tocoa, such a parade was a big deal and definitely had the attention and curiosity of the local media.

So the next night, the white van turned up at the crusade and parked at the back of the field to cover the happenings. It was wonderful having them there, but the best part came when one of the radio personalities raised his hand to ask Jesus into his heart!

CHAPTER 8

KINGS AND CASTLES

WE HAD FOUND A HOME in Honduras. Much of the crusade team growing around us lived in San Pedro Sula, and I had fallen in love with the people. We sensed the favor of the Lord here and knew we would be working in Honduras for years to come.

But after four crusades we also sensed a new challenge: to expand our nets. A passion for souls drew us toward the Dominican Republic.

The decision would stretch our faith and push us beyond our comfort level. But it would also open a surprising door: meeting political leaders and persons of influence. It was a door that would lead into other nations and more significant meetings in the years to come.

IT'S NOT TOO BIG!

The plan was to fly to Puerto Plata and spend the next couple of days praying over towns *beyond* the city limits. Dennis and a pastor already had it mapped out. So when Steve and I arrived, we hit the ground running.

For two days we drove around beautiful countryside, talked to several people, and felt nothing. Facing the possibility of flying home without an evangelistic target, we had to acknowledge none of the smaller venues outside Puerto Plata had panned out. That left us with only one remaining option: the much larger Puerto Plata.

This would mean a shift in our thinking. The places we had targeted in Honduras were towns; Puerto Plata had an international airport. To do an event here would mean a much larger budget, a need for more laborers, and a stretching of faith to embrace the challenges.

In real need of a heavenly perspective, Dennis, Steve, and I took the cable car to the top of a mountain. It was a dazzling view, the city stretched across the valley to the white sand beaches and beyond to the beautiful blue waters of the Caribbean. It was time to split up and prayer-walk the mountain with one burning question to resolve: What about Puerto Plata?

The three of us had this unspoken agreement: If one of us felt NO to a venue, we would back off. Every campaign had to be bathed in unity. So for this to work, the Holy Spirit had to speak to all three of us on that mountain.

I found Steve at a lookout point and asked what he was hearing. He looked right at me and dropped five words of faith and power: "It is not too big!"

Fire flushed my heart in confirmation as if to shout, "Nothing is too hard for Jesus!" Dennis agreed. If the Lord was calling us to Puerto Plata then regardless of size or past experience, this was the place for us!

NOTHING IS IMPOSSIBLE FOR GOD

Nothing is too difficult for God. The statement itself is both a challenge to rise in faith and a call to stand on top of your mountain. It is time to seek the Lord to empower us to walk in the impossible—believers filled with faith, courage, and power.

The Bible is full of such men and women. People who walked with God through the impossible and triumphed! Two such examples are David and Caleb.

David (1 Samuel 17)

For David, it was a giant standing in front of him—bigger, stronger, more powerful than anything the armies of Israel had ever seen. But David did not confront Goliath based on his own strength and ability; he did it because he knew that God was even bigger!

And what God knew about David was this: On the other side of that giant was a destiny that went beyond anything he could ever have imagined! One giant, one God-ordained moment, and one supernatural destiny.

There are giants in the land today that need slaying. Those challenges and the destinies that lie beyond them are reserved for those brave in heart and confident in the Lord their God.

Is it worth the risk? Yes! How much better to risk and fail than to look back on your life having never believed God to do the impossible. It is time to slay those giants and enter the destiny He has prepared for you!

Caleb (Joshua 14)

His inheritance was in front of him in the form of a mountain, full of giants and walled cities. None of that intimidated Caleb, because he knew the promise of God! He had waited a long time and he was ready to act. His faith and fervor were summed up in four famous words: "Give me that mountain!"

Fully aware of the greatness of God, Caleb was certain His plans and promises could not be thwarted. What stood before him (and David) may have looked impossible in the natural, but with God all things are possible! The Lord walked them through the impossible, straight into their divine destiny.

Our hearts should burn to do the impossible with God. To know and love Him gives us strength to believe for things that we could never do or accomplish on our own. If you are pushing and believing for things that do not need the supernatural intervention of God, then stop! You are only robbing yourself of discovering more of His character and nature, and forfeiting the full destiny He intends for you.

The Bible says: "What then shall we say to these things? If God is for us, who can be against us?" (Romans 8:31). And again: You are of God, little children, and have overcome them, because He who is in you is greater than he who is in the world" (1 John 4:4).

Like David and Caleb before us, now is the time to do something great for God! Nothing is too big, because with God all things are possible.

BROWN SOCKS, BLUE SLACKS

Thirty-four people made up our team for the crusade week in Puerto Plata—our largest by far. And when we touched down, several city pastors welcomed us warmly. This, coupled with a local radio reporter who enthusiastically walked with us to the bus and asked everyone for two-minute interviews, only reminded me this was nothing like the smaller towns we had worked in before.

Demand for interviews only increased as the week unfolded. Looking back, one stood out over the rest. It involved a TV interview with the president of the Association of Pastors for Puerto Plata.

The producer had a plan. He lined up four stools, and from left to right sat Steve, me, Dennis, and the pastor. Sound checks finished, everything seemed ready. They framed the set with the cameras and turned on a television so we could see what they were recording. I stole a quick glimpse at the TV as the producer counted down three, two, one. It was a mistake.

I noticed my socks immediately. Of the few television interviews I had personally participated in, almost all of them had framed us waist up or there was a table in front of us blocking our feet. Not that day. Sitting on the stool, my pants pulled up enough to reveal brown socks against blue slacks.

I may have survived the fashion faux pas, except for Josh, a friend and pastor at my home church. He had brought a camera. Smiling at the back of the TV studio, he opted to film his own special documentary—commenting on my wardrobe and zooming in on my slacks and socks for emphasis.

However, Josh had saved the biggest surprise for last. Having finished with his observations on my color combination, he panned slowly over to Steve. Unbelievably, beneath his brown slacks he had on a pair of blue socks—the exact opposite of me. It was more than Josh could resist pointing out, and he opined that a switch in socks would have solved the wardrobe malfunction completely.

We watched his short video several times on the way back to the hotel, laughing at our blunders. But even as this trip would start to crack open the door to meeting with political leaders, it also served to help us get more and more comfortable in front of the television cameras. Both areas would become increasingly important as we continued moving forward.

PRESENTING THE GOVERNOR WITH A BIBLE

Saturday night would be our largest evangelistic thrust to date, with an estimated twenty thousand people. It had been a huge gathering the night before, and that had not gone unnoticed. Calls started coming in from various dignitaries, expressing their intent to attend Saturday night—including the state governor! It was the first time such a thing had happened to us.

It was a perfect night to gather at a national landmark. As I sat in the passenger seat taking in the view as we drove alongside the sea wall and waters of the Caribbean, I wondered what tonight would hold. Quietly, I started whispering, "Thank you, Jesus," over and over again.

We eased up as we reached the police blockade. Identity confirmed, they waved us through and we drove into a sea of humanity. People surrounded us on every side of the vehicle, all heading toward the stage. There was lots of light, pulsating sound, and people everywhere. The atmosphere was electric.

It was a dream venue: the ocean wall behind the stage, the plaza to our right, and gorgeous castle center right. It was spectacular! I got out of the car, navigated through the crowd, and found my family on the other side of the stage. It was the first time Mom, Dad, Alisa, and Riley had all been with me at a LOLI crusade. I was thrilled to experience this with them!

As the night progressed, a pastor told the crowd about the dignitaries present. He invited the governor, a congressman, and a representative from the mayor's office to join him on the platform. After Steve presented the governor with a Bible, the pastors lay hands on and prayed over their political leaders.

It was a divine moment not just for the Christian and political leaders, but for us as well. Indeed, it marked the foreshadowing and beginnings of something larger.

RECOGNIZING POLITICAL AND CHRISTIAN LEADERS

The Bible has a lot to say about political and religious leaders. We recognize and honor rulers and political leaders because the apostle Paul called them ministers of God, men and women called upon to rule wisely and justly as His representatives in their nation (Romans 13).

We also honor Christian leaders because they, too, are ministers of God in the church and community. Their assembling across denominational lines offers a powerful testimony of humility, unity, and faith. And it echoes Psalm 133: "Behold, how good and how pleasant it is for brethren to dwell together in unity. . . . For there the Lord commanded the blessing—life forevermore."

We should pray for both. Paul encourages us to pray for leaders: "I exhort first of all that supplications, prayers, intercessions, and giving of thanks be made for all men, for kings and all who are in authority, that we may lead a quiet and peaceable life in all godliness and reverence. For this is good and acceptable in the sight of God our Savior, who desires all men to be saved and to come to the knowledge of the truth" (1 Timothy 2:1–4).

CYPRUS GOVERNOR AND THE POWER OF THE GOSPEL

In Acts 13, the person wanting to hear more about Jesus is a Gentile governor. His problem: A sorcerer had his ear. And while this account reveals the supernatural power of God and the impact it had on the Cyprus ruler, it also draws attention to three important Gospel principles.

Rulers Are Looking for the Gospel (Acts 13:1–7)
Having been sent out by the Holy Spirit, Barnabas and Saul sailed to Cyprus and preached throughout the island. The Bible says the governor "sought to hear the word of God."

The Roman ruler called for Barnabas and Saul, because he wanted to hear more about Jesus. This principle still applies today. People everywhere are searching, and that includes the most powerful men and women in the world. The Holy Spirit draws all eyes toward Jesus, including rulers hungry to hear and experience the Gospel.

Jesus alone satisfies and rescues from the torment of doubt and darkness. This Gospel power liberates people bound by addiction and satanic blindness. Forgiveness and life in His name are freely available in Jesus Christ!

Rulers then and now are attracted to the demonstration of the Gospel power of Jesus Christ. It happened in Cyprus with Saul and Barnabas, and it continues today.

Satan Does Not Want the Gospel Preached (Acts 13:8)

The absolute last thing Satan wants is for the Gospel to be preached. In Cyprus, a sorcerer stood against Saul and Barnabas—"seeking to turn the proconsul away from the faith."

This is the first battleground issue: prevent the declaration of the Gospel. Satan will do anything in his power to keep a Christian silent, because the Gospel is potent and has devastating effects on his demonic kingdom. His hope is that followers of Jesus will remain quiet. That was not the case with Saul and Barnabas. They didn't shy away!

When someone presses forward in the name of Jesus to share the Gospel with a lost soul, the battleground shifts again. The Enemy of our soul knows how powerful the Gospel is. He tries to minimize the damage using a number of tactics, even removing the person from the conversation. With Barnabas and Saul, the sorcerer interrupted and resisted, trying everything in his power to deter the governor from hearing the Gospel.

The Holy Spirit Makes You Bold (Acts 13:9)

We have a powerful ally in the Holy Ghost! And Saul did not shy away from the demonic response. Instead, he boldly counterattacked.

The Bible says in this passage that Saul was "filled with the Holy Spirit." This made him bold! Saul knew he had been sent out by the Holy Spirit. He knew he was a Gospel agent on assignment and fully empowered by God. All he had to do was act on His authority and power.

Reinhard Bonnke once said in a team devotion that "Father God is fully committed to the Gospel. So when you reach out to a lost soul, all of heaven lines up behind you to see it accomplished!" That is the perfect description of what happened here in front of the governor. Full of the Holy Spirit, Saul rebuked the sorcerer. The resulting blindness of the demonic agent not only demonstrated the authority of the Gospel, it astonished the proconsul.

The ruler believed because of what he saw and what he heard. And the same is true today. Reinhard Bonnke put it this way: "The power of the Gospel is at work in the world (both then and now) so the sacrifice of Jesus might not be in vain."

God works His glorious power in mighty and miraculous ways through people like you and me. Jesus sacrificed Himself so we could receive eternal life—and then partner with Him in the power of the Gospel. And it applies even among governors and rulers of nations.

THE LORD MAYOR OF BELFAST

One of my first experiences with someone of political influence occurred a couple years before meeting Evangelist Bonnke, and it certainly did not end with the same force of inspiration drawn from the story of Saul and Barnabas.

Our student group had accepted an invitation to visit Northern Ireland and spend a week serving one of the local churches. As one of the pastors, I was excited to report to our team that we had received a special invitation to share morning tea with the Lord Mayor of Belfast. No one on the team had experience interacting with political leaders, but having grown up in a Welsh family, I knew enough about hot tea to get nominated to lead the way.

We climbed the grand staircase to the second tier and crossed over to a reception room to await the Lord Mayor. I noticed the beautiful stained-glass window front and center first. Then looking to my left I saw a collection of artifacts and a seal of the city that dated back several centuries. And to my right was a table thoughtfully prepared with tea and biscuits.

The Lord Mayor of Belfast arrived and warmly welcomed us to Northern Ireland. A devout Christian, he commented that his country was filled with religion but lacked faith. He wished our team the best of success and presented us a plaque with the city's Coat of Arms imprinted.

That is when things went awry. Invited to say a prayer for the Lord Mayor and the peace of Northern Ireland, I did—and then acknowledged that we had a small token from Texas to present him with on behalf of our team. However, when I turned and reached for the gift, everything quickly went still and quiet.

Somehow there had been a breakdown in communication and our gift for the Lord Mayor had been left behind. I have no idea what went through the mind of our host, but I was upset, embarrassed, and could not get out of that room fast enough. Whatever level of excitement I had before meeting the Lord Mayor of Belfast was now totally dwarfed by our humiliation and failure.

Walking out of the building that morning, no one would ever have predicted I had a future in meeting with political figures. No one except the Lord Jesus Christ.

The amusing conclusion to the Northern Ireland story is when word got back to the mayor of the small town where we were staying that we had met with the Lord Mayor of Belfast, he quickly invited us for tea. This time we came doubly prepared and blessed him with every Texas souvenir our team possessed.

JAIRUS: A LEADER AND A DAD

On a crowded beach, Jairus awaited the arrival of Jesus. A religious ruler and a man of significance due to his position in the synagogue, everyone there would have recognized him.

Jairus had not come to make a public appearance. His one and only daughter was dying. At twelve years old, there were no more answers, no hope of saving her—except Jesus.

The meeting on the beach between Jairus and Jesus would be more remarkable due to the tension from recent events. Religious rulers had reacted violently to Jesus and cast Him out of a city synagogue. How ironic and humiliating then for Jairus to be the one waiting by the seashore to ask Jesus for help.

Jesus could easily have treated him poorly or ignored him entirely. But one of the amazing things about our Savior: No matter your past, regardless of who you are or with whom you have associated yourself, you are always welcome.

Jairus certainly recognized the consequences as he moved toward Jesus. But he had no other options. The Bible says when he saw Jesus, he fell at His feet and begged! This is not the disposition of a ruler.

No, it reflected the deep desperation of a dad. His act of humbling himself before Jesus would certainly be viewed as controversial by his peers and many of the people witnessing it. But what motivated Jairus that day was something much more valuable than his position or reputation—it was the life of his baby girl!

In the sand before Jesus, Jairus makes a heart-wrenching plea: "Come and lay Your hands on her, that she may be healed, and she will live." Jairus was not only asking for a temporary solution (her healing), but for his daughter to live and fulfill all her days and destiny!

This is exactly what Jesus wants to do for you too—not only to touch you now, but also enable you to move forward into your future. Touched with all our iniquities and struggles, He offers us hope and peace. The Bible tells over and over again that God does not despise the brokenhearted or the hurting. He cares for us. He welcomes us. He loves us!

A Mixture of Truth and Error

Jesus reveals His heart of compassion to Jairus by agreeing to go to his house. As they made their way, a multitude followed, pressing in to Him. It would have been a charged and electric atmosphere, with people wanting to see what Jesus would do. In this environment, a lady reaches out and touches Jesus—and something miraculous happens. The miracle would have ignited the crowd: shouts of joy, rising excitement, and people rejoicing over what had happened.

This happens at mass evangelistic crusades. When the power of the Holy Spirit touches someone and suddenly they can hear or see or walk, people naturally react. In Africa, with even larger crowds, you would hear spontaneous roars in various areas as God moved on the people. The impact then and now would heighten faith and fill hearts with joyous wonder.

But in the middle of the euphoria, a message comes to Jairus from his house. It is devastating news: "Your daughter is dead. Why trouble the Teacher any further?" The statement is a mixture of truth and error. Yes, the little girl had died, and this fact would have devastated Jairus. But notice the error that followed: "Why trouble the Teacher any further?"

This is the kind of advice that only a person who has never been in the presence of Jesus could make. It is an expression of failure, defeat, and utter hopelessness. It is a lie of Satan: Jesus is too busy, or you are not important enough, or there is nothing else that can be done. He floods our minds with lie after lie in order to 1) get you away from His presence; and 2) keep you from calling on Him who can release resurrection life and power into your situation. If there had ever been a time to call upon Jesus, now was that time!

Do Not Be Afraid—Believe!
Jesus was not intimidated by the negative report. The Bible says that as soon as He heard the word that was spoken, He said to Jairus, "Do not be afraid; only believe."

These words of Jesus held resurrection life, hope, and supernatural power. But it was left up to the ruler of the synagogue to decide: Which voice are you going to listen to? Given the choice to choose between the worldly report and the message of the Savior, Jairus made the right decision!

The story ends in powerful fashion. Jesus does exactly what this religious leader had pleaded for. Jesus lays His hands on the daughter, and with just a couple of words her spirit returned.

Like Jairus, we are called to believe in the Lord Jesus Christ. He cares deeply about you—as a dad and mom, as an important leader, as an onlooker in the crowd, as a son or daughter. You matter to Jesus!

SITTING DOWN FOR THE ALTAR CALL
After the governor and other dignitaries made their way off the platform, the mic came to Dennis and me to preach. Even though the hour was later than expected, the crowd remained and listened intently.

Hundreds of people started moving forward in response for salvation. I was tired and decided to sit down on the edge of the platform as people responded. It must have been a divinely orchestrated moment, because as they drew near I instinctively reached out, shook their hands, and wished them well in Jesus' name. People continued to come to shake hands, and suddenly there were a thousand people (or more!) standing around the platform and me!

The whole thing felt so intimate and personal. I was happy they had said yes to Jesus and felt privileged to pray with them!

LAME MAN WALKING

There is much more that could be said of those two nights. Miracles, healing, deliverance from demonic bondage, and joyful celebration.

On Saturday night, a man came up on the platform to share his testimony. When Dennis asked him what happened, he began to cry. Five years earlier he lost his wife in a car accident and was paralyzed. His sister had brought him to the crusade and when the fire of God fell, he stood and started to walk after five years of people telling him he would never walk again!

Nothing is impossible for God! He can unite the hearts of pastors, draw leaders of cities and states, raise up crippled or brokenhearted men, and rescue those bound and enslaved by satanic and sinful bondage. This is Jesus, the one who does so many wonderful things.

COMMISSION TO GENTILES AND KINGS

The Great Commission propels us to reach all peoples, including rulers, kings, and queens. Everyone needs Jesus.

This is demonstrated in Acts 9, where Jesus speaks to Ananias of the calling and commission for Saul: "He is a chosen vessel of Mine to bear My name before Gentiles, kings, and the children of Israel." This text is important for many reasons, but notice the Gospel is earmarked to reach kings!

Throughout the life of the apostle Paul, he witnessed boldly to people of all kinds of classes and strata. In Philemon, his life influenced the destiny of a slave. In Acts 16 and 18, Paul interacted with business professionals like Aquila, Priscilla, and Lydia. Colossians reveals his inner circle included medical doctors like Luke. And many more examples abound.

In Acts 27, he witnesses to the military Roman centurion on the ship taking him to Rome. And prior to boarding, he boldly testified before Governor Felix, Festus, and King Agrippa. No matter Jew or Gentile, slave or king, Paul fulfilled the commission given to him by Jesus.

The same outworking of God's purposes by the Holy Spirit is true today. The call to reach everyone, everywhere echoes just as loudly today as it did then. The Gospel is potent and available to all—rulers included!

THRONE ROOM VIEW OF THE FUTURE

In Revelation 11:15-18, John has seen the unfolding of the future. On one hand he is very much aware the throne room is a place of strength and everlasting dominion. On the other hand he sees God's wrath being poured out against sin and rebellion. It reveals two different perspectives: power above and a purging below.

Declaration of the Seventh Trumpet

Although it seems like everything on earth is in a state of crisis, God still reigns! His power has not diminished and His purposes are about to be established.

The Bible says that with a blast of the seventh trumpet loud noises filled heaven with this pronouncement: "The kingdoms of this world have become the kingdoms of our Lord and of His Christ, and He shall reign forever and ever!"

We have to remember: No matter how difficult the fight or challenging the path, our God wins because our God reigns! The heavenly declaration is that our world is destined for the manifestation of the kingdom of the Lord Jesus Christ.

John is pointing out this dramatic contrast: Though there may be turmoil on earth, there is tranquility in heaven. War may be breaking out on earth, but worship surrounds the throne. This is good news!

Declaration of the Twenty-Four Elders

Once more we see the twenty-four elders falling on their faces—affirming not just who He is but also what He does. This declaration comes first: "We give you thanks, O Lord God Almighty, the One who is and who was and who is to come, because You have taken Your great power and reigned."

This is who our great God is: mighty and glorious! I love echoing this Scripture in prayer: "You, O Lord, have taken Your great power and reigned." It is an eternal reality of His strength and authority, and applied to our outlook or circumstances, it offers hope and a divine perspective.

The second part of the declaration addresses the futility of human rebellion: "The nations were angry, and Your wrath has come." This is a direct fulfillment of the prophecy in Psalm 2 that asks: "Why do the nations rage, and the people plot a vain thing? . . . He who sits in the heavens shall laugh!"

Our God is not intimidated by the plots of wicked leaders or rebellious nations. It is His desire for rulers and nations to walk in righteousness, because sin does not have dominion or the final word. The strength and scope of the Lord God Almighty is vastly superior to sin, death, earthly kingdoms, or anything we could ever imagine.

This glimpse into the throne room should strengthen us, because it offers a view of radical power and strength. Paul understood this when he penned: "At the name of Jesus every knee should bow . . . every tongue should confess that Jesus Christ is Lord" (Philippians 2:10–11). Our future is glorious because our God reigns!

ONE YEAR'S CELEBRATION, ONE YEAR'S CHALLENGE

With the third year drawing to a close, we could celebrate the three opportunities we had to preach the Gospel to win souls in large open-air meetings. There was little time to get comfortable, though, as we sensed the Holy Spirit challenging us to prepare for four evangelistic and compassion campaigns.

The first one would be Puerto Barrios, Guatemala. A place where a special lady named Rosa was about to enter our storyline.

CHAPTER 9

Jungles and Bears

THERE ARE FOUR THINGS that make up the heartbeat of LOLI. The first is evangelism and the second is compassion. The Bible clearly teaches to remember the poor. Jesus was all about people—lepers, tax collectors, widows, prostitutes.

He still is. The barefoot children, the mothers washing clothes along the banks of the rivers, the hungry father in Santa Cruz, the unreached in mountains and jungles. This is our heart-cry: a passion for the lost and compassion for the poor.

ROSA AND HYDROGEN PEROXIDE

It did not take long for Bruce, one of our distribution leaders. and his team to have a life-impacting encounter in Puerto Barrios, Guatemala. It was the beginning of the crusade week, and teams had spread out to different locations with local pastors and translators.

Way up on a mountain road, they met a sixty-year-old widow named Rosa. It was a small village in the middle of nowhere. On the edge of the road, in a tiny hut, with a few random items for sale, Rosa survived.

She had two sons, but they had long ago abandoned her in hopes of making it to California. Rosa was alone.

Bruce and his team connected with her immediately. Rosa was not just another person they would bump into; she had touched their hearts. She thanked them for the food, the prayers, the hugs—but the biggest blessings were still to come.

Someone asked if she wanted a Bible. It had been almost ten years since she had opened one. Part of the problem was her vision; she couldn't see very well.

That is when something wonderful happened. A lady on the team had brought with her an extra pair of reading glasses. And when Rosa put them on she could see perfectly!

The Bible and glasses excited her. But when Bruce pulled out the largest green teddy bear you have ever seen, it was pure joy. This is part of the wonder of missions in the third world: You reap more than you could ever give away as your heart connects with remarkable people like Rosa.

After lots of hugs and pictures, the Texas team did what they do best—they went shopping. It was only a tiny hut with random items, but each happily found something to buy and take with them to remember Rosa. One of the items purchased: a small bottle of hydrogen peroxide.

The team loaded the truck and headed back down the mountain. On their way, though, they came across people gathered in the road. Having a few extra bears and bags of food, they stopped. But what caught the attention of one team member was a lady off to the side of the road. She was diabetic and had suffered a wound on her leg.

This was the invisible hand of God at work. Because the team traveled into the mountains, they met Rosa. Because they connected so deeply with Rosa, they shopped in her hut. Because a member of the team was a registered nurse, she purchased the hydrogen peroxide. And because villagers were standing in the middle of the road, the team stopped and encountered a diabetic lady.

All of that so the team nurse could clean her wound using the hydrogen peroxide bought an hour earlier. This happened so a diabetic lady ultimately could open up her heart and let Jesus in.

THE POOR HAVE THE GOSPEL PREACHED TO THEM!

One of the core passages for Light of Life International is Luke 7:19–23. John the Baptist sends disciples to Jesus with a question: "Are you the Coming One, or do we look for another?"

Having worked many miracles in their midst, Jesus says: "Go and tell John the things you have seen and heard: that the blind see, the lame walk, the lepers are cleansed, the deaf hear, the dead are raised, the poor have the gospel preached to them. And blessed is he who is not offended because of Me."

This is one of those amazing moments where Jesus defines Himself. His answer points out: 1) He wields supernatural power; and 2) He has compassion for the poor.

Time and time again, Jesus demonstrated His authority through miracles, healing, and casting out evil spirits. But His message and ministry among the poor and hurting exemplified a heart of compassion. This is the nature and character of Jesus: strong and powerful, yet merciful and compassionate.

People everywhere need to encounter this powerfully compassionate Savior. If we can introduce them to Jesus through stadium evangelism or by visiting them one at a time in remote villages, the purpose is the same. People need to hear the good news! It is not about the size of the crowd; what matters is the presentation of the Gospel.

SAND IN THE SKY

In the midst of the Guatemala crusade week, Steve, Dennis, and I stopped by the crusade venue to pray. We had finished a radio interview and learned one of the local stations would cover the weekend services live on air and via their website.

The large field was framed by a long wall on one side and a road on the opposite side. Here people would pack the space to hear the Gospel.

Standing there, my heart began to burn for souls and a desire for the message to reach more than just those who would attend. I asked Steve and Dennis to grab some of the sand and rocks on the ground. Together we threw it into the air as a prophetic act and cried out to the Lord to take His Word and carry it beyond this property, this city, and into the nations.

For us it was a prophetic demonstration of our faith for the weekend—and for the future. In time, radio and television would expand from local coverage to much larger audiences. We sensed the Lord stretching us, working in us. So like the sand tossed into the air and carried off by the wind, we were asking Him to carry us and the Gospel message burning inside our hearts beyond our own abilities and into the nations.

ISLANDS AND MACHETES

The week of distribution leading up to the Guatemala crusade continued to be fruitful. One team went house to house in the rain forest and stumbled suddenly on an elementary school. The Christian principal immediately cancelled classes and called for an all-school assembly outside.

About 200 kids gathered to sing songs and hear about Jesus. The team passed out the remainder of their teddy bears, candy, packages of food, and a brand-new soccer ball for the school.

But not all opportunities were what they seemed. It was always exciting to go upriver to an indigenous camp or cross a wooden bridge in the mountains to share the Gospel with a remote people group. So when the invitation came to visit two tribes that lived half an hour off the mainland, it seemed like another exciting opportunity.

The plan had been to ready the supplies on the first day and send teams by boat the next day. But one obstacle after another kept popping up: people running late, bags for the groceries disappearing, random things that forced us to delay our journey out to sea a few days.

The next night I was in a meeting when someone leaned over and whispered, "Did you hear what happened on that island?"

I could not believe my ears! The island tribes were arguing with each other and it had escalated into a savage machete fight. It had turned so nasty, the government had to send in hundreds of militia to quench the violence!

I could not believe the place we had diligently tried to organize an outreach had descended into a brutal tribal conflict. Now I knew why we had hit so many snags along the way: The Lord had intervened to protect us!

I left Guatemala grateful for what He had done and for what had not been done. The compassion efforts resulted in open doors with widows, diabetics, and children. The closed doors reminded me again the invisible hand of God was ordering our steps.

HE DID IT BEFORE; HE CAN DO IT AGAIN!

Do you want to do something eternally significant for God and walk in supernatural power? One of the key triggers is compassion. The Bible speaks plainly of how Jesus loved and cared for people.

In Matthew 9, moments before Jesus calls for laborers to enter the harvest field, He sees the people weary, scattered, like sheep without a shepherd, and is moved with compassion.

In Mark 8, after the multitude has followed Him for three days, Jesus recognizes they have had nothing to eat. He tells the disciples He has compassion for the people and wants to feed them—all of them!

What happens next is an important lesson for us and a remarkable miracle by the hands of Jesus.

Bread in the Wilderness

You have a lot of hungry people and a compassionate Jesus who wants to feed them. Sounds like a recipe for the supernatural! But the disciples' response: "How can one satisfy these people with bread here in the wilderness?"

In the natural it would be impossible to feed four thousand men and their families in the wilderness. But what the disciples did not see was 1) their supernatural past; and 2) the current supernatural opportunity.

Yes, they were in a different place geographically than where the children of Israel had been, but these guys should have known their history, their heritage. They should have remembered in times past God had fed a much larger group than four thousand people in the wilderness.

With a million people wandering in the desert during the Exodus, God fed them manna. The biggest event in the history of the nation involved satisfying multitudes of hungry people with bread in the wilderness!

Jesus could have rebuked the disciples for their lack of faith or not remembering the Scriptures, but He didn't. Instead, He asked: "How many loaves do you have?"

The bread and fish they presented Jesus was more than enough to accomplish the miraculous. It was not a crisis for Jesus but a teaching moment for all of us: He can use what we have!

Jesus has not come to scold us, but to see if we will offer Him what we have. It may only be a whispered prayer to walk in the supernatural and do something eternally significant for God—that is enough to start!

Jesus is the One who does the miraculous work, not us. We cannot save or heal anyone on our own. But we can partner with Him! Offer what you have to Jesus, and you will witness the compassionate and powerful work of the Lord.

The God Who Did it Before Is the God Who Can Do it Again!

How can one satisfy these people with bread here in the wilderness? It would be a good question except for this: The disciples failed to recognize the One who had done it before was the same One standing in front of them!

Wow, how many times have I been guilty of the same thing? In need of a miracle or breakthrough, it is so easy to get overwhelmed by the natural. But we cannot lose sight of this truth: The God who did it before is the One who can do it again!

This truth has helped me so many times in the weeks leading up to the crusades. How empowering and encouraging to know when confronted with financial challenges and no idea where the funds would come from, that we could cry out to the One who had faithfully provided before.

Today, whatever your need or circumstances, you are in the presence of the One who has done it before and can do it again! Maybe you are like the disciples, wondering how to solve an impossible problem today. It could be financial or relational or physical. The good news is you do not have to face it alone. Jesus is standing right here ready to do the miraculous.

The Bible says: "Jesus Christ is the same yesterday, today, and forever" (Hebrews 13:8). Jesus is full of compassion and mighty power. It was on full display in feeding the four thousand then, and it is the testimony of millions more today.

Nothing is too hard for Him. His nature and character as Savior, Healer, Provider, Prince of Peace, Multiplier, Uplifter, and more remain unchanged. Indeed, the God who did it before is the One who can do it again!

BEARS ON A MISSION

Providing food and supplies during the crusade week ultimately paved the way for a new compassion outreach. It started with Alisa and her fourth-grade classroom. Every year, the elementary classes at her school worked together on a missions project for Christmas. And wanting to do something new, and hearing how we collected stuffed animals, the school asked Alisa if LOLI could do something for the Christmas season.

The challenge was even though the ministry was growing, it was still a part-time operation out of our house. Few outsiders would believe it because of the large crowds and scope of compassion during the missions week.

This was nothing less than grace and divine favor, because the reality was we did not have an office building, a staff, or the revenue to take salaries. So in between Alisa teaching fourth grade and me serving on Dad's pastoral team, the Lord quietly continued to carry and build LOLI.

When the school asked Alisa about partnering over the Christmas season, we were flattered but at the same time did not have anything to offer. Instead of looking at it as a negative or getting overwhelmed, Alisa sensed it was the leading of the Lord and started praying for wisdom and direction.

One night, Alisa walked into Riley's room, and an idea popped into her head. The theme from the Indiana Jones movies kicked in, and a paper airplane came soaring out of our daughter's closet. Upon closer inspection, the airplane was actually a note from one of the teddy bears in Riley's closet.

Send-Me-Anna-Jones (as he liked to be called) was a big cuddly bear with a large brown hat. Retired to the closet, he had heard stories that some of Riley's other stuffed animals had gone on exciting adventures to share the love of Jesus with kids in far-off places. That sounded wonderful; maybe he would get a chance to go on one of those divine adventures?

So Alisa brought Send-Me-Anna-Jones to school to see if any other kids had any bears in their closets who might be interested in an adventure. And before you knew it, this tenderhearted bear had recruited 300 friends to go with him to Honduras!

Alisa's dream had come to life as a kids-to-kids ministry. Students brought their teddy bears to school, tied Christmas ribbon around their neck with a small pouch, and put drawings, colorings, or pictures of themselves inside. Each pouch also received a Gospel poem about candy canes.

For Alisa's students, it was a chance to experience the joy of giving at Christmas. Each of them were sending a retired bear from their closet, or a brand-new bear picked out for such an adventure. The bears were ready—each marked for special delivery to a child in Honduras.

SEND-ME-ANNA-JONES

The bears were a big hit in the Honduras orphanages, hospitals, and slums. As Send-Me-Anna-Jones watched his friends find new homes, receive huge hugs, and begin their new adventures, he grew more and more excited about meeting a special little boy or girl. What would he or she be like?

We had one more stop. The dirt road paralleling a brook led into a community of tin-roof houses supported by wooden boards and concrete blocks. We parked our two trucks by a tiny church and got ready.

Almost instantly children appeared out of nowhere! From the bed of the truck, I introduced Send-Me-Anna-Jones and his remaining friends. Steve and Josh climbed up with the candy canes to talk about the meaning of Christmas.

The candy and the bears disappeared quickly, leaving only Send-Me-Anna-Jones. This big brown bear had done a magnificent job bringing smiles to the faces of children in Texas and San Pedro Sula. I quietly prayed for us to find the perfect match for him.

We said good-bye to the kids and headed back toward the main paved road. We had nearly reached it, when I saw her. Beyond the driver's window, a mom was walking with her little daughter. Mom moved awkwardly, her feet inverted so badly the soles of her feet faced upward, meaning she literally walked on the tops of her feet. And to her right she held the hand of one of the most beautiful little girls I had ever seen. Maybe four years old, she had jet-black hair, big brown eyes, and an electric smile. The moment I saw them, I knew Send-Me-Anna-Jones had found a home!

I'm not sure what they thought when two vehicles abruptly stopped near them and a couple of guys jumped out. But all apprehension vanished when they saw Send Me-Anna-Jones. They had come late to the assembly and missed out on a bear. Mom was heartbroken. That is when I noticed a Bible in her other hand, and I knew it was a God moment.

I knelt down before this precious little girl and introduced her to Send-Me-Anna-Jones. I asked, "Could you take care of my special bear?" I watched her eyes dart back and forth between her mom and my daughter's cuddly brown bear, as the wonder of what was happening started sinking into her heart.

I gave her Send-Me-Anna-Jones and put the accompanying big brown hat on her head. It fit perfectly, as if it had been created just for her. I have no doubt it was!

Mom and daughter were beaming, and Send-Me-Anna-Jones seemed very happy too. As we said good-bye and climbed back into the vehicles, I watched them cross over the paved road to the other side where the dirt path resumed. My last glimpse of that beautiful little girl was running down the dirt hill at full speed with Send-Me-Anna-Jones firmly in hand. Grateful, I whispered, "Have fun on your new adventure, Send Me-Anna-Jones!

RED BEAR, BROWN BEAR, OR WHITE BEAR?

As we hauled the overstuffed bears up several flights of stairs in that Honduras public hospital, I kept thinking, *No child deserves to spend Christmas in a hospital bed.* Maybe it was because I'm a dad and I know how much my girls love Christmas. Maybe it was because the hospital conditions were less than ideal and I was nervous of what I was about to see. Maybe it was because these were very poor children, many of whom would not receive anything, even if they were not in the hospital. Whatever the reason, as we prepared to deliver the large bears to sick and hurting kids, I was feeling a wide range of emotions.

It only took five minutes in the first room for the nurses to clear us to visit all the children's areas. Some of the kids had second-degree burns, one suffered from kidney failure due to venomous snake bites, and others had unknown diseases. Despite these serious challenges, the majority of kids were full of personality and thrilled to see the bears. I posted one of my encounters on Facebook:

> *So I walked into the Honduras hospital room and asked this little girl: "Would you like the red bear, brown bear,*

or white bear?" She knew exactly which one she wanted— the big brown bear! She was so happy with the bear, that when we paused to pray, she insisted on holding its hand instead of mine. So I did the daddy thing: I grabbed the other bear's hand, and the three of us prayed to Jesus! . . . I'm sure the Lord would understand!!

Alisa's Bears on a Mission project had impacted my life. Visiting the children with burns from scolding water and seeing the little girl speeding off with Send-Me-Anna-Jones remain lasting images. For Steve, watching a girl at the orphanage choose her bear, take it back to her seat, then hug it tight, pull it out to look at it, hug it tight again, then look at it again in absolute delight left the biggest impression. Surely, this wonderful joy and precious innocence was why Jesus said: "Let the children come to me. Don't stop them! For the Kingdom of Heaven belongs to those who are like these children" (Matthew 19:14 NLT).

THE DISCIPLES' CHALLENGE!

The Bible calls us to be mindful of the poor. When the disciples and Paul met in Jerusalem for a report on the impact of the Gospel among the Gentiles, Paul had many triumphs to share. The disciples and believers in Jerusalem listened to his report and affirmed Paul. Although they were personally compelled to win their Jewish brethren, he had their full blessing to spread the Gospel to the Gentiles far and wide.

There was, however, one addition. The disciples insisted Paul "remember the poor" (Galatians 2:10). Of all the things the disciples could have required of Paul, they accentuated the need for compassion.

This was something Paul was not only eager to do, but something he practiced. In saying farewell to the Ephesian believers, he ended with: "I have shown you in every way, by laboring like this, that you must support the weak. And remember the words of the Lord Jesus, that He said, 'It is more blessed to give than to receive'" (Acts 20:35).

This powerful orator and soul-winner—one who planted churches throughout the known world—retained a heart of compassion for the poor and hurting.

This is why we deliver beans and rice, hand out blankets, provide ice cream, surprise kids in hospitals with huge teddy bears—because sometimes the message needs to be more than heard; it has to be felt. That is the purpose of compassion: for the Gospel to be handled and experienced with their own hands.

NEW GUINEA MAN OF TERROR

One of the reasons missions is so precious and personal to me is the example of my dad. As a missionary in Papua, New Guinea, at a time when few people knew of the place, he cared for the needs of the people and preached the Gospel. Working in part with Missionary Air Federation, planes would land on the rivers with supplies each week, and Dad would haul them into the rain forest.

In a small way the compassion work we do today is an extension of my heritage. His work decades ago may have been more primitive working with the Dani people, but the compulsion to meet the needs of people and share Jesus is the same.

The plan had been to get out of the jungle before nightfall. But tropical rains had changed that. With rainwater rushing down from mountain peaks, banks had flooded and the fast-moving water made crossing impossible. Dad and the missionary working with him were trapped inside the jungle. There was no alternative; they would spend the night among the tribesmen.

They knew about the reputation of the crazy man. The villagers described him as violent and savage. A man so demonized, the elder warriors locked him up at night in one of the huts. Fear of his madness and terror dominated the village.

That night everyone went to their huts, except the two missionaries. They lay down underneath the sky by a small fire and tried to sleep.

It happened very quickly. Punctuating the middle of the night came a blood-curdling scream that woke up everyone immediately. Dad looked up just in time to see this crazy demonized man leaping across the flames at him with arrow in hand. With zero time to react, Dad cried out, "In the name of Jesus!"

It was as if that man smashed into an invisible brick wall. The powerful name of Jesus stopped him midair and he fell to the ground next to the fire.

Men of the village rushed out of their huts to see what happened. They could hardly believe their eyes. This man of terror, who could not be restrained by ropes or held prisoner in one of their huts due to demonic power, lay on the ground whimpering like a small child.

The name of Jesus had spared Dad's life. It also impacted the demonized man and led to several tribesmen believing upon Jesus as Lord and Savior.

JOURNEY INTO THE AMAZON

There are challenges and costs to taking the Gospel to remote places. I learned this on a Peru mission trip a couple of years before meeting Reinhard. Our assignment was to build a church in the heart of the Amazon Basin.

It took some effort getting to the river. We flew into Lima (Peru), transferred to a much smaller plane, bounced around like popcorn up and over the Andes Mountains, landed several times on grass clearings, and finally switched to an even smaller plane to cross from Tarapoto to Yurimaguas.

Dawn on the Huallaga River had nine of us climbing into a twenty-one-foot launch boat. Made of wood, a tin top, and tarp, it seemed like a huge mismatch in favor of the river. If we tried standing up or shifting positions, the long canoe-like structure would rock wildly. So as we set out on the ten-hour journey, our hopes of arriving uninterrupted and during daylight seemingly rested on our balance, a tiny outboard motor, and the fifteen-foot walking stick that all of us were wondering about.

The first couple of hours passed quickly as we took in the beautiful surroundings. Here the river stretched at least a half mile wide. We also passed barges made of round wood tied together and stacked high with banana leaves drifting down to the markets in Yurimaguas.

Splitting off from the Huallaga River, the scenery quickly became more dramatic as the width between banks shrunk to twenty-five yards or less. Visibility also dropped significantly as the water no longer flowed in a straight, forward direction, but in blind, winding turns. I noticed, too, the point man at the front of our boat was on heightened alert, resorting to hand signals to cue the pilot at the back.

The sharp cry from the point man was our first challenge. From one bank to the other stretched dense green reeds protruding at least three feet out of the water. We had one chance to break through it, and our pilot gunned the engine as we headed straight at the blockage. We didn't make it. The reeds entangled themselves around the motor and shut us down. The point man grabbed the walking stick hoping to push us out of the reeds, but the water was too deep. We were stuck.

While the pilot cleaned the motor, we did our best to avoid the reeds and black ants, while also trying to stay as still as possible so as not to turn the boat upside down. It took thirty minutes but our pilot managed to re-fire the motor and we pushed through the blockage.

The river is beautiful. Scores of butterflies, including the large, bright blue ones indigenous to Peru, escorted us up river. Lush tropical trees, colorful fruit, and massive termite colonies several feet high above the ground only served as reminders: We were going deep into the Amazon Basin.

At 1 p.m. the afternoon showers came. We untied the tarps attached to the tin roof on both sides for additional cover, but we still got soaked. However, the stormy weather and the tarps created another problem: a serious loss of visibility. The inability to see, especially oncoming debris in the water, increased the risk.

We felt the submerged log before the point person saw it. The force of the blow ripped the engine right off the back of the boat. We would have been in a colossal crisis if not for two lightning-quick reactions: the pilot hitting the kill switch as the engine fell into the river, and the catlike reflexes of my friend Fons to fish out the disappearing engine.

After all the excitement, the nine of us were hungry. So while the guides worked on reattaching the engine, we feasted on hard-boiled eggs, crackers, and raw potatoes. According to a GPS carried by Fons, the straight line from this point back to Yurimaguas was twenty-seven miles, but factor in all the bends in the river and it had to be a lot more than that.

Despite other challenges along the way, we eventually came around a final curve in the river. There stood a small wooden hut covered with straw and banana leaves, elevated above the water by wooden stilts.

Kids raced to the riverbank to check us out and watch us unload our gear, but soon they were back to playing soccer in an open field.

As light waned, I headed to the creek to bathe. One of the villagers laid several wooden planks across the mud in the shallow water so we could kneel down and splash ourselves. Some of the braver guys just waded into the water, but I had too many ideas about piranhas, alligators, and snakes to venture in.

Nighttime in the jungle is dark and full of exotic sounds. But you should see the sky! I stood transfixed by the galaxies shining overhead, the jaw-dropping handiwork of our Savior.

Dinner that first night was around a wooden table with a kerosene lamp in the middle. It was just enough light to see our food and one another. The beating of drums promptly ended dinner and summoned us to the evening service on a dirt path that led back down to the river.

The kerosene lamps provided light to see the silhouette of the pastor as he led the villagers in song. I stood next to one of the guys on our team, listening to them sing. He said, "Miles into the Amazon Jungle and the name of Jesus is being lifted up!" Indeed the Gospel is bearing fruit in all the world, impacting tribes and nations!

TROUBLE IN THE AMAZON

We had come to assist in building a church that could double as a meeting site for area tribes. The building was coming along and with the two-story skeleton frame in place, we started hauling the wooden beams that would support the trusses up to the second deck and nailing them into place. It was hot and tiring, and everyone was ready to break for lunch. That is when I heard the commotion. Something terrible had just happened.

One of our guys hit a nail, and a shard of tempered steel fractured off the head of his hammer. The fragment had pierced his right eye.

The good news was we had a medic on our team. He immediately examined the eye using his microscopic glasses. The bad news: Only an eye specialist could remove the debris. Otherwise fluid might drain out and cause permanent damage.

Three of us made ready to leave camp and make the long journey back to Lima. The medic reiterated no one but a specialist should touch the steel shard, even if it meant flying home to Texas.

Heading back we were in a smaller and much faster launch boat on loan from a man in the village. In addition to the three of us, we had two villagers to navigate the river and two translators.

The heartbreaking reality was our friend was in pain, and we had a long way to go. We read the Psalms and sang to pass the time. Looking out at a rainbow stretching across the jungle, I quietly wondered how this would all turn out.

We reached our first destination in three hours. You are definitely deep in the jungle when it takes that long to reach the first available site where you can radio an emergency. Sixty minutes later a large, high-powered Red Cross vessel intercepted us in the wide waters that flow back toward Yurimaguas.

The bigger boat had a cot to lie down, where the oldest nurse wanted to pull the splinter out. But there was no way we were going to let that happen, especially with the boat bouncing up and down as we raced through the water.

It only took six hours to make the journey back to Yurimaguas. With the sun setting, though, there were no flights to Lima or anywhere else, as the small airport shut down at dark. We were stuck.

As a last resort, we called the Regional Security Officer at the US Embassy. We would have to wait until morning, but a private charter would be sitting on the runway ready to go wheels up at 9:30 a.m.

The next morning we arrived in Lima with a medical staff ready on the runway to transfer us to the eye clinic *next* to the hospital. The RSO had firmly instructed the only other option than flying home was that clinic. But something was lost in translation upon landing, and we were rushed directly into the hospital emergency room.

When we realized what was happening, we raced out of the hospital. We could not come this far and get it wrong. Finally we made it to the clinic.

After a DVD imaging scan, eye drops, and a booster shot, the eye specialist was ready to proceed. The jagged sliver she pulled out of his eye was the size of her finger nail and required four stitches to close the cut.

She wanted to follow up in the morning, but we already had a ticket booked to fly him home to Dallas that night. When she objected, she said there was only one doctor in the world she would release him to for follow-up care. When she said the clinic was in Dallas, Texas, we knew this was the invisible hand of God at work.

A faster ride down the river, the Red Cross, the Embassy, the best eye specialist in South America, and now a follow-up physician who lived in our hometown—only the Lord could do that! And yes, the eye healed perfectly.

WHATEVER YOU DO, DO IT IN THE NAME OF JESUS!

The work of compassion can take many forms in the four corners of the world. It may be building projects, digging water wells, providing medical care, distributing Bibles, or training up indigenous leaders.

It may involve food or stuffed animals. The key to any compassionate endeavor, however, is that it be done in the name of the Lord Jesus Christ. If so, it becomes more than a humanitarian effort. It gains eternal significance as an extension of His love and compassion.

CHAPTER 10

PRAYING AND PREACHING

AFTER GUATEMALA, we returned to the Dominican Republic for a second crusade. Our hopes and expectations were sky-high as our first trip there had impacted our lives and ministry in a prophetic and powerful way.

We opted to go all in, bringing Pastor Misael Argeñal from Honduras and my dad to speak at a pastors conference during the crusade weekend. If there was ever a time I wanted things to go well, this was it because of my high regard for both men!

WHAT A DIFFERENCE A NIGHT MAKES

As if I was not already intimidated by our conference speakers, the mayor and general of the military joined us Friday night. Never before had dignitaries sat on the platform, and I felt out of sorts preaching with them sitting so close. It turned out to be the least of my concerns.

I was preaching to a brick wall. Following unexpected guest performances and multiple announcements, the choir (which was supposed to remain in front of the stage) dispersed as soon as I received the microphone. Worse, they had retreated behind the platform to socialize.

And when the moment arrived to call for salvation, ushers started stacking chairs and clearing out the people because of the imminent threat of rain. It was the oddest service I could remember, and it left me frustrated and tired.

The next morning Pastor Misael met Dennis to give some timely encouragement and advice: "Never let the evangelist get up to speak in a cold atmosphere. It's important to come in an atmosphere of worship!" It was a sound point—when the microphone came to us, all eyes needed to be fixed on Jesus.

What a difference a night makes! This time the choir filled the area in front of the stage during the preaching, which engaged them in praying and receiving from the Lord. It also enabled our team to move behind the stage with some of the intercessors to pray throughout the message. With fewer performers, there was a greater intensity in worship, and we could sense the hunger of the people as they reached out to the Lord.

I preached on the fire of the Holy Spirit and, unlike the night before, I could feel a strength and boldness flowing out of me. When the power of God fell, it sounded like an explosion! People everywhere were crying out before the Lord, and God's glory washed over the multitude, triggering miracles and healing. People were saved, delivered, filled with the Holy Spirit, and caught up in the presence of the Lord.

WHEELCHAIR SURFING ABOVE THE CROWD

I handed the microphone to Steve and he started making prophetic declarations over the people and praying out in the Holy Spirit. I embraced the pastors on the stage and prayed over them—it was so powerful. That is when I turned around and saw it.

An empty wheelchair was being passed above the heads of the people. It looked as if it was surfing on top of the crowd. And it was coming straight toward us!

When the call for Holy Spirit fire went out, the LOLI team started working its way through the crowd, laying hands on the people. Three teenagers encountered a lady in a wheelchair. The sense of electricity and power moving through the crowd finally led one of them to look at her and cry, "Stand up!" When she stood to her feet, the people nearby got even more excited. Could she walk?

Once she started moving toward the platform, someone grabbed the wheelchair and held it up for all to see. It was like lightning hit the crowd! It was an explosion of faith and excitement. Everyone was pulsating with joy over what the Lord had done.

DARKNESS AND DEMONIC POWER SHATTERED

At the same time, a young girl was violently reacting to the presence of the Holy Spirit. She started beating on one of the guys praying for her, then her eyes rolled back in her head.

Something wonderful happened at that moment: Jesus touched her! Darkness and demonic power was shattered, and the peace of God flooded her soul for the first time. The transformation was amazing: Her face changed and her eyes cleared. For the longest time all she did was hug her mom and the people who had prayed for her. The Lord Jesus Christ had set her free!

MIRACLES ARE GOD'S ADVERTISING AGENT

Miracles are a divine advertising agency; they emphasize the greatness of God! They relate to His lordship and serve as powerful reminders that we are standing in His presence.

Many times it is a miracle that triggers faith in the heart of an unbeliever, moving him or her to invite Jesus into his or her own life. Many times at the crusades, people who said no to salvation during the invitation linger and watch. Hearing the testimonies of healed bodies, freedom from witchcraft, reconciliation of broken relationships, and others asking Jesus into their hearts draws them to Jesus. This is the powerful nature of signs and wonders: They confirm the Word of the Lord!

However, miracles do not necessarily change the will of *every* person. Signs and wonders stimulate our mind because they confront us with the demonstration of the supernatural. But the choice to bend our will and submit our heart is both personal and deliberate.

This is what happened in Acts 3–4. Peter and John told the lame man by the temple to rise up and walk in the name of Jesus—and he did! The rulers, scribes, and high priest gathered in response to the miracle: "When they saw the boldness of Peter and John, and perceived that they were uneducated and untrained men, they marveled. And they realized that they had been with Jesus. And seeing the man who had been healed standing with them, they could say nothing against it" (Acts 4:13–14).

The religious leaders couldn't deny a notable miracle has taken place their midst, but it did not change their minds about Peter and John—or Jesus! In fact, they reacted harshly. They said this: "That a notable miracle has been done through them is evident to all who dwell in Jerusalem, and we cannot deny it. But so that it spreads no further among the people, let us severely threaten them, that from now on they speak to no man in this name" (vv. 16–17).

Peter and John would have none of it! Walking in the power of God, they had seen the miraculous and experienced the fire-power of the Holy Spirit. There was no way they were turning back, and God used their lives to dramatically shake the city.

We are called to do the same thing. Miracles remain one of God's advertising agents. They follow the preaching of the Gospel and are used to bring transformation and joy. Like Peter and John, you serve an awesome and fiery God. And like Peter and John, the resurrection power that lives and dwells within you can impact lives and shake cities and nations for the glory of His name!

BUILDING AN ARMY OF INTERCESSORS

The lessons learned from the second Dominican Republic outreach led to a new strategy: growing an army of local intercessors. We wanted them around the platform, and if possible around the crowd. With a gaze fixed on Jesus and the advancement of His kingdom, the more intercessors we could recruit and deploy, the better! This became our strategy moving forward.

We quickly discovered people wanted to unite to pray for their homes, churches, neighborhoods, leaders, and country. It connected us with them in new and wonderful ways. The intercessors took their job seriously. They stood on top of mountains and at the gates of their cities to plead the blood of Jesus for their communities. They walked around the venue praying for a harvest of souls, gathered at churches to fast and pray, even held all-night vigils for revival and breakthrough.

We had never held intercessor rallies—until now! It soon became the first thing we did when arriving in a city for a crusade week. We would share our hearts and they would start praying—over our families, our health, our destinies, everything!

Those services were never the same. One time they grabbed Dennis and me by the hand and pushed us into the center of the room. They lifted up our hands, and the entire roomful of people closed in on us to intercede on our behalf. Another time, the lights went out and everyone turned on their phones, held them above their heads, began marching around the room, shouting praise and singing songs. And one time the place grew quiet and reverent as the people slipped to their knees to pray. Regardless of how it looked, the addition of local intercessors had sharpened our focus, and we were a stronger unit because of it.

PICTURES FROM THE THRONE ROOM

Being an intercessor means you have a great passion for the Lord Jesus and the things that move His heart. You carry an insatiable appetite to draw near Him, to take on His character and nature, and to exalt His holy name.

One of my favorite passages to talk to intercessors about is Revelation 4. It is a glimpse of the ongoing prayer movement taking place around the throne of God. And it is a call for us to join in.

Consider for a moment the throne, the rainbow, the sea, the lesser thrones, the lamps, the creatures, the elders, and the Supreme Sovereign. It is a powerful picture of worship and intercession.

The Throne

The first thing John sees is a throne. It is not just any throne; it is one occupied by the founder and ruler of the universe! It's a place of power, authority, and a reminder of the greatness of our God. Everything around the throne is a reflection of His strength and character, and all of it is spectacular because He is Spectacular!

Rainbow of Promise

The throne is encircled by a rainbow, which is an expression of promise. This was initially communicated to Noah in Genesis following the flood. Every time he would see a rainbow, it would remind him that God had made a promise to him and the people on the earth.

On earth the rainbows we see are half circles, but around the throne the circle is full and complete. The Bible echoes this. Here we see in part, but one day we will see in full. As intercessors we have to pray for the part we know to come to fruition. But we also need to remember the promises of God are much bigger than our perception.

Ephesians 3:20 says He "is able to do exceedingly abundantly above all that we ask or think." Also 2 Corinthians 1:20: "All the promises of God in Him are Yes, and in Him Amen, to the glory of God." This is good news because each of us today has promises hanging over our lives. It is the throne of God where every promise is made and through which every promise will be fulfilled!

Hebrews 4:16 encourages us: "Come boldly to the throne of grace, that we may obtain mercy and find grace to help in time of need." And again in Ephesians 2:8: "For by grace you have been saved through faith, and that not of yourselves; it is the gift of God." How awesome to have an invitation to come before this mighty throne—a place of power, a place of promise, and a place of amazing grace!

Sea of Glass

Another astonishing thing about the throne of God: In front of it is a sea of glass like crystal. Despite the energy and power flowing from the throne, the entrance to it is a place of complete rest and peace. This is very encouraging because no matter what the strife or turmoil abounding in our lives or around the world, we have access to a place of total power and total peace.

We see this throughout the book of Revelation. On earth turmoil and warfare are breaking out, but when you look at the heavenly picture it is one of peace and worship. No wonder Paul could say repeatedly: "The peace of God . . . will guard your hearts and minds" (Philippians 4:7). This is why Jesus could say: "My peace I give to you; not as the world gives do I give to you. Let not your heart be troubled, neither let it be afraid" (John 14:27).

The throne of God is not only a place of power and promise but also a place of peace. It is a place before the Lord Almighty, who occupies this throne. So as we come to worship and intercede, we can claim the promises, the peace, and the power of God for our lives, our families, and the nations for the glory of His name!

24 Lesser Thrones

Around the great throne are twenty-four lesser thrones occupied by twenty-four elders. Each elder is clothed in a white robe and wears a gold crown, signifying purity and dignity.

Purity comes through the blood of the Lamb. He alone is the One who can wash us white as snow. Isaiah declared: "Though your sins are like scarlet, they shall be as white as snow; though they are red like crimson, they shall be as wool" (Isaiah 1:18).

Dignity is the gift of the Holy Spirit, who lifts us up in heavenly places through Christ Jesus. Jesus clothes us in robes of righteousness and makes us priests before our God (Revelation 1). So we can come boldly before the God of this great throne, cleansed by the blood of Jesus and crowned with the right of authority!!

7 Lamps of Fire

There are also seven lamps of fire burning before the throne—representing the seven-fold Spirits of God—underscoring the fact that "our God is a consuming fire" (Hebrews 12:29). Yes, we serve an awesome God!

Moses had a glimpse of this greatness in his encounter with the burning bush. The purpose of this encounter was for the fire in the bush to become the fire within the heart of Moses. And when that happened, Moses stepped into his destiny: to confront Pharaoh and lead the children of Israel out of Egypt.

We see a glimpse of His character and nature on the day of Pentecost when 120 flames sat on top of the heads of each follower of Jesus in the upper room. Once again when the fire of God filled the hearts of those disciples, something inside was changed and they moved forward with boldness, authority, and supernatural power.

All of this reminds us that our God is awesome! He is wondrous in power, glorious in might, and absolute in holiness.

4 Living Creatures
Around the throne, we are also introduced to the four living creatures. These are the beings who lead forth in declarations of worship. Each have six wings, are full of eyes around and within, and have the resemblance of a lion, a calf, one with the face of a man, and a flying eagle.

This is not the only passage we see these creatures in Revelation, but when we do encounter them they are always serving as DECLARERS! These living creatures cry out: "Holy, holy, holy, Lord God Almighty, who was and is and is to come!" Not only is this declaration true, it is unique because it represents the only time in Scripture one of the aspects of God's character is heralded three times.

The first thing declared by these creatures is the holiness of God. The word *holy* in its Hebrew context literally means "radically different." Our God is radically different in every way! He is radically different because He holds all power. He is radically different because He holds all peace. And He is radically different because He is the Holy, Holy, Holy One.

24 Elders' Response
Notice how the declarations of the four creatures trigger a RESPONSE in the hearts of the twenty-four elders. It is the essence of worship: responding to revelation! An encounter always brings forth a resonance

from deep with the human heart. Like the elders, we, too, can respond: "You are worthy, O Lord, to receive glory and honor and power; for You created all things, and by Your will they exist and were created."

This is the privilege given to us! Whether you are a Declarer of His character or a Responder to His presence, there is a place for you around the throne of God. He is the focus of it all!

The Supreme Sovereign

Everything John sees is amazing. But when he looks upon the One who sits on the throne, he realizes the limitations of his humanity. After all, how do you describe the Supreme Sovereign?

John tries by comparing Him to the most precious and beautiful of jewels. But it is impossible to capture the fullness of His majesty and splendor. He is awesome and worthy of every declaration and response, every word of praise and worship.

This is the throne room, a place we have access to today because of Jesus. It is dynamic, alive, and full of energy. It is a place as intercessors and believers we can enter for power, promise, peace, and worship.

PRAYING AND PREACHING

One of the most vivid lessons I learned with Evangelist Reinhard Bonnke was the balance between prayer and preaching. I witnessed up close how he employed each of these elements in his life and calling. Both key a healthy and advancing Christian walk for us as well.

Prayer is deeply personal and most often private. It is a place where we spend time talking and interacting with God. Sharing our faith, on the other hand, is often more open and visible. It is where we relate to others what Jesus has done for us—and can also do for them.

Spending time alone with the Lord *and* talking about Him triggers power! Doing both not only sharpens our faith, it enriches our lives.

The key, as Reinhard would say, is not living lopsided but maintaining a proper balance in our Christian walk.

I watched him demonstrate this from the stage on many occasions. It was both humorous and deeply convicting! He would start with his *right* leg, identifying it as the prayer life of the believer. He would stomp the right leg up and down to emphasize its power.

Then he would move over to his *left* leg, indicating it as the preaching life of a believer. He would stomp the left leg hard against the platform to emphasize its power. After hearing the echo of the platform underneath the weight of each stomp, there was no way you could miss the point that both legs contained tremendous power.

Then with determination, Reinhard would powerfully stride across the length of the platform, shouting out this cadence: "Pray (stomping down on the right leg)—and Preach (stomping down on the left leg). Pray and Preach, Pray and Preach, Pray and Preach," all the way across the platform. This was the balanced walk God intended for all of us: to pray and to preach!

Next he illustrated what happened when a believer did one or the other only. For those who liked to pray but remain silent, Reinhard would lean on his right leg only and hop across the platform. (I was always nervous he might lose his balance and fall over, but fortunately that never happened.) And to demonstrate those who liked speaking but spent little time quiet before the Lord, Reinhard would lean on his left leg only and hop across the platform.

I smiled every time he demonstrated the lopsided Christian life, because it looked so out of sorts leaning and hopping across the stage. But the principle always impacted me. Power flowed through a balanced life!

Now more than ever, we need to live out the balanced Christian walk. My hope is this will stir your heart to go deeper in prayer and fellowship with the Holy Spirit, and that those prayer-closet experiences will light a fire in your soul to broadcast the Good News everywhere.

RUNNING OFF THE PLATFORM

We finished the year with two crusades in Honduras. In La Entrada, not far from the Copan Ruins, a large field in the middle of a neighborhood made up the venue. With houses squaring it off on three sides, we faced a surprisingly nice problem: We ran out of room!

People sat on cars, families stood on balconies, and others stood in alleys leading away from the field, hearing but unable to see. It was densely packed with people hungry for Jesus!

Some of the occult activities we were appraised of during the week burned in my soul and compelled me to preach on Dagon and the supreme authority of Jesus Christ over darkness and witchcraft. I also knew for the first time I had an army of intercessors crying out for souls at that very moment. It moved me deeply as people pushed forward to receive Jesus as their Savior.

I had never run off the platform before. But the response motivated me to get on the ground with the people as fast as possible. I know it alarmed a few members of the team, but I love Hondurans and wanted to touch or hug as many of them at the altar as I could. No other decision in their lives would carry as much significance as the one to say yes to Jesus!

The presence of the Holy Spirit swept over the thousands of people jammed on that field. Our team of altar workers tried to move through the crowd, laying hands on the people, but it was nearly impossible. It was so dense from the hunger of the people that the team could not work their way front to back. Instead, they were forced to move diagonal or sideways.

There were so many miracles and testimonies in La Entrada as people pressed in to receive a touch from the Lord Jesus. Like so many of the previous crusades in Honduras, we left rejoicing over the power of God and even more in love with the people.

SEVEN TYPES OF PRAYER

Prayer is divine interaction between you and God. Even as we daily interact with friends in various ways from Facebook, to coffee at Starbucks, to an intimate dinner, it is the same in communicating with God. There are various forms and levels.

Common Prayer

Common prayer is the elementary level. These are learned prayers, something said in a congregational or family setting. The classic children's bedtime prayer from the eighteenth century: *Now I lay me down to sleep . . .* or the Irish blessing: *May the road rise up to meet you, may the wind always be at your back . . .* or the thirteenth-century prayer of Assisi: *Lord, make me an instrument of your peace*, are examples of common prayer. Like a nursery rhyme, these prayers are easily learned and easily recited.

They may not have been common when first spoken. But with time and reciting them over and over, they tend to become common.

The essence of this type of prayer is determined by if it comes from the heart, or only from the mouth. If I'm just quoting someone else, it is common prayer. These kinds of prayers, though, can become more than that if they come from the heart.

Conversational Prayer

Conversation prayer is the causal level. These are often inward sighs, such as a student whispers before an exam: "Lord, help me," or when a person is heading to an appointment and breathes out: "I need you today." These prayers can happen anywhere, at any time. Nothing intense or dramatic, just quick communication bursts from earth to heaven.

Contractual Prayer

Contractual prayer is praying the promises of God. These take the Word of God and call eternity into time. Praying the words of Jesus: "Your kingdom come. Your will be done on earth as it is in heaven" is a form of contractual prayer.

In Acts 4, the disciples came together in the middle of a crisis and applied Psalm 2 to their situation. Activating God's Word in prayer, they asked for boldness and power. And the Bible says when they finished, "the place where they were assembled together was shaken" (v. 31).

Compassionate Prayer

Compassionate prayer is the outpouring of one's heart—the desperate cry of the soul. Jesus exemplified this form of prayer in the Garden of Gethsemane, where He prayed so earnestly that "His sweat became like great drops of blood falling down to the ground" (Luke 22:43). These prayers range from deep desire to intense desperation.

Creative Prayer

Creative prayer is praying in the Holy Spirit. The Bible says "For we do not know what we should pray for as we ought, but the Spirit Himself makes intercession for us with groanings which cannot be uttered" (Romans 8:26).

Paul encouraged believers to pray and sing with the spirit and with understanding (1 Corinthians 14). Both are vital for our spiritual health and development.

Celebratory Prayer

Celebratory prayer is the sound of victory! It is jubilant declaration, extolling the majesty and wonder of His name. Shouts of thanksgiving and praise for His goodness and greatness are examples of celebratory prayer. It is the remembrance of who He is and what He has done for us.

Collective Prayer

Prayer not only functions powerfully in private but also corporately. Many of the most intimate revelations of prayer come when we hear others pray. Something begins to stir inside as we hear others pray, releasing a fiery hunger to minister to the Lord like that too. In these moments, prayer is not taught, it is caught!

This happened to the disciples. They would have known the common prayers of their day, but it didn't register like the prayers of Jesus. The words that came out of His mouth were unlike anything they had ever heard before. It made them hungry!

This is part of what prayer is supposed to do in a corporate sense: draw us to the Lord Jesus Christ and to kindle fire inside us and stir up the passion to call upon His name. As Jesus prayed, His candor and intimacy with the Father, coupled with His fervor and authority, moved the disciples to crave a similar prayer life. And just as it pleased Jesus to teach them how to pray in new and wonderful ways, He wants to do the same with us today!

UNABLE TO SPEAK

The year had raced by, and a new emphasis on developing a stronger prayer and intercession focus had resulted in increasingly more powerful crusades. One thing we loved about Honduras was ministering in remote places—areas that people rarely went to. Yoro was such a place. And we were about to experience a mighty demonstration of the love and power of God.

Thousands gathered to hear the Gospel in an open field. I asked Steve to pray for me moments before preaching on the fire of the Holy

Spirit, because one of the leading pastors with whom we had come to love and respect came from a non-Pentecostal background. But when the call for Holy Spirit fire went up and the pastor saw the power of God sweep across the people, he grabbed the microphone and started pleading with everyone: "Receive it, receive it, receive it!"

Testimonies flooded the platform: pain gone, skin conditions healed, deaf ears opened, people set free from demonic bondages. And the presence of the Holy Spirit only continued to mount in intensity. It reached the point that many who came up to testify could not even speak!

People fell to the ground under the weight of His marvelous presence. It was so strong, I told the leaders on the platform not to touch anyone. And still people continued to fall to the ground!

Eventually they were helped up and given another opportunity to speak, but they still could not. They ended up leaving the platform without having been able to say a word.

One young lady finally did manage, trembling, to utter one phrase: "The power of God is so strong" . . . and this testimony is absolutely true. Jesus is magnificent!

CHAPTER 11

FIRE STARTERS AND RAIN CRUSADERS

NOW THAT WE WERE DOING crusades year-round, we were running into more and more weather issues—specifically rain. After months of work, fundraising, and prayer, the last thing we wanted to see were storm clouds roll in.

RAIN CRUSADERS

But as we moved into our fifth year, the reality was we had encountered a lot of rain. Pastor Andrew McMillan from Colombia sent a lighthearted email saying as much as he rejoiced over the souls and miracles, he thoroughly enjoyed reading our weather updates. It seemed he took the greatest joy when we preached in downpours! It had happened so many times, he finally called us the "rain crusaders."

The remarkable thing about these stormy episodes is how intentional the move of God had been. Despite driving rains, heavy winds, even thunder and lightning, some of the most supernaturally charged nights took place in the worst of conditions.

It reached the point we finally determined in our hearts that when the rain came, the fire of God would fall as well.

THE NIGHT IT RAINED AND FIRE FELL

The first time we came face-to-face with a heavy rainstorm was in Siguatepeque, Honduras. It was our third evangelistic rally, and news of stormy weather approaching only added to the trouble brewing.

Opposing voices demanded we take down the stage, insisting we find a different venue. When that had failed, they went on local television and radio to announce the event had been cancelled.

And if that had not caused enough chaos, they spontaneously organized a free concert with a popular Honduran band on the same night as the crusade. Never had we faced such an avalanche of resistance. So to hear we now faced a possible rain out on Saturday night only darkened our outlook.

The team gathered to pray that afternoon, and right on cue the heavens opened and the rain began to pour down. After all we had battled, it seemed uncanny that now was the moment for a rainstorm to blow through. It was awful, made worse by the fact that the harder we prayed for it to stop, the fiercer the rain pounded down outside.

I finally got up and walked out of the room. I had to find a private place to ask the Lord what was going on. Looking out a hotel window at the rain, I poured my heart out.

No, the rain did not stop, but the Holy Spirit whispered a word of hope, direction, and reassurance into my heart. Those several minutes alone with the Lord changed everything.

I walked back into an apprehensive meeting room and went on the attack. I had come to peace with the rain, I announced, and we had a lot to be thankful for. The crusade had been paid for, the Gospel had gone out the night before, and if necessary we could always come back. No matter what happened the rest of the day or night, we would leave victorious and full of peace.

Immediately the tension and anxiety broke. The prayer focus shifted away from the rain to praying out Scriptures over the city. And, wow—the declaration of the Word of God was powerful! Not only did it refocus us as a team back to souls, it readied us for an amazing night ahead.

Despite the rain, we loaded up the vans. I had no idea if anyone would turn up in such bad weather conditions, but even if only one came, I pledged to preach my heart out!

It was heartwarming to see umbrellas and raincoats. Someone even turned up with an accordion! Everything was drenched, so we had no band to lead us in worship. The accordion was a last effort by one of the musicians to engage the crowd. Seriously, we had no business conducting a service that night. Except that people came!

Dennis and I took to the pulpit, and the rain came down harder. No one moved. It occurred to me if these precious people were willing to get pounded by the elements to hear the message, then I had an obligation to preach it. So with no Bible or notes, I stood under an umbrella and preached on the fire of the Holy Spirit.

I learned later the umbrellas for Dennis and me were not a merciful courtesy but to protect the last two working microphones. We were barely making it.

Finished, I cried out for God to answer with Holy Spirit fire. It was as if lightning fell from the sky, hit the stage, and leaped into the crowd.

The only way I was able to later describe the intensity of that moment was to use an Old Testament story. In the biblical account judgment burst forth from the tabernacle, and the priests ran into the crowd to get ahead of it so it would stop. But this was not judgment; it was healing, redemption, and Holy Spirit fire! The altar workers did not go into the crowd to stop it but kept praying for more.

I could feel the intensity of it and cried out to the altar workers, "Hurry, hurry, hurry!" They ran in among the people, and many of the men, women, and children were already on their knees in the mud! The response to the presence of God was extraordinary.

A man asked if he could share his testimony from the night before—how the Lord had opened his ear to hear. He said liquid had oozed out of one ear, and as he wiped it away the Lord healed him instantly! He had endured the rain all night for an opportunity to glorify God.

The moment he finished testifying, the power of God hit him harder than anything I had ever seen before. He spun 360 degrees and was driven backward. It was like a tidal wave crashed into him, literally lifting him up and throwing him on his back.

His head slammed into the stage. It was so violent, so forceful, that when he hit the stage I was concerned. We were all concerned. But he was fine. Josh went over and asked about his head, to which he replied, "Not my head—Jesus healed my ear!"

Drenched and exhausted, I climbed into the car where Dad had spent most of the evening because of the conditions. He listened to Dennis, Alisa, and me chatter about what we had seen. Then, typical of my dad, he added a benediction: "The night it rained and the fire fell." It was a perfect summation of what had just happened, and a prophetic word for many of the evangelistic events to come.

YOU SHALL RECEIVE HOLY SPIRIT POWER

"You shall receive power when the Holy Spirit comes upon you; and you shall be witnesses to Me" (Acts 1:8). As a spirit-filled believer in Jesus, you become a channel of His power, His compassion, His ministry to forgive, and His ability to save, heal, and set free. Understand when Jesus said you will receive power, He meant it! You have an important assignment on this planet, and He has given you His Spirit power to fulfill it!

Who is the Holy Spirit?

He is God. The God of the Bible is awesome! The Holy Spirit is the essence and expression of God. One of the characteristics ascribed to God is as all-consuming fire (Hebrews 12:29). This is evidenced throughout Scripture: from Abraham's altar, to Moses' encounter at the burning bush, to Solomon's dedication of the Temple, to Elijah's triumph on Mount Carmel. And it is certainly true of the upper room.

In Acts 2, on the day of Pentecost, 120 people were present when the Holy Spirit came. Cloven tongues of fire sat on each of them. The divine purpose of the fire was firstly to purify the disciples. It was fulfillment of the words of John the Baptist concerning Jesus: I indeed baptize you with water . . . but He will baptize you with the Holy Spirit and fire" (Matthew 3:11).

The divine purpose of the fire was secondly to empower the disciples. This is what Jesus meant when He said, "You shall receive power when the Holy Spirit has come upon you" (Acts 1:8).

We see this in the lives of the disciples. After Pentecost, they walked in the power of the Holy Spirit, always preaching salvation, praying for the sick, casting out demons, and reaping the joy and favor of God.

The same can be true for us! This life-transforming experience is a promise from Scripture: "The anointing which you have received from Him abides in you" (1 John 2:27).

When the fire of the Holy Spirit comes on you, it will remain on you forever. It will impact your life and ministry, because it is the power of God living within you! You will not have to ask for a new anointing, because the flame of the Holy Spirit will never stop burning. Instead, the fire of the Holy Spirit will blaze so strongly inside of you, your life will make an eternal impact!

The Holy Spirit is the Anointer, and the Holy Spirit is the Anointing! The Lord Jesus ignites a flame to continuously burn inside you, always remain fresh, and always remain active.

Answered Prayer of Jesus

The life in the Holy Spirit is a gift. It's not because we deserve it, it is because we need it. It is the fulfillment of the promise of the Lord Jesus Christ, who said: "I will pray the Father, and He will give you another Helper, that He may abide with you forever" (John 14:16).

Jesus said, "I will pray!" Each time fire falls, whether it be in the crusade services in Africa or Latin America or anywhere else in the world, it comes in direct answer to the prayer of Jesus. The fire power of the Holy Spirit comes because Jesus already prayed for us. This fire is available for you!

After the fire fell in the upper room, Peter stood up with the other disciples and explained the supernatural workings of God. Their boldness and passion that morning was an expression of the authority of the Holy Spirit. They were unmistakably on fire for God.

What started that day continues through today. As the prophet Joel says, in the last days, "I will pour out My Spirit on all flesh" (Joel 2:28). It is the divine intent and purpose to set every heart and congregation ablaze for the glory of His name.

The heavenly Father wants to use and release through you these wonderful gifts. They are the expressions of the Holy Spirit given to those who ask Him. The Bible says, "The manifestation of the Spirit is given to each one for the profit of all" (1 Corinthians 12:7).

The Holy Spirit enables us to honor and exalt the Lord Jesus, and partners with us in prayer. The Bible says, "The Spirit also helps in our weaknesses." That when we do not know what we should say, "the

Standing ready to collect Evangelist Reinhard Bonnke's jacket (2004).

In traditional African clothing with Evangelist Reinhard Bonnke and Peter Van den Berg (2004)

Encountering Jesus in Santa Ana, El Salvador (2010). This young man was the first to reach the platform in response to the call for salvation.

Preaching in the rain in Puerto Barrios, Guatemala (2008). This was our 7th LOLI crusade. By this point, we were getting used to Central America showers!

A Beautiful Smile in La Lima, Honduras (2010). One of my favorite pictures from our first ten years of ministry

Gospel campaign in Cofradia, Honduras (2011). Despite the threat of stormy weather, people came to experience the presence and power of God.

Bears on a Mission in San Pedro Sula Hospital (Christmas 2011). Red bear, white bear, or brown bear? This little girl knew immediately which one she wanted!

Send-Me-Anna Jones finds a new home (Christmas 2011)

Meeting with Honduras President Porfirio Lobo Sosa at the Casa Presidencial (April 2012)

Endorsement of Honduras Prays by President Porfirio Lobo Sosa (April 2012)

Honduras President Porfirio Lobo Sosa at Honduras Prays in San Pedro Sula (July 2012)

Call for Holy Spirit Fire at Honduras Prays (2012)

Response to the Call for Salvation at Honduras Prays (2012)

Praying for revival with Alisa at Nicaragua Prays (2013)

Nicaragua Prays Crusade in Managua, Nicaragua (2013)

Panama Prays Crusade on Friday night in Colon, Panama (2014)
We gathered in Panama City the next night - hosting Gospel campaigns on both the Atlantic and Pacific sides of the Panama Canal.

Meeting with Nicaragua Minister of Government
Ana Isabel Morales Mazum (2014)

Praying for the Panama President Juan Carlos Varela (2015)

Talking with Panama President Juan Carlos Varela (2015)

Spirit Himself makes intercession for us with groanings which cannot be uttered" (Romans 8:26). The gift of the Holy Spirit enables us to worship in spirit and truth and to witness in the power of His might. All this in answer to the prayer of the Lord Jesus!

Activated Power Source

In the Great Commission, Jesus said Go! So when we step out in faith to do something for Jesus, the fire power of the Holy Spirit kicks in. Supernatural power is released as God confirms His word with wonders and signs (Mark 16).

Remember Jesus said: "You shall receive power when the Holy Spirit has come upon you; and you shall be witnesses to Me" (Acts 1:8). Part of that promise is we will speak in other tongues as the Holy Spirit gives us utterance (Acts 2:4). The fire of the Holy Spirit comes directly from heaven, connects with our spirit, and releases our tongue to pray in a new language. The spiritual connects with the physical, the heavenly with the earthly. The result is a release of supernatural power!

Speaking in tongues simply connects your spirit to the source, which is the Holy Spirit. You become a conduit for the Holy Spirit. It does not matter if you feel anything, because it is not about feelings or emotions, it is about being connected. Power flows because you are connected to the source!

Consider an electrical switch. Power is always available, but only when you turn the switch on does the light bulb actually come on. We are anointed for action: to preach the Gospel, pray for the sick, and exercise authority over the demonic. When we take action, the switch is flipped and the power flows!

You may be aware of the Holy Spirit resting on you right now. It is His desire to set you ablaze for the rest of your life. It will operate every time you do something to glorify Jesus. You have the power and anointing to affect your world!

You are empowered to be a witness for Jesus—for people to be saved, healed, and delivered. In generations past, people who were filled with the Holy Spirit stepped boldly out of their comfort zone and impacted history. You are a candidate today—it is your calling; it is your destiny!

TWO CONDITIONS TO RELEASE THE FIRE OF THE HOLY SPIRIT

If you are hungry for the fire of the Holy Spirit to be released in your life, then you can receive it right now. There are just two simple conditions:

> *First,* you must know that the blood of Jesus has washed your sins away! Only the blood of Jesus makes you worthy to receive the fire and power of the Holy Spirit. This means Jesus is alive in you, that you are clean from a life of sin and darkness. Without the blood of Jesus, there is no release of Holy Spirit fire. It is the blood of Jesus first, then Holy Spirit fire.
>
> *Second,* you must come trusting and receiving. Even as you received the gift of salvation, you receive the free gift of the Holy Spirit.

The fire power of the Holy Spirit is received as a love gift from the Father. It will impact your life and ministry to boldly testify on His behalf. This gift will fill you with supernatural joy, and you will pray in a new language as the Holy Spirit prays through you!

ROOMING WITH SMITH WIGGLESWORTH

One of the surprises of my family heritage was learning about an acquaintance my grandfather John had with another evangelist: Smith Wigglesworth. This man shook the United Kingdom with his fiery preaching, and remarkable miracles often broke out at his meetings. So when Dad told me he had memories of Wigglesworth staying in their home while growing up, I wanted to know more.

My grandfather worked first as an architect building underground bridges in the coal mines of Wales. Conscripted during the First World War, he endured eighteen months of imprisonment in Turkey. Returning home, he rededicated his life to Jesus and committed himself to church planting and pioneering. It was as a pastor and mentor to other young men that John became acquainted with Smith Wigglesworth.

During that time, itinerate ministers stayed in homes of area pastors. On several occasions Dad's childhood home transformed into a bed-and-breakfast to host visiting preachers—and a couple times that included Smith Wigglesworth.

Their paths crossed again at a Welsh convention. In those days, long weekend gatherings were a huge attraction, usually around Easter or Pentecost. People came from surrounding villages to hear speakers like Smith Wigglesworth and other area pastors.

That particular weekend Smith Wigglesworth was scheduled to preach the night service, and John Evans was slotted in the morning. One small problem: John lost his voice the night before.

The solution to such a problem was patently obvious to his famous roommate: John needed to stay up all night and pray. And he should keep praying until his voice returned! Well, who was my granddad to argue with Smith Wigglesworth?

The next morning John spoke without any vocal problems. But the irony of it all was Smith Wigglesworth was scheduled to speak again the next day—and this time his voice had gone hoarse after preaching the night service. To which my grandfather was more than happy to pass on a tried-and-true piece of advice. And that is exactly what Smith Wigglesworth did.

THIS GIFT IS FOR YOU!

My favorite Smith Wigglesworth story was when he spoke at a convention held in Crosskeys, South Wales. It was a service attended by my dad and granddad.

Smith Wigglesworth stopped in the middle of his message and said, "The Lord has a gift of healing for someone present." He immediately asked everyone who needed prayer to come forward.

He went to the first person and said, "The gift is not for you, but I'll pray for you." He moved to the second person and said, "The gift is not for you either, but I'll pray for you." This dialogue repeated itself throughout the entire line until he had prayed for everyone.

Looking out at the audience, he asked if there was anyone else sick who had not come forward. A lady with a form of palsy stood up. She had remained in her seat, because hundreds of times people had prayed for her and nothing happened.

Smith Wigglesworth walked over to her and said, "This gift is for you!" Stretching out the palm of his hand toward her, he said, "Take it!"

As the lady reached out and touched his hand, the power of the Holy Spirit healed her instantly.

THE NUDGE OF THE HOLY SPIRIT

One time after Dad shared this story, I just could not stop wondering what it must have felt like to stand there knowing it was a supernatural moment. Extending his hand in faith to that lady and watching the power of God touch her. It simply overwhelmed me, and an immediate hunger to walk more closely with the Holy Spirit intensified inside me.

At that very moment the Lord spoke to my heart: The release of the supernatural is not based on human inventiveness but an acute awareness to the *nudge* of the Holy Spirit. A nudge—followed by an immediate obedient response.

This is a place squeezed between *divine intention* on one side and the *marvelous outworking of it* on the other side. What a place to stand—in between the nudges of the Holy Spirit and the outworking of His remarkable grace and mercy!

This was seen repeatedly in the life and ministry of Jesus, constantly responding to the compulsion of the Holy Spirit to do the will of the Father. In John 4, the Holy Spirit nudged Him to take a different route back home, so "He left Judea and departed again to Galilee. But He needed to go through Samaria." It led to an encounter with a woman at the well, which not only held personal significance for her but multiplied dramatically to reach scores of others in her community. All of this because of a nudge!

Such awareness and submission to the Holy Spirit releases the supernatural. It may be a rapid expansion of the Gospel or a divine manifestation of healing, but all of it is an act of God's grace, who wills and does it for His good pleasure (Philippians 2:13). The Holy Spirit is active in our world today. My prayer is that all of us would live with an acute awareness to His nudges and see His glory. This nudge is for you—take it!

A CLOUD OF WITNESSES

When I hear these stories, my heart shouts, *That's my Jesus!* But these are only a few that cry out from a cloud of witnesses who have boldly gone before us. Hebrews 12 urges us: "Since we are surrounded by so great a cloud of witnesses . . . run with endurance." Lock your eyes on Jesus!

These are heroes who went before us and walked according to the nudge of the Holy Spirit. There are millions of them, and all are reminders that God uses people to set communities, generations, even continents ablaze with revival fire.

I don't want to be like those who prayed for that lady and nothing happened. No, I want to walk in the nudging of the Holy Spirit, to preach Jesus Christ boldly, to lay hands on the sick, to influence nations for His glory. I want to do my part, to one day join that cloud of witnesses with a testimony of the greatness of God!

Charles Finney

One of the most famous American revivalists, Charles Finney was full of the fire of the Holy Spirit. Radical in his generation, he preached salvation, personal holiness, and the power of the Holy Spirit. A nation shaker, Charles Finney is credited with triggering the Second Great Awakening in the United States during the nineteenth century.

A well-documented revival story came during his visit to New York, where he went to look through a factory. He noticed there was some agitation among the workers—in particular a small group of women busy weaving. Finney described it this way: "I went slowly towards them. They saw me coming, and were evidently much excited. One of them was trying to mend a broken thread, and her hands trembled so that she could not mend it. I approached slowly, looking at the machinery, as I passed; but this girl grew more and more agitated, and could not proceed with her work. When I came within eight or ten feet of her, I looked solemnly at her. She was quite overcome, sunk down, and burst into tears. The impression caught almost like powder, and in a few moments nearly all in the room were in tears. This feeling spread through the factory. The owner of the establishment was present, and seeing the state of things, he said to the superintendent, 'Stop the mill, and let the people attend to religion; for it is more important that our souls should be saved than that this factory run.' . . . We did so, and a more powerful meeting I scarcely ever attended. It went on with great power. The revival went through the mill with astonishing power, and in the course of a few days nearly all in the mill were hopefully converted" (Charles Finney, *Autobiography,* English version, p. 154).

This is the power of revival; it not only touched the lives of the people in the mill that day, but just reading the testimony sparks fire inside our souls. No wonder he could say, "Revival comes from heaven when heroic souls enter the conflict determined to win or die—or if need be, to win and die!"

What a war cry for our generation! To be full of Holy Spirit fire, unrelenting in our passion to holiness and humility, so desperate to know Jesus and make Him known. Who knows—maybe God wants to use you to unleash the next Great Awakening!

John Wesley

Another fiery witness for Jesus, John Wesley lived during the eighteenth century. His passion for evangelism was so strong he annually covered an estimated 8,000 miles on horseback preaching the Gospel. A history maker, Wesley impacted two continents and founded the Methodist movement.

You can feel the heat in Wesley's charge: "Give me one hundred preachers who fear nothing but sin, and desire nothing but God, and I care not a straw whether they be clergymen or laymen; such alone will shake the gates of hell and set up the kingdom of heaven on Earth."

I think of the first generation of believers who turned the world upside down, because they exemplified this type of charge. And it begs the question: where are the one hundred men and women today—radical for God, hungry for holiness, and filled with Holy Spirit power?

John Wesley also said: "I set myself on fire and people come to watch me burn; I burn with passion, enthusiasm, dire devotion towards God, and a Holy Hatred of the world and every form of lukewarm religion." This is the portrait of the one hundred. No compromise, eyes locked on

Jesus, and revival burning in their soul. Yes we need one hundred history makers. The burning question is: will you be one of them?

George Jeffreys

A bold and gifted speaker, George Jeffreys set Europe ablaze with the fire of the Holy Spirit. People came by the thousands to hear him preach, and salvation, miracles, and healing characterized his meetings. A nation shaker, George Jeffreys founded the Elim Foursquare movement in the United Kingdom.

My dad and granddad attended one of his tent meetings in Cardiff, Wales, and it left an impression upon my dad, who was only a boy at the time. George Jeffreys was preaching on hearing the voice of God and as an illustration picked up his Bible. He raised it up to his ear and began fanning through its pages. As he continued "listening," Jeffreys asked dramatically: "What are the pages saying to you?"

As a seven-year-old boy, Dad was mesmerized by it all and could not wait to get home. He wanted to hear what his Bible had to say to him! He rushed to his bedroom, found a Bible, and quickly started fanning the pages by his ear. After several attempts he returned to his dad, disappointed, and announced that his Bible was broke and not working.

Revival breeds that kind of childlike hunger for the Word of God—an urgency to pick it up and see what the Holy Spirit has to say. The book may not speak audibly as you fan its pages, but the words of Scripture are fire to our soul, shaping character and purpose. *What are the pages saying to you?*

These are just three witnesses out of a multitude of those who have gone ahead of us. They walked in supernatural authority and personal holiness—and impacted their generation and world for the kingdom of God. This is the challenge they left us, and it is the call of Hebrews 12: Run the race of faith! "Since we are surrounded by so great a cloud of witnesses, let us lay aside every weight, and the sin which so easily ensnares us, and let us run with endurance the race that is set before us, looking unto Jesus, the author and finisher of our faith" (Hebrews 12:1-2).

FAITH VERSUS BELIEF

There is a critical difference between faith and belief, and we need to know the difference. Belief is so safe, so passive, and usually so conventional. Our world does not need more belief systems—it is full of them. What our world (and the church) desperately needs today is the demonstration of faith!

Biblical faith by nature is active, bold, and sometimes way out of the box. The difference between holding on to belief points and walking in the demonstration of resurrection life is an important distinction. It may be impossible to imagine living like that on our own, but remember nothing is too difficult for God!

The call today is to rise higher in faith and look beyond the obvious. While the world continues to deteriorate, the power of God continues to manifest itself. And this is the promise: What is in front of us is greater than what now lies behind.

In Luke 5, we see the faith of a group of men and a paralytic. The men knew Jesus would touch their friend if they could only get to Him. With people packed around the house, they became aggressive in faith, destroying their neighbor's roof in order to lower their friend before Jesus. When Jesus saw their faith, He said to the paralytic: "Man, your sins are forgiven you." When the religious leaders mentally objected, He said to the paralytic: "Arise!"

There were many people in that room who had a strong belief system. Pharisees believed in the law, believed in the covenant, and even believed in the supernatural. But as far as faith was concerned, their belief system was rooted in the past, not the present.

But the men and their paralytic friend went beyond the philosophy of belief; their faith triggered boldness and action. They didn't just believe that Jesus could, they knew He *would* heal their friend! And what happened? The paralytic went home both forgiven and healed. Faith had transformed his life!

This is New Testament Christianity: people living as demonstrations of the touch of Jesus. This was the testimony of the early disciples: people took note that they had been with Jesus. Walking in the supernatural and aching for the holy presence of Jesus is normal Christianity. It is time to shift from traditional belief to transformative faith in the word and work of Jesus!

COSTA RICA DOWNPOUR

We had seen the Lord do some incredible things in the four years prior. But as we arrived in Costa Rica, it was about to rain down again in every way imaginable.

Holding a crusade on the Pacific Ocean, it should not have come as a surprise to hear the report of rain. Once again, we faced the prospect of a wipeout on Saturday as coastal storms hammered the area.

For three hours straight that afternoon, it poured. The scouting report indicated the crusade field was *underwater and transformed into a swamp.*

The rain had lightened up at the start of the service, but the report was true: The field was an absolute mess with water six inches deep in many places. Mud and bugs were everywhere. But that was only half the story.

The real news, though, was standing in the mud, drenched by the rain, people all over the grounds were worshiping Jesus! It was so radical. Some were even kneeling in the mud with hands lifted high, completely oblivious to anything or anyone else except the Lord Jesus Christ.

Such hunger and abandonment hit me hard. How was I supposed to speak to them when all that was screaming inside me was *I want to love Jesus like that!*

That night there was a fervency, an electricity in the crowd as I spoke about the fire of the Holy Spirit. When the moment came to call for fire, the altar team lined up at the front of the platform to go lay hands on the people. This time, before a cry went up for fire, before our team began moving through the crowd, the power of God dramatically fell on our gathering. Everywhere, people started going down in the mud, untouched.

The heavenly response was nothing short of astonishing! People fell forward, facedown in the water underneath the power of God. Ushers and security staff raced to pull their faces out of the water. People came up speaking in tongues! Testimonies of addicts set free, necks healed, backs healed, eyes healed, and hands healed flooded the platform.

A young girl came forward, trembling. She testified: "Tonight I was baptized in fire." The worship leader asked, "What do you feel?" For a moment it appeared she could not answer him. Her response was not in Spanish or English—it was her new prayer language from heaven! As she prayed in tongues, she could no longer stand but simply fell onto the platform under the glory of the Lord.

Another person came to the platform to testify, but the presence and power of the Holy Spirit was so strong on her, she could not speak at all. The rain kept coming, but the fire of God poured down even more upon the people.

Watching all of this, my heart finally could not take it any longer—it was exploding inside. I handed the microphone to a pastor and slipped to the back of the platform. I lifted my face toward the sky and cried out, "Me too, Lord, touch me too!" It was raining, but all I could see was Him.

BEING ON FIRE FOR JESUS IS MORE THAN A SPIRITUAL GIFT!

The fire of the Holy Spirit is contagious. It stirs deep things inside, increasing our passion for Jesus and motivating us forward to go after the impossible for God. Revival fire melts us, purifies us, and empowers us.

This is the nature and character of God: "God is a consuming fire" (Hebrews 12:29). When His flame settles inside our heart, our life takes on His fiery nature and character. Being on fire for God is more than a spiritual gift—it's the essence of who we are in Christ Jesus!

The coming of the Holy Spirit accentuated this—that we would live lives ablaze, filled with power. The Bible tells us that "You shall receive power when the Holy Spirit has come upon you; and you shall be witnesses to Me" (Acts 1:8). Traits of fire and power are clearly tied to the sharing of the Gospel. No evangelism; no fire power!

Maybe that's what attracts us to the revivalists or explains why we love reading the book of Acts so much. Their lives were extraordinary—bold, full of faith and power! The Holy Spirit bears fiery witness to their testimonies, creating an attraction or longing for our lives to look like that.

Here is the good news: We were created and redeemed to live extraordinary lives too! The Holy Spirit came to set us ablaze for Jesus and His Gospel so the nature and character of God could shine brightly through us.

CHAPTER 12

TREASURES IN EARTHEN VESSELS

EVEN AS WE WERE growing our reach into other nations like Dominican Republic, Guatemala, Costa Rica, and El Salvador, we never lost sight of Honduras. We returned every year to do at least one evangelistic and compassion campaign.

Part of the reason for staying active in the country was our love for Honduras and the spiritual hunger of the people. Practically, though, it made sense, as Dennis and our entire Central American team lived in San Pedro Sula. So if we did an event outside of the country, we tried to do the next one in Honduras for the sake of their families.

GENESIS OF SOMETHING BIGGER

Getting our guys home each night to their wives and kids while working in country meant targeting the large communities in and around San Pedro Sula.

This strategy, based primarily out of a desire to honor the family unit, ultimately unlocked a massive door that changed how we operated.

We did not see it right away, but as we built relationships throughout San Pedro Sula, the Holy Spirit was laying a foundation for what would become *Honduras Prays*—an evangelistic and prayer emphasis that would usher LOLI onto a national platform.

It was nothing short of the invisible hand of God directing our movements. Over the next three years, we would host seven crusades in the largest communities of San Pedro Sula and forge hundreds of relationships with pastors, hotel and restaurant managers, political leaders, and members of the media. From those three years, a dream began to sharpen in focus—one for the communities, the city, and the nation of Honduras.

MY SEIZURE IN VILLANUEVA

The first of the seven communities was Villanueva, directly to the south of San Pedro Sula. It was close enough for the Hondurans to sleep in their own beds and for our Texas teams to stay at a hotel in the city. But the first step toward *Honduras Prays*—an assignment we did not even know about yet—was about to come under siege in dramatic fashion.

It was Saturday night, the second night of the crusade. The last of the evangelistic meetings, and the atmosphere was electric. Thousands of people filled the soccer field, and the growing intensity and anticipation was palpable. Fireworks exploded into the night sky as the people celebrated.

Enlace Honduras asked for a quick TV interview. It was the last thing I did before climbing the steps onto the platform.

I took the microphone at 7:30 p.m. and began to preach. *Wham!* The initial blast of weakness hit me hard, halfway through the message. It came unexpectedly and left me dizzy and light-headed.

I stepped behind the podium and leaned on it for support, trying to recover. *What just happened?* I tried to be as casual as possible, as I certainly didn't want to raise any alarm or suspicion that something was awry.

I focused hard on my notes, breathed in, and determined to push ahead. *Wham!* A second and much stronger wave of weakness hit me, and instinctively I knew I was in serious trouble.

I stopped abruptly, turned, and walked to the back of the platform to where Steve was on his knees praying. I yelled, "Steve, take it!" He took the extended microphone and started moving toward the front of the platform.

I barely made it much farther. I sat in a chair at the very back of the stage and made a mental note that Alisa was by my side. I leaned forward—and everything went dark.

I had suffered a seizure in the middle of the crusade. Evidently, it was quite the effort by several Villanueva pastors to move 200-plus pounds of dead weight from the stage into the back of Dennis's SUV. There was confusion for several minutes as some of the leaders thought I had been shot. Others asked if they should stop the meeting.

But driving away from the venue, Alisa asked Dennis, "What's happening now?" Dennis replied, "What do you want them to do?" Alisa responded urgently, "The crusade can NOT stop!" Her forcefulness caught Dennis by surprise, but he immediately phoned the leading pastors and exhorted them to redouble their focus in prayer, in faith, and in ministry.

Forty-five minutes later, I woke up with my head on Alisa's lap. We were racing back to the hotel after an unsuccessful stop at a local doctor's clinic. A staff of medical professionals assisted me to my room, propped me against some pillows on the bed, and checked my vitals. By that time, whatever had happened to me had lifted entirely. I was recovering.

Meanwhile back in Villanueva, Steve finished the message and the Gospel went forward in great power. Nita New noted what happened when I left: *The people are to be commended for their response of faith. After it became apparent that Stephen was not coming back, we led everyone in prayer for him and they prayed fervently!* As encouraging updates on his condition were received they were shared with the people, who applauded enthusiastically each time. Everyone stayed, the Holy Spirit moved, and victory was won! . . . Afterwards, we learned articles of witchcraft were found underneath the stage and in the field. It was reported that on Friday night, one had told a security guard that the event was not be finished on Saturday night—that it would be shut down. Thanks be to God, He has delivered us from the power of darkness and given us victory in Jesus' name! Lives were changed as salvation, healing and a move of the Holy Spirit swept across that field.

RETURNING TO VILLANUEVA

We flew home the next day. I was thrilled by reports of repentance, miracles, and people receiving the baptism of the Holy Spirit. But it was hard to leave, because inside it felt like I had failed. The weekend lacked closure, and I certainly did not classify it as a success with such a public collapse. I hurt inside and out.

I had barely returned home when I said to Alisa, "I have to go back to Villanueva!" I needed to see the pastors again. I had to return to the scene where I had been carried off. And I wanted to finish my message!

Steve and I flew back a couple of weeks later. Dennis had organized a meeting with several pastors at Wendy's. Some of them were afraid I had come back to shame them for what happened—that somehow they should have covered/protected me better. How ironic that despite a strong victory, the Enemy of our soul had snuck in and wounded our spirits. We all felt lousy, convinced we had let one another down.

Lunch brought healing and a new perspective. The Lord vanquished all the lies and darts of the Enemy, and used the situation to forge a stronger bond between us. I hugged each of the pastors and walked out of there revived!

I still had one more item on my checklist: revisit the venue. Dennis, Steve, and I drove to the field. Two youth teams were engaged in a competitive soccer match. We parked the car, got out, and waited.

My chance came at halftime when the teams cleared. I went straight to the spot where the stage had been set up. I found it ironic that it was located in the same place on the field where I had been hurt years ago in University (just inside the penalty box). Undeterred, I started speaking on the fire of the Holy Spirit—from the point where I had been dramatically interrupted.

I am certain the coaches and players on the sideline were startled and wondering what in the world was going on. One minute they had been playing soccer, the next a Texan was on the field shouting in English. It did not matter. The message was not for them anyway. Rather, it was a declaration of victory to unseen observers.

I wanted every demonic entity in Villanueva to know that what had happened on Saturday night was not a setback—it was an advancement for the Gospel. Instead of fear, faith started rising in my heart along with a fresh boldness and determination to win more souls in Jesus' name!

I had come to the end of my message. Despite the players and onlookers, I cried out for God to send His flame and ignite revival in Villanueva, in San Pedro Sula, across Honduras, and to the ends of the earth. I said amen, and the three of us headed back to the car. I was alive and full of fire!

Something broke through that day. This is what made Villanueva special. It was a place of revelation, a place of testing, and a place of great victory.

WHAT-IF-NOT COUNTERATTACK

It could have turned out much differently. Some saw the seizure as an indicator I should reconsider international evangelism. With some of our remote venues and risks involved, surely it made sense to consider something safer and much closer to home.

One friend awkwardly noted: "If people knew you suffered from seizures, no one would risk taking you with them." I'm sure he did not mean it as harshly as it came out. But he might as well have screamed, "Stephen, you're a liability!"

I heard the whispers. Why did it happen? What if it happened again? What if this, what if that? So many questions! Yet how could I stop doing what the Holy Spirit clearly had orchestrated?

I retreated to something my mom and dad taught me long ago. The what-ifs will always come to flood your heart and mind, and create fear and uncertainty. But we are not without options. In the name of Jesus we have a supremely powerful counterattack to the what-ifs in life: What-if-NOT!

This was not the time to yield ground to the Enemy or become paralyzed by fear and doubt. No way! Now was the time for boldness and faith. The Bible promised: He who had begun this good work *in me*—He would be the One faithful to see it through (Philippians 1:6, my paraphrase).

I decided right then in the name of Jesus the "what-ifs" would have zero power over me. And that is why I returned to Villanueva—to declare out loud, "What-if-NOT!"

Looking back, Villanueva was a battleground, one to quench a divine strategy for something much larger. All of it could have been forfeited by swirling doubts and fears due to my collapse. To have done anything other than counterattack in Jesus' name and trust God with my human limitations would have meant forfeiting *Honduras Prays* and beyond.

Whatever challenge you are facing today, you can overcome any obstacle, doubt, or fear. When the Enemy, the world, or anyone else for that matter says *you can't* to the dreams to do something significant for God, remember you have a counterattack. *Yes you can in Jesus' name!*

TREASURES IN EARTHEN VESSELS

God is an equal-opportunity employer. He does not discriminate based upon our condition. He can use anyone—meaning He can use you to do something great for the kingdom of God!

Do not let the devil or anyone else say you cannot make the critical difference in your neighborhood, your work environment, your family, your school, or your generation because of a perceived weakness or limitation. The truth is most people cannot identify with your mountaintop achievements or successes. But all of us can identify with one another's weaknesses.

No matter the frailty or failure, the Lord Jesus will use it for His good if we will let Him. My dad coined a phrase decades ago: "Failure is not fatal in God and failure is not final in grace." He can use you!

The Bible says, "But we have this treasure in earthen vessels, that the excellence of the power may be of God and not of us" (2 Corinthians 4:7). What a promise! It does not matter the size or shape or even the condition of the earthen vessel. What makes the critical difference is the treasure contained inside.

The treasure is the Gospel and the power of the Holy Spirit. And moments like Villanueva serve as holy reminders that we are all fragile—unlikely candidates to host such beauty and power. But it is also what makes the work of God so remarkable. It means He can use anyone, because the power and presence is the treasure inside!

I WILL BE WITH YOUR MOUTH

One example of God using an earthen vessel is the life of Moses. When a bush in the wilderness suddenly burst into flame and remained unconsumed, the Bible says Moses turned to observe it. He left a changed man. The conversation between Moses and God in the desert not only changed a man, it liberated a nation.

This conversation out of Exodus 4:12–17 is powerful because it reveals a passion of God to recruit and deploy earthen vessels for His glorious purposes. And it highlights the vessel can have flaws, even physical limitations for God to choose and send out on divine assignment. So let's walk through these six verses and glean some of the things that changed a man and ultimately a nation.

A Great Commission (v. 12a)

The purpose of this supernatural conversation between God and Moses is this: a call to action. God sums it up into a couple of words: "Now (therefore), go!"

This charge is similar to what Jesus said to His followers: "Go therefore and make disciples of all the nations" (Matthew 28:19).

For Moses, it is a rescue mission for Israel. Go! Remind the children of Israel of My covenant—and the promise of freedom from slavery.

For the followers of Jesus, it is a rescue mission for the world. Go! Tell people everywhere of My cross and resurrection—and the provision of freedom from sin.

Both the Old Testament and New Testament accounts reveal an encounter with the King of Glory. And in both cases, the encounter results in a commission to Go Somewhere and Do Something!

The same applies today. A genuine encounter with Jesus will transform you and usher you into a kingdom assignment. You can be a global-changer! It starts by saying yes to Him and His Great Commission.

I Will Be With Your Mouth (v. 12b)

Immediately following the call to action, God tells Moses: "I will be with your mouth and teach you what you shall say."

The accent is not just on Moses going. It is imperative that as Moses goes, he also speaks! The promise of God was as Moses opened his mouth in obedience to the commission, the Lord Himself would get personally involved in the presentation.

This was also true with the disciples. Jesus told them ahead of time not to worry about what to say in front of leaders, because the Holy Spirit would teach them. "When they bring you to the synagogues and magistrates and authorities, do not worry about how or what you should answer, or what you should say. For the Holy Spirit will teach you in that very hour what you ought to say" (Luke 12:11-12).

For Moses and the disciples, the commission to GO and SPEAK was couched in a commitment by God Himself. He was not sending them out alone. He pledged to see the commission through to the very end!

What an encouragement to know that Jesus promises not only to be with us but also with our words. The devil knows this and fears the words of our testimony. So he battles hard to stop people from stepping out into their divine commission *and* opening their mouths.

Thank God For Unanswered Prayer (v. 13)

As the conversation nears its end, Moses learns the time of Israel's deliverance has arrived, and the Lord wants to use him to do it. So how does he respond to this amazing prospect and supernatural invitation? By asking God to send someone else instead! Moses' own words: "O my Lord, please send by the hand of whomever else You may send."

God commissioned Moses to Go and Speak. He promised to be with him as well as the words of his mouth. And Moses wanted no part of it, pleading with the Lord to send someone else.

Can you imagine what would have happened if the Lord had said okay? Think about the tragic implications if God had consented. Moses would have missed the ten plagues, the glorious Exodus, the Red Sea parting, forty days and nights on the mountain of God, receiving the Ten Commandments, and much, much more. If the Lord had agreed to his prayer, Moses would have missed out on a destiny as remarkable as any in the history of humanity.

Whatever he was nervous about, it failed to compare to what God had prepared for him and the nation he would help rescue. For Moses, the ultimate reality was this: Thank God for unanswered prayer!

God, who sees everything from the end to the beginning, had something special and extraordinary in mind for Moses. God's revealing Himself in the bush was more than a calling; it was an invitation into a life and relationship. More than redeeming his past, it would change his present and future into something more than he could ever have hoped for or imagined!

The same is true for us. God wants to reveal Himself as a God of fire, passion, and power—to offer us a life and relationship that far exceeds what we could map out or deploy on our own. The commission is to GO, to SPEAK, and to TRUST. The Lord is more committed to you (and your future) than you are. And like Moses, we can likely say: Thank God for unanswered prayers!

A God of Fire (v. 14a)

Look for a moment at the lengths God takes inviting Moses to partner with Him in national deliverance and a personal relationship. He sets a bush on fire, keeps it ablaze supernaturally until Moses notices, calls out to him, reveals His name, and commissions Moses to be His personal ambassador.

When Moses requests He find someone else, two things immediately happen: 1) the Lord gets angry with Moses; 2) the conversation becomes one-sided—with God doing all the talking.

The Bible says: "So the anger of the Lord was kindled against Moses." Why such a strong response from the Lord? I think part of the answer is due to how serious God takes the destiny of individuals and nations.

He was committed to liberating the children of Israel, and He was fully committed to using Moses as His vessel. His hot response to the reluctance of Moses makes this very clear.

God is passionate about revealing Himself to us. He may or may not use a fiery bush, but He is intentional about personal relationships and our partnering with Him.

All we need to do is look at the lengths Jesus took to make it possible: the humiliation of the cross. So when we hold on to our lives for sinful and selfish pleasures, or outrightly reject His Commission, we affront the divine agenda and supernatural destiny prepared for us.

A God of Mercy (v. 14)

"Now the anger of the Lord was kindled against Moses, and He said: 'Is not Aaron the Levite your brother? I know that he can speak well. And look, he is also coming out to meet you. When he sees you, he will be glad in his heart.'"

This is the mercy of God. Instead of letting Moses walk away from his calling or punishing him due to his objections, the Lord brings Aaron alongside him, so that together they can walk out the revelation from the fiery bush. Even though Aaron does not see the burning bush, his heart is glad when he hears God will deliver His people—and willing to serve alongside his brother.

Notice the Lord tells him: "I will be with your mouth *and* with his mouth, and I will teach you what you shall do" (v. 15, emphasis mine). Yes, God has provided Moses with a helper in his brother Aaron, but the assignment remains unchanged.

In the New Testament, the Holy Spirit linked Paul and Barnabas together for the first missionary journey. God had prepared something remarkable for Paul, but it took a Barnabas coming beside him and believing in him to set things in motion.

So what kind of person are you? Some people have an obvious calling hanging over their head. They are visionaries and leaders, but they rarely can do it all on their own. Others are enablers and encouragers. They add strength and help others move forward into what God has assigned them. The truth is we can be both!

Do the Miraculous (v. 17)

The conversation concludes with: "You shall take this rod in your hand, with which you shall do the signs." The promise was that supernatural power would go with him back to Egypt. For Moses, it would start with the plagues—a powerful rebuke against the gods of the land. And it would continue through the Red Sea and beyond.

The same type of promise is given to us in Mark 16. As we go into the world on His behalf as kingdom agents, He promises to do the miraculous as confirmation for us too. He was greater than every god then, and He is greater than every name today. This God of Fire is the God of the Miraculous, and His promise is to go with you and your mouth.

PEOPLE WHO ARE A LITTLE LESS THAN PERFECT

Moses had reservations based on his past and his speech, but God had no issue partnering with someone a little less than perfect. What an encouragement!

God can use any of us to show His power and declare His greatness. As one of those less-than-perfect vessels, I am aware He could have chosen someone stronger, someone without risks or limitations, to send into mass evangelism. But He sought me out, then sent me out!

The Bible says: "God has chosen the foolish things of the world to put to shame the wise, and God has chosen the weak things of the world to put to shame the things which are mighty" (1 Corinthians 1:27). It is just like Jesus to use people who are a little less than perfect, kind of rough around the edges and disqualified in the eyes of experts.

You do not have to be perfect, talented, wealthy, beautiful, famous, or anything our world esteems. You only need Jesus! This is what makes the Gospel and the work of the Holy Spirit strong and powerful. It shines through the weakest and most broken among us!

PICKPOCKET TRANSFORMATION

A few months after Villanueva, we returned to Honduras for our second crusade in the San Pedro Sula area. Not far from the airport, Rivera Hernandez was known for its violence and gang activity. It was not the most dangerous community in San Pedro Sula, but it definitely landed on the top-five list of places you wanted to avoid after dark.

It was during our week here that we met a young man from Villanueva. His story touched my heart, because it linked to the previous campaign.

He had come to the Villanueva crusade, but not to find God. He had no interest in healing or praying for his community or any kind of spiritual development. He was a thief—a pickpocket artist who saw the crowd as an opportunity. If things went well, he would sneak in, grab what he could, and disappear.

But as he worked his way through the crowd something unexpected happened—something that had never factored into his plan. The message started to penetrate his defenses, and he found himself listening to the Gospel.

Finally he gave up maneuvering through the crowd and joined them in giving his full attention to what was being said. The Gospel washed over this young man, and he fell under the conviction of the Holy Spirit.

He started moving through the crowd again—this time forward—not to steal but to start a new life with Jesus.

This pickpocket had come to steal and remain hidden but left transformed with a testimony of grace and salvation. Instead of leaving with a few coins, he had discovered a treasure much more valuable: eternal life through the Lord Jesus Christ!

PSALM OF THE CROSS

Before David concludes the prophetic Psalm of the Cross, he zeroes in on two things: remembrance and reverence. "All the ends of the world shall remember and turn to the Lord, and all the families of the nations shall worship before You. For the kingdom is the Lord's, and He rules over the nations" (Psalm 22:27–28).

The World Shall Remember Him for What He Did

The psalmist declares that in the annals of human history one event will stand out in their remembrance—an event so remarkable, so passionate, so impressionable, it will never be forgotten or dismissed. What was he prophetically pointing toward? The death and resurrection of our Savior, Jesus Christ!

To understand the magnitude of the event described, note the significance of the cross in Roman times. A Roman cross consisted of two wooden beams secured together by ropes. Its purpose was to inflict the most excruciating pain on the victim and to serve as a warning to others.

To the Jews, crucifixion was more than the most painful way to die; it was also associated with a curse. Deuteronomy 21:23 notes: "He who is hanged is accursed of God."

The act of crucifixion was often preceded by brutal flogging. The victim then had to carry the horizontal beam to the execution site, where the soldiers nailed the person to the cross via the wrists and feet. But it was not the nails or beating that brought death; it was suffocation.

In addition to the screaming pain of a filleted back and punctured hands and feet, victims had to contend with the horror of trying to catch their breath! To inhale oxygen, it meant pushing oneself up on the nails while rubbing one's back up against the wooden beam, before collapsing downward to hang on the cross again. This merciless cycle often lasted for days. Only when the victim became too weak to push up any longer did he or she suffocate and die. This is why the soldiers sometimes broke the legs of the condemned—to hasten death.

It is this prophetic portrayal of love and sacrifice by Jesus the Christ that the psalmist calls us to remember and respond to. Consider his description: "They gape at Me with their mouths, like a raging and roaring lion. I am poured out like water, and all My bones are out of joint; My heart is like wax; it has melted within Me. My strength is dried up like a potsherd, and My tongue clings to My jaws. You have brought Me to the dust of death. For dogs have surrounded Me; the congregation of the wicked has enclosed Me. They pierced My hands and My feet; I can count all My bones. They look and stare at Me. They divide My garments among them, and for My clothing they cast lots" (Psalm 22:13–18).

As these words reflect the agony and heartbreak of what Jesus would suffer, the cry of Messiah comes from verse one: "My God, My God, why have You forsaken Me?" (Psalm 22:1). These, of course, are the words echoed by Jesus on the cross as He bears the full weight and judgment of our sins. He is completely alone and condemned—and He dies.

It is this demonstration of love—the death and resurrection of Jesus—that the psalmist calls the whole earth to remembrance! No longer would the cross be seen as a warning to Roman citizens or a curse to Jewish onlookers. Because of the passion of our Savior, the cross would be remembered and recognized as the gateway to everlasting life!

Jesus was forsaken so we might be received. Jesus suffered condemnation so we could receive mercy. Jesus died and rose again so that we might have life. And like the hymn, we can sing: "We will remember, we will remember, we will remember the works of Your hands. We will stop and give You praise, for great is Thy faithfulness!"

The World Shall Reverence Him for What He Did

Having drawn our attention to what the Lord has done, the psalmist draws our attention away from the suffering Savior to the sovereign Lord. From the earthly to the heavenly; from the cross to the crown! And in doing so he calls us to reverence: "You who fear the Lord, praise Him! All you descendants of Jacob, glorify Him, and fear Him, all you offspring of Israel!" (v. 23).

The implication of the cross forces every individual to make a decision. It can be ignored, it can be rejected, or it can be received. However, it is only through the cross of Jesus that sins can be forgiven and pardon received. Only by the resurrection of Jesus will one find meaningful and everlasting life.

In Acts 26:18 the message of the cross is heralded as redemption for humankind: "To open their eyes, in order to turn them from darkness to light, and from the power of Satan to God, that they may receive forgiveness of sins and an inheritance among those who are sanctified by faith in [Jesus]."

If there has ever been a time to take another look at the love of Jesus through the cross, now is that time. If there has ever been a time to turn from sin and self to receive Jesus, now is that time. If there has ever been a time to come before Him and give Him reverence, now is that time. The amazing thing about a relationship with Jesus—is Jesus. Thank you, Jesus! And the reality is: One day every knee will bow and every tongue will confess that Jesus Christ is Lord! What a day that will be.

CHAPTER 13

OLD DISCIPLINES AND NEW SURPRISES

IT WAS NOT that I had never fasted before. Prior to Reinhard, though, it was not a regular part of my life. Nor did I realize just how powerfully connected fasting was to my personal growth and development in the Lord.

I started fasting before each of our LOLI trips. Initially it was three days, then a week, and later it stretched to two weeks. Surprisingly, I found myself looking forward to these times. There was a sweetness about it—a special time carved out only for me and Jesus.

It no longer was about the crusades, really; it was about drawing near to Him and shaking off much of the world's entanglements. It left me feeling totally clean, alive, and focused. Fasting was sharpening my spiritual preparation, and I was growing in faith and power because of it.

MY 40-DAY-FAST JOURNAL

As I looked at the approaching 2010 New Year, I started thinking about what the next ten years would look like. The prior six years had blown my mind. And now new challenges, new dreams, and fresh opportunities awaited. I felt a sacred anticipation stirring in my heart.

The Holy Spirit began whispering to my heart about starting the year and decade off with a 40-day fast. It was a radical idea, because I had never made it through three weeks! But the closer I got to the end of the year, the more and more the call to fast 40 days grew in intensity. By the time New Year's Eve arrived, I had no choice; the Lord wanted me to trust Him.

Day Two

The Lord spoke to my heart out of Mark 10. I was reminding Him I had never fasted half that distance before, and I already had serious doubts about making it through the week. But then I read verse 27: "With men it is impossible, but not with God; for with God all things are possible."

I know the context of this passage has absolutely nothing to do with fasting. But when I read verse 27, it was as if the Lord was speaking directly into my heart, saying: *I know your limitations and fears, Stephen, but I am able to not only bring you through a six-week fast, but over the future challenges as well.* It humbled me and strengthened my faith to press onward.

Day Ten

I finished speaking in the Sunday morning service when the pastor approached me with a huge smile. He had a surprise. It turns out our friends had prepared a Tex-Mex lunch in our honor.

I love fajitas. The smell of steak, chicken, and all the fixings left me shaking my head at the cruel humor of it all. Only in the middle of a fast would such a once-in-a-lifetime meal suddenly pop up.

Day Nineteen

I had outlasted every fast personally attempted. The Holy Spirit had brought me to a deep place, but my resolve was about to be seriously tested.

That night I sat in a board meeting with my dad. I began to physically go downhill fast. More than having a hard time focusing on conversations, I did not feel right inside. I excused myself and went to the restroom to splash water on my face.

When I returned, Dad took one look at me and asked if I was okay. No, not okay! I felt faint, dizzy, and just needed to get out of there. I left and went home.

Before reaching bed, the call from family and close friends to break the fast was in full swing. The sudden weakness and vulnerability I felt earlier that night had scared me—and them too! My resolve wavered severely as the Enemy played on my fears.

Alisa sat down next to me and asked, "Stephen, did the Lord call you to this?" She encouraged me not to make a fear-based decision. That led to a long conversation and a serious assessment of my personal condition. But I knew the answer to her question.

It was something I had known for months. Yes, I had been called to fast. It was not my idea or intention to start the year and decade out this way; it was His! So yes, I would push through.

Day Twenty-One

After a day and a half of struggle, something broke. I don't know if it was getting past the halfway mark, but I woke up with renewed energy and an enthusiasm for the journey. The Lord was working in me for good, and I could not see me quitting now.

Around Day Thirty

Steve and I traveled to a campus in the Northwest. It was several days of church services, campus chapels, office hours with students, and times of prayer. The schedule was taxing, and often I had to retreat to my room to rest. But that was the last of the major battles; the Lord was bringing me through it!

The Final Days
These were some of the most amazing I've ever experienced. I felt so close to Jesus. It is hard to explain, but my love for Him was abounding! My delight in Him and what He had forged inside me flooded my soul with faith and absolute joy.

The Last Day
After the sun had set, I retreated to my room one last time—to kneel down and give thanks. There was so much gratitude and awe in that moment. Lots of tears too. But as I committed the forty days to Him, I felt His pleasure and nearness and a whole lot more. It had been worth it all!

FASTING IN THE NEW TESTAMENT

Fasting is a vital part of our personal development. It is a source of power, it unlocks supernatural doors, and it produces fruit that remains. Examples abound in the Bible of those who discovered the divine purposes linked to prayer and fasting. Look at three from the New Testament.

Fasting in the Life of Jesus—a Source of Power
The Bible says after Jesus was baptized, He was "led by the Spirit into the wilderness, being tempted for forty days by the devil. And in those days He ate nothing" (Luke 4:1-2). The very first thing Jesus did in launching His public ministry was to obey the leading of the Holy Spirit by committing Himself to an extended fast.

The Holy Spirit not only led Him there, the Holy Spirit kept Him there! Despite an onslaught of temptation by Satan near the end, Jesus remained resolute, and the Bible says "Jesus returned in the power of the Spirit to Galilee" (Luke 4:14).

The example of Jesus reveals that fasting is very important, especially if you are engaged in ministry. And from verse 14, we learn it triggers supernatural power! This is one of the reasons our teams fast before the crusade week; we need breakthrough in the seen and unseen world.

The start of His ministry is not the only time we see a connection between Jesus and fasting. He accented it immediately after the transfiguration. The disciples, who had already been casting out demons and healing the sick, had been unable to help the deaf and dumb boy terrorized by a demonic spirit. Jesus rebukes the wicked spirit and restores the boy to wholeness! Later, Jesus explains to His disciples, "This kind can come out by nothing but prayer and fasting" (Mark 9:29).

This is a clear teaching of the Lord Jesus: There are certain things in the realm of the supernatural that are triggered through the discipline of prayer and fasting. If you want to grow in your relationship with Jesus and increase in power in witnessing, then fasting is essential to experience breakthrough.

Another teaching from Jesus on fasting is in Mark 2. The Pharisees ask why His disciples did not fast like them? Jesus replied the time would come when He would go away, and His followers would "fast in those days" (Mark 2:20).

That day is right now! As His followers, it is part of His plan for our lives to pray and fast so that we might walk intimately with Him and experience the power of the Holy Spirit in our lives. Every time you set aside time to fast and pray, you are fulfilling the words of Jesus!

Fasting in the Life of the Apostle Paul—Destiny and Open Doors
A large portion of the book of Acts is dedicated to the life and ministry of Paul (formerly called Saul). It is one that took him through Asia Minor and to Europe with the Gospel. A life defined by sea adventures, earthquakes in jail, amazing miracles, visions, and a network of deeply personal relationships. So what served as the launching pad for these missionary journeys and supernatural experiences? Fasting!

The Bible tells us Paul, Barnabas, and others had gathered together to seek the Lord. "As they ministered to the Lord and fasted, the Holy Spirit said, 'Now separate to Me Barnabas and Saul for the work to which I have called them.' Then, having fasted and prayed . . . they sent them away" (Acts 13:2–3).

In the middle of fasting (accented twice in these verses), the Holy Spirit set Paul and Barnabas apart and commissioned them to the first missionary journey. Who could have imagined this formerly violent and angry man would not only find Jesus but now would be used by the Holy Spirit to pen many of the New Testament books, open the door so the Gospel could go to Europe, and work so many mighty miracles? Jesus did. And for Paul the promotion came through fasting!

This is not the first time we see the connection of Paul and fasting. In Acts 9, he encounters Jesus on the road to Damascus. For three days, Saul fasts and prays—that God would send someone to open his blind eyes and show him what to do (vv. 6–12). The Lord answers his prayers and gives prophetic insight into what He has in store for him.

Fasting empowers and advances us in the purposes of God. It allows us to hear the leading and direction of the Holy Spirit, activating destiny in our lives. In cataloging the marks of the ministry, Paul mentions the highs and lows in advancing the Gospel. In it he includes fasting as part of his remarkable experience (2 Corinthians 6:5).

Like Paul, the Lord has a supernatural destiny for our lives, and fasting is one of the keys for it to be revealed and activated. And like Paul, whether you are hurting and blind, or hungry for more of God, it is always a good time to seek the Lord!

Fasting in the Life of the Roman Centurion Cornelius— Revelation and Lasting Fruit

A biblical example of someone (other than Jesus or Paul) who was committed to fasting was Cornelius. He was a Gentile and an officer in the Roman military. The Bible describes him as generous, devout, and a man who feared God (Acts 10).

Notice it was during a time of prayer and fasting an angel appears, commanding Cornelius to send for Peter.

Peter arrives and immediately points out how unlawful and unfit it was for him to be standing in the house of a Gentile. But the Holy Spirit had told him to come without doubting—and he had come. Now he wanted to know why he had been summoned.

Look at what Cornelius says: "Four days ago I was fasting... a man stood before me in bright clothing, and said, 'Cornelius your prayer has been heard, and your alms are remembered in the sight of God'" (Acts 10:30-31). So Peter starts recounting the Gospel message, and while he was still speaking, the Holy Sprit fell on the entire household of Cornelius—and the Gentiles gathered there started speaking in tongues!

The outpouring of the Holy Spirit on Gentiles astonished the Jewish brethren and revealed a glorious fact. The Gospel of Jesus Christ was for the Jews—and Gentiles! Peter would return to Jerusalem with this report: "If therefore God gave them the same gift as He gave us when we believed on the Lord Jesus Christ, who was I that I could withstand God? When they heard these things they became silent; and they glorified God, saying, 'Then God has also granted to the Gentiles repentance to life'" (Acts 11:17-18).

An angelic visitation, the outpouring of the Holy Spirit on his household, and the glorious revelation that the Gospel included the Gentiles flowed through a military man committed to fasting and prayer.

Cornelius was not a church leader or an apostle—just a God fearer! His example teaches us fasting is not just for the Lord Jesus or church leaders; it is the privilege of every believer whose heart burns for more of God.

Fasting is not only biblical, it is life transforming. It deepens intimacy with God, releases power, unlocks divine purpose, and births fruit with immediate and eternal consequences. If there has ever been a time to seek the Lord, today is that day!

FACING DEATH THREATS

We returned to Costa Rica in 2010 to do a three-night crusade. It was the first time we had returned to an area or done more than two services. There was excitement in the air and everyone felt good moving forward. Then we received news that changed everyone's mood considerably.

Several hours before the Friday service, Dennis and I met away from the others underneath the palm trees by the beach. He said we had received death threats by a local gang.

This caught me completely by surprise. Though after what happened in the rain the last time we were in Costa Rica, I probably should have anticipated some pushback. Dennis had more: "Last night gang members turned up at the venue with guns, warning people to stay home and delivering this message: 'Stop the crusade or else!'"

We had never received threats before, so it took me a few minutes to process the ramifications. What about the team, my pregnant wife and family, the pastors who had pleaded with us to return? It was not a simple decision.

Steve joined us, and we decided on two things: increase security and quicken our spiritual response. I knew in my heart this wasn't about human beings; we were being challenged by principalities and powers that did not want the Gospel to advance any further. So on a spiritual front, we alerted our network of intercessors, asking them to cry out for our safety and for a spiritual breakthrough.

We also had to tell the team about the threats. I talked with Alisa and my parents first, then met with the LOLI team.

That meeting was remarkable. Each person listened carefully to the threats, and I answered a couple of serious questions. Then it was time to fight!

We engaged in warfare through prayer and the declaration of the Word of God. Over and over, the promises of God were uttered. One person would lead out: *"For God has not given us a spirit of fear, but of power and of love and of a sound mind"* (2 Timothy 1:7) and pray that promise over our crusade situation. Then another: *"He who is in you is greater than he who is in the world"* (1 John 4:4) and declare victory over the Enemy. Then another: *"Yet in all these things we are more than conquerors through Him who loved us"* (Romans 8:37) and exalted the name of Jesus. Still more: *"No weapon formed against you* shall *prosper"* (Isaiah 54:17); *"When my heart is overwhelmed; lead me to the rock that is higher than I"* (Psalm 61:2); and *"If God is for us, who can be against us?"* (Romans 8:31). On and on the team proclaimed Scriptures over this situation.

The Word of God is so powerful! The presence of the Lord grew so strong in our midst, that when it came time to load the vehicles, no one would stay back.

This was the first time we had personal bodyguards. But leaving for the crusade venue, our strength and confidence came from an awareness of a much larger, invisible security force. I had come to preach the Gospel—and the kingdom of God was ready to advance!

WHAT DID THE AMERICANS GIVE YOU TO DRINK?

My favorite testimony of those three nights came from Carina, one of the ladies who helped prepare our meals at the rental property where our team stayed. She came on Saturday, having interacted with many team members and hearing them pray upstairs throughout the week.

Something had started burning inside—and ultimately, it drew her to the crusade.

Carina knew she needed Jesus. And when the call for salvation came, she responded.

She was glowing when she arrived back at the house. The American team, Honduras staff and family, and several Costa Rican pastors had gathered outside by the pool to rejoice over the evening. Steve and I were cooling off in the pool when an idea suddenly sprung up in our conversation.

Steve got everyone's attention and asked if anyone wanted to be baptized. That is when Carina stepped forward and announced that she had invited Jesus into her heart that night at the crusade—and yes, she definitely wanted to be baptized!

Completely dressed in the clothes she wore to the crusade, Carina walked down the pool steps and into the water. Pastor Dennis gladly shared with her the significance of water baptism, and Steve assisted.

When she came up from under the water, you could have heard the roar a half mile away! It was such a wonderful time of celebration, and made the decision to move ahead with the crusade that weekend even sweeter.

The next morning she told us about what happened when she arrived home to her husband soaking wet and full of joy. He took one look at her and asked, "Why are you wet—and what did the Americans give you to drink to make you so happy!"

We just laughed and rejoiced even more with her. Jesus truly had made a large impression!

SPIRITUAL WARFARE 101— THE SUPREMACY OF JESUS

The Bible tells us we fight an unseen Enemy who is powerful and ruthless: "We are not struggling against human beings, but against the rulers, authorities and cosmic powers governing this darkness, against the spiritual forces of evil in the heavenly realm" (Ephesians 6:12 Complete Jewish Bible).

We have a real Enemy who looks for every opportunity to negatively impact our lives. Not restricted to a particular attack, he can lash out at you physically, emotionally, financially, spiritually, and various other ways.

The Enemy is bigger than us and more powerful than us. To try to oppose him in our own strength is futile. Satan is brighter and more experienced, and he is totally ruthless. He has not come to bless your life but to "steal, and to kill, and to destroy" (John 10:10).

His mission for you is bondage and everlasting darkness. This is the bad news regarding spiritual warfare: There is a real and dangerous adversary.

But I have great news. Our Lord Jesus Christ reigns supreme, and the Enemy of our soul is a defeated foe! The Bible says the Enemy has been crushed under the weight of the authority and power of God, through the blood of Jesus. The reality of the cross is Jesus not only conquered sin, He also conquered Satan and every stronghold!

The Bible says: "For Christ also suffered once for sins, the just for the unjust, that He might bring us to God, being put to death in the flesh but made alive by the Spirit, by whom also He went and preached to the spirits in prison, who formerly were disobedient . . . through the resurrection of Jesus Christ, [He] has gone into heaven and is at the right hand of God, angels and authorities and powers having been made subject to Him" (I Peter 3:18–19, 21–22). This is exciting news: Jesus died, descended into hell, declared His triumphant victory to all the spirits of darkness, and has risen again! Again, the Bible declares: "Having disarmed principalities and powers, He made a public spectacle of them, triumphing over them" (Colossians 2:15). You can have confidence in the Lord Jesus Christ because He has crushed the darkness and paved a way for us to also live victoriously!

SPIRITUAL WARFARE 102— ARSENAL OF THE BELIEVER

Jesus has not left us ill equipped. Instead, we have a massive cache of weapons to not only ward off every scheme of the Enemy, but to powerfully advance His kingdom. Our Christian duty is to "be strong in the Lord and in the power of His might" (Ephesians 6:10). This passage reveals that we have a large spiritual arsenal that God has given us to live valiant and overcoming lives.

The Belt of Truth

The belt of truth defends us from assaults against our values. Make no mistake: The Enemy wants to blur truth, not broadcast it. If he can diminish godly conviction and erode biblical principles, then it is to his advantage.

The Bible urges us to know the truth and hide it in our hearts. Instead of blending in, you can boldly stand up and stand out for Jesus!

Truth brings freedom (John 8:32), keeps us from sin and deception (Psalm 119:11), and draws us toward righteousness and holiness (Ephesians 4:21–24).

» "You shall know the truth, and the truth shall make you free" (John 8:32).

» "Your word I have hidden in my heart, that I might not sin against You" (Psalm 119:11)

» "The truth is in Jesus: that you put off, concerning your former conduct, the old man which grows corrupt according to the deceitful lusts, and be renewed in the spirit of your mind, and that you put on the new man which was created according to God, in true righteousness and holiness" (Ephesians 4:21–24).

The Breastplate of Righteousness

The breastplate of righteousness protects us from the attacks aimed at the heart. If he can crush your dreams, dampen your fiery resolve, or cripple you with fear, it is again to his advantage.

Reinhard liked to say: "The anointed ones become hot when others are cold and frozen because of the burning flame inside their hearts." This undiminished flame is the power of God in action. No wonder the Enemy wants to quench it!

A holy and humble heart leaves no place for the evil darts to penetrate through this powerful breastplate. Here are a few verses on the strength of righteousness:

- » "The work of righteousness will be peace, and the effect of righteousness, quietness and assurance" (Isaiah 32:17).

- » "For You, O Lord, will bless the righteous; with favor You will surround him as with a shield" (Psalm 5:12)

- » "In the way of righteousness is life, and in its pathway there is no death" (Proverbs 12:28).

Feet Fitted With the Gospel of Peace

Our adversary has a plan for your feet. He hates pure and godly environments. He works hard to entice our feet to wander and linger in places that cause moral and spiritual decay.

The Holy Sprit has a purpose for our feet, too, and has supernaturally fitted them with the preparation of the Gospel. This means as a child of God, every place your feet tread falls under the dominion of God! Even as God spoke to Asher that his feet would be like iron and brass, so the Holy Spirit will strengthen and empower your feet.

Our feet have an assignment: to go and share the Gospel! Here are a couple of verses worth knowing about your feet and the Gospel of peace:

> » "How beautiful are the feet of those who preach the gospel of peace, who bring glad tidings of good things" (Romans 10:15)

> » "Asher is most blessed of sons; let him be favored by his brothers, and let him dip his foot in oil. Your sandals shall be iron and bronze; as your days, so shall your strength be" (Deuteronomy 33:24–25).

The Shield of Faith

The shield of faith protects us from attacks on our outlook. The Enemy wants to sabotage our faith and paralyze our forward movement. If he can flood us with fear and doubt, then it is to his advantage. But the Holy Spirit has given us an enormous shield! It not only knocks down every challenge, it also gives us confidence to move ahead.

My parents hammered this into me: Never lay down your shield! Confronted by the what-ifs of life, they always countered with the divine view: What-if-Not! Instead of thinking defensively, it was an opportunity for God to show Himself faithful and strong!

That is what makes our God-given shield so powerful. If you are under attack by *what if this* or *what if that*, lift up your shield, dig your feet into the ground, and declare in Jesus' name: "What-if-NOT!"

The former defeats us—those demonic darts of fear and doubt that sabotage all our strength and resolve. But the later mobilizes us, turning the attack back against the Enemy. No matter the what-ifs, do not lay down your shield!

This weapon also applies to the unity of believers. In ancient Rome, soldiers of the battalion carried large hooked shields and connected them together. So the united front line would move forward with this huge wall of armor protecting them.

The army that followed then linked their shields together and held them above their heads. They were not only protected from the arrows of their enemies, it provided confidence moving forward.

This is a picture of the church: united and strong! Each of us has a shield, and collectively the shields link together to move forward in might and supernatural strength. Here are a couple of verses to remind us of the essence of faith and the shield we carry:

> » "Faith is the substance of things hoped for, the evidence of things not seen" (Hebrews 11:1).
>
> » "Above all, taking the shield of faith with which you will be able to quench all the fiery darts of the wicked one" (Ephesians 6:16).

The Helmet of Salvation

The helmet of salvation defends us from the assault on our minds. The Enemy is determined to pollute our minds through what we see, hear, and experience. The Bible teaches us to take every thought captive, to cast down vain imaginations, and to set our minds on things above.

The Bible has a lot to say about the warfare that occurs between our ears. Here are some promises and instructions for winning that battle:

- » "You will keep him in perfect peace, whose mind is stayed on You, because he trusts in You" (Isaiah 26:3).

- » "Set your mind on things above, not on things on the earth" (Colossians 3:2)

- » "For the weapons of our warfare are not carnal but mighty in God for pulling down strongholds, casting down arguments and every high thing that exalts itself against the knowledge of God, bringing every thought into captivity to the obedience of Christ" (2 Corinthians 10:4–5).

- » "Finally, brethren, whatever things are true, whatever things are noble, whatever things are just, whatever things are pure, whatever things are lovely, whatever things are of good report, if there is any virtue and if there is anything praiseworthy—meditate on these things" (Philippians 4:8)

The Sword of the Spirit

The sword of the spirit empowers us against the assault on our understanding. It is not the plan of the Enemy for you to know and apply the Scriptures. He resents and fears its authority. The Enemy gains an advantage if we lack understanding and wisdom, because the Word of God is so potent!

Acting in agreement with the Spirit of God brings victory to the life of the believer. My mom summed it up best when she noted there are only two weapons you take up: the shield of faith and the sword of the Spirit.

It's instinctual and automatic to react and protect ourselves. But it is an act of the will to go on the offensive. Both weapons are there for us to pick up, but the choice is ours.

It is time to grow in faith and the empowerment of the Word of God. It is time to move forward in Jesus' name!

HELLO, ANNA!

The Holy Spirit was working in our lives and ministry in preparation for something glorious. But it was also a time for something—or rather, someone—new!

Alisa was expecting our second daughter in May, and we were busy making room for Anna. Yes, the next crusade was in June, but it was far enough away I could enjoy a couple of weeks with Anna before stepping away briefly. Riley had come a week early, so if Anna did the same I would have nearly a month before the crusade.

The first date we wondered about was our anniversary. If she came early enough, we could actually share our wedding anniversary with Anna! But the day passed and it started looking more and more like she would arrive on the actual May 25th due date.

With Alisa deciding on a natural delivery at a birthing center, there was little to do but count down the days until May 25th. But when we blew by the due date, I started to get nervous. Not so much for Alisa and Anna, because I was reassured everything was fine, but now we were inside two weeks until I was supposed to fly to El Salvador.

One week later, I started wondering what was going on in there with Anna. She was definitely coming out on her terms, and it started to look like I would be missing a flight. But the next morning, Alisa woke up at 6:30 a.m. in labor.

When Anna had finally decided to come, she had come fast. We barely had time to dress, gather our stuff, and head over to the birthing center. Watching Alisa give birth naturally to our daughter was one of the most amazing things I have ever seen. And by 9:30 a.m., Anna had arrived!

The Lord had blessed us by increasing our family with Anna. We did not know it, but He was also birthing something in Light of Life International—something that would expand our boundaries as a ministry as well.

CHAPTER 14

CALLING ALL SOULS

2010 WAS A PIVOTAL YEAR for us on many fronts. The Lord had laid a foundation for the future through fasting and prayer, and Alisa had given birth to Anna. We also came out of El Salvador with a growing awareness that the opportunity to reach for something beyond us was opening before us in Honduras. It was a pie-in-the-sky dream, something mentioned a few years ago to Dennis in a Puerto Plata cable car, an impossible what-if idea. Yet my soul was on fire—as if God was daring us to believe Him for San Pedro Sula NOW. Yes, it was a city many times larger than any crusade we had ever undertaken, but the Lord was revealing a plan built on relationships that would culminate two years later in *Honduras Prays*.

It would be an amazing journey, one that would include five crusades in the next eighteen months in the greater area of San Pedro Sula, Honduras. It would deepen our love for the city, sharpen our focus and remind us vividly of the significance of souls and the power of redemption.

ANTONIO'S PORCH

We started in La Lima. During the last day of distribution, Steve went with one of the teams. The people they encountered were both hungry for the food and to hear the Gospel.

Steve had approached Antonio with food, and the opportunity opened to share the Gospel right there on his front porch. He began to talk about Jesus. It was not too long, though, before Steve noticed Antonio was not the only one listening. In fact, the more he talked, the more he realized a small crowd was gathering around him.

At first it was two young guys lingering in the front yard. Then he noticed a young man leaning on the fence. Then Steve noticed a couple of vendors lingering in the middle of the street. And finally he realized there were others watching intently from the other side of the road. He was literally surrounded!

Steve responded to this growing audience by widening his speaking area, turning in one direction, then back toward the other. By doing so, everyone, from Antonio on his porch to those across the street, could hear what he was saying.

Steve gave a bold altar call right there: "If anyone wants to make a profession of faith in Jesus Christ, come to Antonio's front porch!"

The owner, the two guys hanging out in the front yard, the young man leaning on the fence, and one of the vendors responded immediately. Steve prayed with them, and when he opened his eyes something had changed. Instead of five men, there were now six! In the middle of the prayer, another man had rushed to the porch to rededicate his life to Jesus.

DOUBLING OF THE PARCHMENT

There is a rabbinic interpretation of Isaiah 40:2, and it speaks to the power of redemption: "Speak comfort to Jerusalem, and cry out to her, that her warfare is ended, that her iniquity is pardoned; for she has received from the Lord's hand double for all her sins."

In the ancient Middle East there was a procedure called the "doubling of the parchment." It was common if a person fell into debt and was unable or unwilling to pay the debt, the person who was owed the money had the right to publicize it.

To do so, he would write the amount owed on a piece of parchment, sign his name, then nail it to the doorpost of the debtor for all to see. By law, the debtor was not allowed to remove it.

If there were other unpaid debts, they could be added to the list, accompanied by a signature below. Thus the list could grow increasingly long. You can only imagine the embarrassment and pain this caused members of the family who lived in the shadow of the parchment attached to their door.

There were two ways to resolve the parchment. One was if the individual paid off the debt, which was usually not possible. The other was by an act of benevolence.

If a benevolent person saw the parchment nailed to the doorpost and wanted to help, there was a legal procedure to follow. First, one had to add up the debts listed on the parchment. Then one had to pay the debt.

Next, the benevolent person would take the parchment and "double" it over. This indicated the price had been paid in full, and the debt which was once exposed for all to see was now totally covered. Last, the benefactor signed his or her name on the outside of the doubled parchment.

The parchment now took on a new meaning. Instead of being a document of shame and a means of embarrassment, it became a badge of honor. It indicated that someone cared enough to pay the debt in full.

This is exactly what Jesus did for us! In the words of the old Gospel hymn:

He paid a debt He did not owe
I owed a debt I could not pay
I needed someone to wash my sins away
And now I sing a brand new song
Amazing grace all day long
Christ Jesus paid a debt that I could never pay

The apostle Paul put it this way: "[He] wiped out the handwriting of requirements that was against us, which was contrary to us. And He has taken it out of the way, having nailed it to the cross" (Colossians 2:14).

Our sin, shame, and guilt were on full display for all to see—until Jesus came and doubled it over! The power of redemption is this: Our debt has been paid in full, and the resurrection of Jesus Christ is our receipt!

SECOND-ROW SALVATION

After the La Lima crusade week, we went to Puerto Cortes, the shipping channel on the coast. Once again, we witnessed redemption on full display.

A small rural church had asked if a couple of people could share in their midweek service. One of the pastors with us from Texas agreed and after preaching a Gospel message gave an invitation for salvation. No one responded.

He moved on to pray for the needs of the people, but something was gnawing at him. All night he had felt drawn to a young man sitting on the second row. So when he had a moment, he walked over to the young man.

The pastor asked if he was a Christian. "No," replied the young man. The pastor asked if he wanted to make that decision tonight. "No," came the response. Instead of walking away, the pastor asked the young man one more question. Could he pray for the Lord to bless him? This time the young man said, "Okay."

When the pastor said amen, he thanked the young man and turned to leave. But this time it was the young man who had something to say. He reached out and grabbed the Texas pastor and said, "Now I'm ready!"

The pastor started to pray for him right there on the second row, but the young man stopped him. He stood up, exited the row, and walked to the front, as if responding to the summons earlier. There at the altar, he surrendered his life to Jesus.

CHAMELECON MASSACRE

By the time we finished the crusade week in Puerto Cortes, the choice in front of us was clear. If we were ever going to believe for a mass crusade in San Pedro Sula, it would be in 2012, in partnership with the churches and communities that received and embraced us. The Holy Spirit had given us a clear mandate: Finish canvassing the city in the suburbs and inner city, and He would take care of the rest.

The four neighborhoods already covered were Villanueva, Rivera Hernandez, La Lima, and Puerto Cortes. That left three more significant areas to serve, including the most dangerous one of all.

Chamelecon held the notorious reputation as one of the most violent, dangerous, and gang-infested neighborhoods in all of Honduras. None of us had any desire to put ourselves in harm's way, but Dennis and Steve agreed we had to at least drive through it once (during the day) before we could justify skipping it.

As we entered the neighborhood, driving down the main road, we came upon a mural on the wall parallel to us. Looking out my passenger window, it held my glance and I asked Dennis if it had any significance.

It did. The mural memorialized those who died in a massacre a few years ago, when gang members stopped the bus in this very spot. They boarded it and opened fire, killing mostly children and mothers.

Something immediately rose up inside me as I heard the story. I cried out, "The devil is a liar!" There was no way we could scratch this place off our list. The Holy Spirit was calling us to come here—to the place where the blood of innocent people had been shed.

The Gospel had to be preached here to rebuke the evil and plead the blood of Jesus over this community that lived under the shadow of darkness. How many families had been pained by this darkness? I kept hearing over and over in my heart, *The spilled blood of Jesus, the spilled blood of Jesus—it alone has the power to heal the brokenhearted, release forgiveness, and crush the Enemy.*

This is the message of redemption. Only Jesus can take your pain, the darkness and bondage, any curse, and bring freedom, wholeness, forgiveness, and a life flooded by His light and everlasting love. There is great power in the blood of Jesus; it is the purchasing price of our salvation!

POWER OF FORGIVENESS

The apostle Paul preached in some of the most difficult places in the world. That included Corinth, a place marked by prostitution, gambling, alcohol, and greed. For months, Paul labored to plant a church, but after he left it was taken over by impostors with a new and misleading gospel.

Things went from bad to worse, when a visit to Corinth turned into great personal sorrow and hurt, leaving him hesitant to return. Titus later went in his place with a letter to the Corinthians, and the church listened. They repented for their actions and, after inflicting punishment on the intruders, asked Paul to return.

Instead of plotting revenge on his adversaries, Paul extended forgiveness and called the Corinthians to do the same. So how can we walk in the same type of victory that Paul did? Look at three things that Paul understood about forgiveness:

Forgiveness Has No Limits or Exceptions (A lesson From Jesus)

The message of forgiveness was a major theme of the ministry of Jesus. When Peter asked how many times should he forgive someone, Jesus replied, "Seventy times seven." So is the magic number 490 times? No, He was making a point that forgiveness must remain unlimited and offered freely.

He followed these remarks with the parable of the king who forgave the massive debt of one of his debtors. But the forgiven man left the presence of the king and soon demanded his neighbor repay a minor debt or face punishment. The king heard about it and was furious with the lack of compassion shown by the one who had just received forgiveness of a much greater debt!

As beneficiaries of His forgiveness through His death and resurrection, we must forgive others without limits or exceptions. Jesus states this expectation in the prayer He taught the disciples: "Forgive us our debts, as we forgive our debtors." Freely we have received forgiveness, and freely we must extend it.

Forgiveness Provides a Powerful Christian Witness (A lesson From Acts 7)

Paul knew extending forgiveness to someone who had hurt/wronged him would also point the Corinthians to the cross. It provides us the ultimate example of true love and forgiveness—and His example motivates us.

Luke 23:34 reads: "Father, forgive them, for they do not know what they do." In the midst of the violence and humiliation, Jesus affirms what He talked about and remains perfect and pure!

People identify with pain and revenge. The common response to violation is to inflict a greater level of pain and misery. But this continuous cycle of vengeance never ends and the pain never goes away. But Jesus said forgive them!

Forgiveness stands in stark contrast to the ways of the world. And it provides a powerful Christian witness to neighbors, friends, and coworkers, because they see the difference!

They may empathize with your pain and hurt, but forgiveness confounds them, because (apart from Jesus) they cannot comprehend why you would do such a thing. But guess what? The resulting freedom in your life attracts them, because they, too, want to be free.

In Acts 7, an angry mob drives Stephen out of Jerusalem to stone him. Moments before his death, he looks up and sees Jesus standing in front of heaven, awaiting him. He cries out something familiar to those Jerusalem walls: "Forgive them!"

Stephen followed the example of Jesus. He may not have known the impression his words and actions in those dying moments would leave on the young man guarding the coats of those throwing the stones. But after the young man's conversion, the grace and compassion in which Stephen forgave the murderous mob must have helped Paul in forgiving the Corinthians.

Empowered to exact his revenge, Paul chose the example of Jesus and Stephen instead. He forgave the wrongdoers.

Forgiveness Prevents Satan From Taking Advantage of Us!
Paul understood the crippling effects of an unforgiving heart. The lack of forgiveness would only empower Satan to further hijack their relationship and destroy the church in Corinth.

The plan of Satan is to take advantage of an unforgiving heart. He wants to pour in rage, confusion and bitterness. The refusal to forgive is a tool he can use to destroy your life or ministry.

Look what Paul said. "I have forgiven that one for your sakes in the presence of Christ, lest Satan should take advantage of us; for we are not ignorant of his devices" (2 Corinthians 2:10–11)

God's plan for our lives includes forgiveness. It has no reservations, broadcasts a glorious testimony, and releases victory over Satan and his schemes. There is power in forgiveness in the name of Jesus Christ!

MEETING THE PASTORS ASSOCIATION OF SAN PEDRO SULA

Before gathering at the site of the massacre to preach the Gospel, Dennis, Steve, and I sat down for breakfast with the Pastors Association of San Pedro Sula. This was a critical meeting of introduction. Representing the evangelical pastors in a city with a population of over one million, their blessing to do a crusade in this city would mean the support of hundreds of churches. No decision would be made that day, but the importance of a good first impression would go a long way to securing a partnership for next year.

Outside on the patio area of the hotel, Dennis introduced us to the four men and three women. We shared some background information and our heart for Honduras—especially the San Pedro Sula area in which we were currently working.

They received us warmly. No resistance to a 2012 city-wide campaign emerged, and we left encouraged by the initial meeting.

Returning inside the hotel, I noticed someone sitting by the window having tea. It was someone who knew the dream in my heart, someone who had been praying for us during the meeting just like he always did every morning and night. It was my dad. Seeing him there felt like confirmation.

FRIDAY NIGHT IN CHAMELECON

That night thousands gathered in the place of the massacre. Two of our guests from breakfast—the president and vice-president of the association—also came. Seeing them there made me feel even better about our meeting.

We had come here with two purposes in mind: plead the blood of Jesus and preach hope and reconciliation. The LOLI team and local pastors assembled on the platform to pray for Chamelecon. As Steve prayed corporately for transformation, we knelt down to plead the blood of Jesus for cleansing and healing.

Thanks to William, the younger brother of Dennis, we were able (for the first time) to stream the crusade live on our website. This was exciting because anyone could see the compassion and power of our Savior from anywhere in the world. We also received lots of attention from the secular media because of the dangers and history connected to Chamelecon.

I spoke on the radical conversion of Saul. Dennis made the salvation call, and a flood of people responded—one of them a recognizable gang member. As I looked out at the people coming, I could see beyond the crowd the wall and the mural. In a place where the Enemy had brought so much fear and darkness, the Lord Jesus was pouring out His light, salvation, and even joy.

RADICAL CONVERSION OF SAUL

The testimony of Saul's conversion and calling burned in my heart, especially for the young people of Chamelecon. Without a dramatic encounter with Jesus, many end up in gangs, on the streets, even dead. So that first night I spoke about what happened to Saul to make this point: Nothing compares to living radically for Jesus!

The Contrast

Saul (later called Paul) was a religious zealot, a man more interested in tradition than truth, dedicated to destroying any belief system that would question the veracity of his own. Having been active in Jerusalem, Saul sought to spread his hostility and rage to Damascus and was intent on destroying the Christian faith and arresting its leaders.

This is the same struggle facing our world today. The problem is not political or economic. It is a spiritual conflict! Call it the spirit of violence, or humanism, or fear, or whatever you want. All share this agenda: to negate the message of the Gospel.

Saul left Jerusalem breathing threats of terror against the church. But something happened along the way. Certainly, the Saul who left Jerusalem was not the same man who reached Damascus.

Instead of charging the city, he was led in by the hand. Instead of inflicting harm on believers, he needed help from a leader of the local church to find wholeness. What a contrast!

The reason is well-known intellectually: he had a blinding encounter with Jesus. But to appreciate what really happened, you need to have experienced Him yourself.

Everyone who has had a genuine encounter with the resurrected and glorified Lord Jesus Christ knows that He changes everything! This is what happened to Saul. His encounter radically changed his behavior, rearranged his priorities, redirected his passion, and revealed a new direction.

This new Saul would no longer persecute the church but emerge as one of its greatest pioneers. Instead of fighting the spread of the Gospel, he took it far and wide.

The same is true for every person who encounters and believes on Jesus Christ. There is a new beginning—full of dynamic opportunities to spread the Gospel.

The Calling

The life of Saul is often celebrated due to all that took place after his encounter. But when he walked into Damascus, he was blind, led by the hand, and totally oblivious to the magnitude of the call resting on his life.

Things had radically changed. Saul definitely knew Jesus was alive! The Gospel was true and the grace of God had been administered to him. But now what?

The Bible says Saul sought the Lord. And while he fasted and prayed, the Lord started talking to Ananias about him. This is the key. When we turn our hearts to seek the Lord, He responds. Sometimes He answers directly; sometimes He works indirectly. But the Lord always hears and He answers.

Ananias received instructions from the Lord: *Go to Saul!* He received an address and the name of a person with whom Saul was staying. He was told to lay hands on the eyes of Saul and promised the power of God would open them. Who could resist such a divine assignment? Ananias did—at least initially.

Ananias had a problem with the past. More directly, he had a huge problem with Saul's past, and it hindered him from responding in the moment. Unaware of the call hanging over Saul, Ananias was fearful to move forward.

The principle is this: Failure to function in the present (based on the past) has the potential to frustrate the future. Not just yours, but others as well.

So the Lord tells Ananias again: *Go to Saul!* The command this time is not just to loose Saul from his blindness but also to release him into destiny.

The Bible records it this way: "Go, for he is a chosen vessel of Mine to bear My name before Gentiles, kings, and the children of Israel" (Acts 9:15).

This revelation must have shocked Ananias. It would have been a big reach for him to believe Saul was the ideal candidate to reach the Jews with the Gospel...but the Gentiles? This divine strategy had not yet been openly revealed. Peter would have to visit Cornelius later and witness the outpouring of the Holy Spirit on his household for the Jewish leadership in Jerusalem to realize the Gospel of Jesus Christ also included Gentiles.

The Lord was telling Ananias the Gospel was for everyone. And Saul had a role in its expansion.

This fact remains true today: The Gospel is viable for every man and woman, Jew and Gentile. And like Saul, we have a major responsibility to spread the Good News.

The Certification

Ananias obeyed the heavenly voice, and four supernatural events followed.

The first miracle was *Identification*. Ananias greeted his former rival with Brother Saul! What a remarkable turn of events. Only a short time earlier he wanted nothing to do with him, but now Ananias recognizes Saul as his brother in the Lord. This is one of the hallmarks of the Gospel—it joins and unites people together!

The second miracle was *Impartation*. Ananias laid his hands on the eyes of Saul and "immediately there fell from his eyes something like scales, and he received his sight at once" (Acts 9:18). Saul could see!

This must have been an incredible moment for both men. Saul had waited three days for Ananias, a man promised by the Holy Spirit to come lay hands on him. What anticipation must have exploded within him when he heard that someone by that name was at the door!

For Ananias, to stand in the same room with someone he had mistrusted, even feared, then reach out and touch him in Jesus' name must have been overwhelming. What a powerful testimony of obedience and faith!

The third miracle was *Ignition*. Saul's eyes had opened, but something was still needed: to be filled with the Holy Spirit. This was a spiritual miracle and mandate. It empowered Saul as promised by Jesus prior to His ascension: "You shall receive power when the Holy Spirit has come upon you; and you shall be witnesses to Me in Jerusalem, and in all Judea and Samaria, and to the end of the earth" (Acts 1:8).

What had happened for the disciples and others now happened to Saul. And for Saul to be what God wanted him to be, and for Saul to do what God wanted him to do, he needed to be filled with the Holy Spirit.

The final miracle was *Immersion*. A well-trained rabbinic scholar, Saul was dying to the old life to rise to the new challenge. It was not just an indication of conversion; it was an indication of his dedication to the will and work of God.

These four supernatural events triggered dynamic action. For Saul: "Immediately he preached the Christ in the synagogues, that He is the Son of God. Then all who heard were amazed, and said, 'Is this not he who destroyed those who called on this name in Jerusalem, and has come here for that purpose, so that he might bring them bound to the chief priests?'" (Acts 9:20–21).

This is the testimony of a radical! He encountered Jesus, received a calling that was certified by miraculous power, and moved forward in Holy Spirit boldness.

The same is true for all who have encountered the risen Lord Jesus Christ. The One who calls us emboldens us through the Holy Spirit. And like Saul, we are radically transformed and boldly live for Him alone!

YOU ARE ONE OF GOD'S INVESTMENTS

After the Chamelecon crusade, we moved to a community on the outer edge of San Pedro Sula. Cofradia is rural and full of hardworking people. It was also one of the last two neighborhoods on our checklist.

Sitting in the office with one of the area pastors, he asked if we wanted to take some time to pray. That morning I was tired, hungry, and yearning to return to the hotel. So no, I really did not want to pray. But when his wife joined us next door in the prayer room, they insisted on praying for each one of us. I never would have anticipated what was coming next.

I don't remember all of what came out of his mouth, but I will never forget these words: *"Stephen, the Lord has invested a lot in you—and He is expecting a yield!"*

That caught my attention, because it was the first time I had ever heard someone refer to me as one of God's investments. As if I was part of His portfolio! The idea that God had been investing in me with the express expectation of a return hit me hard.

Yes, I received Jesus into my heart at age four, later baptized in the Holy Spirit, surrounded by mentors during my teenage years, and had been supernaturally put on this path. All of that had landed me here today in Cofradia, Honduras!

But was I a good investment? I thought about economics and the idea of putting money away over a long period of time to maximize the return later. I thought about the ups and downs of the global economy—some investments are profitable, others turn out to be unreliable. And it all got me thinking: If Jesus is expecting a yield, then please help me, Holy Spirit. Help me to live a life that is eternally profitable!

The same is true for you and every believer: The Lord is investing in us! He made the ultimate investment by laying down His life on a cross for our sins—that we might be redeemed, that our lives would no longer be marred by sin, that our lives could reflect His glory. He has poured His Spirit into us so that we may daily commune with Him, grow in Him, and be used by Him.

Every time we pray, there is a return. Every time we meditate on His Word, there is a return. Every time we share our faith, there is a return. Every time we sing out His praise or turn our attention toward the Lord Jesus Christ and His Kingdom purposes, there is a return! Our lives were purchased to make a difference now—and bring Jesus an everlasting return!

OFFICE OF THE EVANGELIST

I asked Reinhard once about the role of an evangelist. His response was simple: "The office of evangelist is to open the door so *everyone* can do the work of evangelism."

I asked Dad to expound on this idea, and he said the early church understood this. They talked about Jesus everywhere to everyone. Biblical examples abound: Ethiopian treasurer, a Roman centurion, in synagogues, by riverbanks, in jails, before kings, to the Jews, to the Greeks, to the Gentiles—everywhere. They made no distinction over the message. Each believer had a testimony, a story, a reason to tell somebody about this amazing Jesus!

In 1 Corinthians 12, it is interesting that two of the ordained gifts are not mentioned. Paul lists apostles, prophets, teachers, helps, etc., but makes no mention of the ministry gifts of pastors or evangelists. Did he forget?

Not likely. As the church continued to grow, it was basically taking care of itself with an emphasis on exhorting, comforting, and cheering—which would be pastoring. And since everyone was evangelizing, he did not need to point out evangelists either. It was natural that every believer would share his or her story.

As the church became more organized, Paul clearly delineated five specific ministry expressions: apostles to govern, prophets to guide, pastors to guard, teachers to gird, and evangelists to gather (Ephesians 4). But the administration of these gifts was *not* to release the church from its first and primary responsibility of spreading the Gospel. It was, however, to provide added stimulus and direction in the outworking of it.

Finally, near the end of his life, he voiced concern about the ongoing expression of evangelism. To one of his sons in the faith Paul urged: "Do the work of an evangelist, fulfill your ministry" (2 Timothy 4:2-5). We must do the same.

THE GREAT OMISSION

Arguably the biggest challenge facing the church today is the Great Omission—the lack of personal conviction or urgency to share the

Gospel with those who are lost. The list of excuses is long and monotonous: Some say it is not their spiritual gift, others do not feel qualified, and a few think it should be left to the professional ministers.

The reality is the Great Omission is an indication of fear or act of disobedience. It not only hurts the cause of Christ, it jeopardizes the well-being of many souls and stunts a person's own spiritual growth and vitality.

Being used by the Holy Spirit to lead a soul into the kingdom of heaven increases your passion, fills your heart with praise, and heightens your sense of worth as being a servant of the King.

The value of the Great Omission is well known to and greatly appreciated by our Enemy. The last thing he wants is for a Christian to activate his or her faith by sharing the Gospel. The Bible is true in saying: "They overcame him by the blood of the Lamb and by the word of their testimony" (Revelation 12:11).

Sharing your personal experience with Jesus releases enormous spiritual power! An example of this is the blind man in the Gospels: "There are many things I do not know. But this one thing I do know: I once was blind, but now I see!"

Now is the time to reverse the Great Omission lifestyle. Take the challenge: Pray for souls and share your story. The Gospel is not weak. It transforms present conditions and future destinies. This is the hour for them to hear it from you!

COFRADIA CROWDS, SOULS, AND INTERCESSORS

The street was lined on both sides with buses and cars as we neared the field on Friday night. People were everywhere, densely packed on every inch of the grounds. It was one of the largest—if not the largest—turnout we had ever seen in Honduras.

People flooded the area in front of the platform in response to the salvation call. They came until there was no more room, and then they still kept coming! At the same time behind the stage, something powerful was happening. Intercessors from the United States and Honduras were united, fervently calling all souls to come to Jesus. I could hear them in English, in Spanish, in the Spirit bombarding heaven for the lost.

This was followed by prayer for healing, miracles, and supernatural breakthrough, with testimonies of joy and victory following. The week in Cofradia had filled our hearts with faith and fire—and the best was yet to come.

CHAPTER 15

SHOUTING IN THE HOUSE

IT HAD BEEN AN AMAZING JOURNEY. And by the looks of it the road was about to get steeper. I knew we were about to step beyond our comfort level, to risk everything, and believe for the impossible.

It would seem foolish. Except looking back at the road we had traveled so far, it was full of hurdles overcome, miracles beyond comprehension, and divine interruptions by the invisible hand of God. The journey had broken us, empowered us, and revealed in us the nature and character of God.

No way we could ever forget the awe and majesty of King Jesus or the mighty exploits He had done. Nations and generations needed to hear the reports of who He is and what He was doing. We needed to keep them at the front of our minds and on the lips of our mouth, not just as a reminder of from where He had brought us, but also to strengthen our hearts for the road ahead.

As we look back at some of the testimonies, I hope your heart will ring: *That's my Jesus!*

THE MAN NEXT DOOR

In Costa Rica, we sent a team to minister in a midweek service. Like many neighborhood churches in Central America, the doors and windows remained open throughout the service. This helped circulate a breeze inside and let the sounds from the service drift outside.

A young man on our team preached and made an appeal for salvation. No one responded. The service ended, and the team prepared to head back to the hotel.

At that moment, a man walked into the church. He asked to talk to the pastor and guest speaker.

That night the preaching of the Gospel had carried beyond the church, into the street, through the walls of the house next door, and upstairs into a bedroom. There, a man lay dying in his bed, listening.

If not for the message sent from the dying man, the team would have left thinking little or nothing had happened. They would not have known the eternal impact of the Gospel that night. While it was true no one in the *their* building had responded to the call for salvation, the man next door in his upstairs bedroom did!

This is the nature and reach of the Gospel. Once verbalized, it finds its way into all kind of unsuspecting places for the glory of God. Like the man next door, there must be many testimonies waiting to be revealed in heaven, when little or nothing seemed to have happened when we shared the Gospel. But unknown or unseen to us at the time, someone else was listening, watching, and receiving. This is the potency of the Gospel of Jesus Christ!

A GOD OF ARCHES

The church was packed. The few hundred chairs set up were not nearly enough. Those who could not get in overflowed onto the road to hear the Gospel message! It was burning hot inside, everyone dripping with perspiration. All of it brought a palpable sense of anticipation.

I spoke on Peter's confession of Jesus. Scores of young people responded to a call for salvation, including several men from outside. People wept at the altars as we drank in the presence of the Lord.

Many came forward for healing. Steve shared about a lady who had flat feet and came to one of the crusades. Nothing happened. She returned home and went straight to bed.

The next morning something had happened. She woke up with arches in her feet! The Lord had performed a miracle for her—not at the crusade, but at home while she slept.

Steve's testimony prompted a mom to bring her baby girl, who had also been born with flat feet, to the altar. I put my hands on her left foot, and Dennis started to pray.

Almost immediately Mom and Grandma started to sob. There was a commotion around us, but I kept my head down and continued praying. Dennis finally touched me on the back and said, "Stephen, look at her feet!"

I pulled my hand away. She now had arches!

RADIO POWER

In Honduras, we received an invitation to do an hour broadcast on a local radio station at six o'clock in the morning. Ray, one of our faithful volunteers, said he would do it.

Ray shared some of the things he had experienced on LOLI trips and at the end, led the radio listeners in a prayer for salvation. He signed off, returned to the hotel for devotions, then loaded up his group for a day of distribution.

Meanwhile William was on a team headed up to a mountain village.

There in the middle of nowhere, he saw a man standing by a wire fence. William asked if he was a Christian, and the man said yes!

The man started gushing how this morning had changed his life. He had heard a man from Texas on the radio speaking about the power and compassion of Jesus. It impacted him deeply. So when the man on the radio invited listeners to pray with him to receive Jesus as their Lord and Savior, he did!

When William later returned to the hotel, he had a big surprise for Ray. Not only had he met someone who had listened to the radio broadcast, but that man had committed his life to the Lord because of it!

ETERNAL CROWNS

We must live our life with a view toward eternity. Everything we say and do in public and private will one day be reviewed and in certain cases rewarded by the Lord Jesus.

The Bible says there are crowns given to reward faithful people. The meaning of the Greek word *stephanos* is "crown," and here are several of the eternal crowns awarded those who faithfully look toward eternity.

Crown of Life for Perseverance

"Blessed is the man who endures temptation; for when he has been approved, he will receive the *crown of life* which the Lord has promised to those who love Him" (James 1:12, emphasis mine).

This is the crown awarded to those who remain steadfast in the midst of trial and temptation, demonstrating a persevering love for the Savior. This should be something we all can strive for, because the Lord Himself helps us overcome temptation and stand firm in our faith.

The Bible says: "No temptation has seized you beyond what people normally experience, and God can be trusted not to allow you to be tempted beyond what you can bear. On the contrary, along with the temptation he will also provide the way out, so that you will be able to endure" (1 Corinthians 10:13 complete jewish bible).

Crown of Life for Martyrs
A special honor is reserved for those who face trials at a much higher level. It is mentioned in Revelation as a crown of life for martyrs, reserved for those who faced death and did not cling to this life.

Jesus speaking to the persecuted church says, "Be faithful until death, and I will give you the crown of life" (Revelation 2:10). Facing tribulation, sufferings, and imprisonment, Jesus exhorts them to remain faithful even if it costs them their lives. The Bible says, "In the world you will have tribulation; but be of good cheer, I have overcome the world" (John 16:33).

Looking at church history, more people have given their lives for faith in Jesus Christ over the last one hundred years than the entirety of the first nineteen centuries! Do not let that scare you. Rather, take a moment to evaluate your love for Jesus. Let Him strengthen you to live, and if necessary die, for your faith. Paul exhorts us this way: "For to me, to live is Christ, and to die is gain" (Philippians 1:21).

Crown of Righteousness
Paul wrote: "There is laid up for me the *crown of righteousness*, which the Lord, the righteous Judge, will give to me on that Day, and not to me only but also to all who have loved His appearing" (2 Timothy 4:8, emphasis mine).

In wrapping up one of his final letters, Paul realizes his life is drawing to an end. He is not discouraged. Instead, he is looking forward to meeting the Righteous Judge (King Jesus) and receiving his reward.

And in the verse before he writes, "I have fought the good fight, I have finished the race, I have kept the faith." For those who can say the same thing, having a burning desire to see the Lord, this is part of your reward!

The Complete Jewish Bible says the crown of righteousness is reserved for them who have "longed for him to appear." This should be the cry of all of our hearts: Even so, come, Lord Jesus!

Soul Winner's Crown

Paul wrote to the Thessalonians: "When our Lord [Jesus] returns, what will be our hope, our joy, our crown to boast about? Won't it be you? Yes, you are our glory and our joy!" (1 Thessalonians 2:19–20 cjb). This is the soul winner's crown!

The Bible has a lot to say about winning souls: "The fruit of the righteous is a tree of life, and he who wins souls is wise" (Proverbs 11:30).

James wrote: "If one of you wanders from the truth, and someone causes him to return, you should know that whoever turns a sinner from his wandering path will save him from death and cover many sins" (James 5:19–20 cjb).

All who lead people away from death and into eternal life with Jesus Christ will receive this crown. But this reward comes with a very special bonus. More than the crown, all the people your life impacted will be there to personally say thank you!

Crown of Glory

Peter wrote: "When the Chief Shepherd appears, you will receive the *crown of glory* that does not fade away" (1 Peter 5:4 emphasis mine).

This is a crown prepared for pastors and those who shepherd the people of God. Peter urges these overseers to be both examples and servant-leaders to the believers. The reward for such a faithful work is the crown of glory!

There is also an implication in faithful work for those using the gifts and calling God has given for His kingdom, glory, and ministry.

Look at the parable of the talents. The reward was given to the ones who were faithful and fruitful. To the one who did nothing, the talent was taken away. He did not receive anything from the Lord.

Twenty-Four Elder Crowns

Some of my favorite passages in Revelation are the glimpses we see of the twenty-four elders around the throne casting their crowns before the King of Glory. Our ultimate motivation for winning these crowns should not be for the sake of the reward. It should be for the privilege to present before Him something of eternal worth.

Indeed, when we see Jesus we will want to offer Him everything. This is one of my prayers: to live life in such a way as to have something of eternal value to lay at His feet in worship.

JESUS GREATER THAN VOODOO

Step by step the team moved carefully over the stream, using the large rocks that pushed out of the water as a guide. On the other side, just three houses inside this tiny Dominican Republic village, they encountered Nina.

She accepted the beans and rice but wanted to know why they had come to her village—to her door! When one of the men mentioned the name of Jesus, she cried out, "No, No, No!"

Something was not right. She was weeping but resisting the words and care of the team. Someone asked if they could pray for her, and again she cried, "No, No!"

Walking away from her house, no one had a peace about the meeting with Nina. Something bigger was going on behind her refusals. One of the lady pastors from the area turned back to find out.

Nina finally explained. The day before, a spiritualist had come to their village. He was a voodoo doctor many of the villagers went to for advice. He had spoken harshly to Nina and the others. If they encountered Americans the next day, he said, they must say NO or face grave consequences.

Such a threat had bound her in terrible fear. It only multiplied when she opened her door to a team of Americans!

The pastor listened then explained to Nina she had a big decision to make. The Gospel held the power to free her from all fear and bondage of Satan. It could turn her from darkness to glorious light. But the decision was hers. She could say yes to Jesus or continue living under the terror of satanic agents.

Nina said yes! And when she put her trust in the Lord Jesus Christ, her boldness broke an unseen blockade in the village. The spell was gone as people in six of the next thirteen houses renounced voodoo and submitted themselves to the lordship of Jesus Christ.

This is the glory of the Gospel message: Jesus is greater than voodoo! If you are ensnared by witchcraft, black magic, occult rituals, or any form of darkness, you are not without hope or a remedy. Cry out to Jesus. He will save you!

MARRIAGE RECONCILIATION

It was a painful secret. A Honduran man who led worship in his church, and even helped us prepare the crusade choir, was not all he appeared.

He had been separated from his wife for over a year. On the outside, everything seemed okay but on the inside his choices and secrets were eating him alive.

He was a prominent leader at the crusade. But when the convicting power of the Holy Spirit fell on him, he broke down in tears. He asked his wife to forgive him and for permission to return home.

Watching the restoration of this young couple triggered a powerful response with others on the platform. Husbands and wives started moving quickly to each other. One of our leaders put down his microphone and ran to the side of the stage to hug and hold his wife!

It was the first time I had ever seen anything like this. Clearly the Holy Spirit was sending a powerful message for husbands and wives to reaffirm their love and affection for each other.

BLIND EYES OPEN

At the same crusade, an usher brought an elderly lady forward for prayer. She was blind, with cataracts visible on both eyes.

Freida, one of our intercessors, laid her hand on the eyes of the elderly lady and started to pray. She had never seen blind eyes open, but as soon as she removed her hand, something glorious had obviously happened.

The lady could see! Not only could she identify the colors on the usher's blouse, she was able to reach up and touch Freida's face. The bright lights of the platform stung her eyes for a few minutes, but the cataracts were gone and the pupils were clearly visible.

The next day, Freida asked if she could tell me about what happened. We were on our way to the airport and had stopped for lunch at Pizza Hut. As she told the story, tears started flowing down her face, and the presence of the Lord washed over me and those in our booth. I had seen eyes opened in Africa and Latin America but always from the platform. But Freida had put her fingers on blinded eyes, and the Lord Jesus Christ had healed them right in front of her.

We were all weeping now. Not just because of what Jesus had done for a blind lady, but also for the fire of the Holy Spirit burning a desperate desire for more of Jesus inside our souls.

TRANSFORMATIONAL GENERATION

I was a teenager when I first heard Dad teach that the world was predominantly gray in color. Yes, there was a black diabolical side, contrasted by a strong vibrant white-hot element of believers in Christ. But for the most part, people liked to live in the neutral, comfortable gray zone.

Dad predicted the dark would get darker and the light would grow brighter. The result would be clear: The gray would be swallowed up, forcing our world, our culture, our generation, our families to gravitate toward one extreme or the other.

The Bible echoes this: "The words are closed up and sealed till the time of the end. Many shall be purified, made white, and refined, but the wicked shall do wickedly; and none of the wicked shall understand, but the wise shall understand" (Daniel 12:9–10). This is happening today before our eyes.

Yes, wickedness is expanding, but there is good news too. God is positioning a Transformational Generation. Joel 2 describes the era of this generation: "I will pour out My Spirit on all flesh; your sons and your daughters shall prophesy, your old men shall dream dreams, your young men shall see visions.... It shall come to pass that whoever calls on the name of the Lord shall be saved" (Joel 2:28, 32).

We are seeing the Spirit of God poured out among the nations in high volume. More and more people are encountering God and experiencing times of refreshing. It is an exciting time to be on the earth!

This Transformational Generation is preparing the way for the Lord's return. And three characteristics stand out for these white-hot Christian believers.

Passionate for Jesus
Transformational People will be passionate about the Lord and the things of the Lord! This passion involves prayer and fasting, radical worship, and spreading the story of what Jesus has done. This balance

in the Christian walk, private prayer and a public witness is empowering and contagious!

The life of Daniel is a great example. It was his custom to turn his face toward Jerusalem and pray three times a day. He did this every day. His relationship with God enabled him to speak before people of influence and to inform them there was only one true God. Sometimes this led to promotion, but it also landed him in a den of lions. Regardless of his state, the faith and passion of Daniel was undeniable: "The people who know their God shall be strong, and carry out great exploits" (Daniel 11:32).

Transformational people cannot help but be passionate. As they walk on earth, their spirit is in tune with heaven. They see, walk, and live differently. Or as Paul said: "The love of Christ compels us . . . that those who live should live no longer for themselves, but for Him who died for them and rose again" (2 Corinthians 5:14–15).

Purity and Character Matter
Transformational People pursue purity and character—before the Lord and in the world. They fight for purity—in body, mind, heart, and soul.

If you take a neutral stance on purity today, you will get run over. Peter summed it up this way: "Be holy, even as the Lord your God is holy" (1 Peter 1:15–16, my paraphrase).

Consider a smoke-filled room. If you walked into a smoke-filled place and spent even a minimal amount of time crossing from one end to the other, by the time you exited, you would smell of smoke. Your clothes, hair, everything would be saturated by smoke.

The same is true with the filth and dirt of this world. It permeates and pollutes. But the blood of Jesus and the washing of the Word of God have the ability to make us clean.

The reason character matters so much is that it speaks to integrity, trustworthiness, humility, and consistency. The Holy Spirit wants to create in us a shining character that reflects the nature of the Lord Jesus. In a world that champions success and glorifies accomplishment, it is imperative that Christians win with character!

It will not benefit anyone to make it to the top only to lack the character and moral integrity to stand in such a place of prominence or influence. It hurts everyone—the people who supported you along the way, yourself because of the humiliation of the fall, and it enhances the ammunition for critics of the Gospel.

Transformational People tenaciously pursue purity and embrace character, for they know its fruit remains. Or in the words of DL Moody: "If I take care of my character, my reputation will take care of me."

Awareness of the Presence and Favor of God

Transformational People walk with a prophetic awareness of His presence and favor. One of the words used to describe a prophet is *Nabi*. It literally means "one who walks very close to God, or has an intimate relationship with God." Abraham was not simply a friend of God; he was called a Nabi!

Another expression of prophetic awareness and divine favor is cognizance. The Bible is full of exhortations to get wisdom and gain understanding. "The sons of Issachar who had understanding of the times, to know what Israel ought to do" (1 Chronicles 12:32).

These characteristics attach themselves to Transformational People. They walk close to God and are released to impact nations and generations through the power of the Holy Spirit.

The power of God is being poured out around the world. Transformational People are living in the middle of it! You were created to be a part of this Generation—to love Jesus passionately, to walk intimately with Him, to exemplify His character and nature, and to live a life that would cause your peers to rise up and call you blessed of the Lord!

I THOUGHT THIS ONLY HAPPENED IN THE MOVIES!

Jesus loves teenagers, college students, and young adults. Many have never seen healing, miracles, deliverance, or even salvation. Yet Jesus desires our lives to be full of Holy Spirit fire, walking in His supernatural power and promises. He wants young people growing in faith, believing for impossible things, with a hunger to spend time with Him in prayer and the Word.

In Honduras, a couple of college students were part of a team that went to a midweek service in the country. It was a small church with only a few people attending that night. It also turned out to be an expression of something sinister and demonic.

In the middle of the service, three demon-possessed girls burst into the church. They were screaming and completely wild. People were shocked, paralyzed by fear. The pastor reacted immediately by dismissing the service and urging his congregation to go home.

It frightened one of our college students, who came back and said, "I thought this only happened in the movies!" Our pastors and leadership team prayed for her and encouraged her with Scriptures, but the encounter left her unsettled for the days leading up to the weekend crusade.

When the power of God fell upon the crusade gathering, the team started moving through the crowd. In the midst of praying for people, this college student unexpectedly came face-to-face with one of those who had terrorized the service.

This encounter had a much better ending. Pastors and intercessors surrounded the girl, rebuking the demonic. The Holy Spirit touched her, restoring her to soundness of mind and heart and freedom.

The college student who had been frightened earlier in the week saw this transformation. One year later she came back for a second mission trip. She even brought a special recruit—her mom!

The supernatural power of God is life transforming. The Holy Spirit cancels fear and draws our eyes to an awesome Jesus—to come alive in worship and evangelism. This is our destiny!

POWER IN THE NAME OF JESUS

There is great power in the name of Jesus. Acts 19 tells a story about the seven sons of Sceva. They thought they could cast a demon out of a man "by the Jesus whom Paul preaches."

One demon versus seven men—what a complete mismatch! These sons were not dealing with just a man, but a supernatural force inside him who was bigger than all of them combined.

Even more troubling was their using the divine name as a mantra or talisman—as if the name of Jesus were an omen.

The supernatural power of God does not flow based on how you pronounce His name. The authority and nature of God acts because of the relationship you have with the Lord Jesus Christ!

The power is in the person of King Jesus! You must believe in His Name. And in believing in His name you put your complete trust in the person and work of Jesus the Christ.

Because you put your trust in Him, what you do, what you say, what you are then becomes an extension of who He is, what He says, and what He does. So that even as Jesus went expressing the heart of the Father during His life and ministry, we now have the privilege to likewise express the heart of the Lord Jesus.

TIMELINE/WE ARE CLOSERS

If I asked you: "Given the opportunity to live anywhere along the timeline of human history, what time frame would you choose?" Would it be during the biblical histories or something more recent? For me, with the exception of walking the planet when Jesus did, I would vote for right now!

Many of the prophetic indicators point to this generation as being the "last days." Who would not want to be a part of such an exciting time? Knowledge and information is exponentially increasing. Technology, social networks, and travel have vastly reduced many of the obstacles of sharing the Gospel around the world.

Israel reborn after 1,900 years. A massive outpouring of the Spirit of God globally resulting in an unprecedented harvest of souls and mighty signs and wonders. All of it echoes loudly: We are living during one of the most spectacular times in human history!

What an awesome time to live for Jesus. Stretching out the human timeline from Adam through the book of Acts through the Reformation and all the way to today, it puts us at the end. Or put another way: We are closers!

Even as a baseball manager calls a specialist—his top reliever—to close out the game in the 9th inning, so the Lord has given us the privilege to live and experience the end of a much larger and glorious storyline.

He could have dropped us anywhere on the human timeline—and all of it would have been important. But He chose us to live on the earth today, to be a closer in these last days. You are very special indeed!

These are prophetic times. Jesus is coming soon! We have been positioned on this planet to preach the Gospel to every creature in all four corners of the earth.

This generation has the tools to do it. It gives us a cause, a purpose, a destiny. We were handpicked for today! Our assignment: Preach the Gospel until He returns!

The Bible says: "This gospel of the kingdom will be preached in all the world as a witness to all the nations, and then the end will come" (Matthew 24:14). These are exciting times, and we have a prophetic assignment. We are closers!

CHAPTER 16

WALKING INTO DESTINY

IT HAD BEEN FOUR YEARS. Four years since the Puerto Plata crusade in Dominican Republic. We had taken the team to the top of the mountain for devotions and to show them where God first challenged us: *It's not too big!*

It was the ride back down on the gondola when the Holy Spirit revealed a desire for something even bigger. I looked at Dennis and asked, "What would it take to host a crusade in San Pedro Sula, Honduras?" It was the first time we had ever talked about it. At ten times the size of Puerto Plata, it seemed like a ridiculous thing to ask. But in my heart, I saw us doing an evangelistic crusade in Dennis's and William's hometown.

YOU ARE A CRUSADE EVANGELIST

The quest for what would be called *Honduras Prays* (July 2012) began in earnest the spring of 2011. At the invitation of Pastor Misael Argeñal,

Steve and I arrived in San Pedro Sula to attend his annual city crusade. Held in the Olympic Stadium, the site where the national soccer team competed for entry into the World Cup and Olympics, it was an amazing venue.

We parked next to the stadium and got out of the car. The moment I looked up at the structure of the underbelly of the stadium, I started having flashbacks to Africa. How many times had I accompanied Reinhard into a large venue to listen to him preach the Gospel?

Being here jarred something deep within me, something I did not understand fully at the moment. By the time we passed through the private entrance and made it to our seats by the stage, I knew the Holy Spirit was stirring something deep inside my soul.

We had arrived a couple of hours early to greet Pastor Misael and join in praying over the evening. My seat was between Steve and Dennis, and there I closed my eyes and started to pray quietly in the Holy Spirit.

Almost immediately, I became oblivious to my surroundings. I entered into a very deep place of intercession, where time disappeared and the Lord Jesus began to work inside me.

I was no longer aware of being in Honduras. Instead, in a mystical way I was back in Africa, looking down on one of the fire conferences. I saw two figures praying fervently from the stage. I knew exactly where we were. And suddenly I realized one of them was me!

Instead of watching the service continue, an invisible hand lifted me off the stage and put me in the San Pedro Sula Olympic Stadium. Clearly I heard the Lord say, *You are first and foremost a crusade evangelistic minister. I have called you to preach the Gospel to the nations.*

That deep place of intercession impacted me on so many levels. It reminded me the Lord had orchestrated my leaving Africa and CfaN. It reinforced to me the Lord had called me to Honduras and Latin America. And prophetically it announced: Here in San Pedro Sula—even in this

Olympic Stadium—I was exactly where I was supposed to be, doing exactly what I had been authorized to do.

I didn't recognize it at the time, but the Lord Jesus had just confirmed *Honduras Prays*. It was an assignment that would lead me right back into this stadium fifteen months later for our first national mass crusade!

I DIDN'T ASK STEVE TO PRAY FOR HIM!

It is so important to listen to the Holy Spirit. After having such a deeply personal revelation, I should have been laser-like in tune with every divine hue and movement of the evening. But the very same crusade that moved me to tears and awe also resulted in some stern correction and instruction.

Due to the focused prayer time, I had not noticed Pastor Misael's other guests sitting in our section. So when Dennis leaned over later and whispered that sitting right behind me was a well-known evangelist also ministering in Latin America, I suddenly felt insecure and threatened.

How absolutely incredulous that just one hour earlier I had been involved in deep intercession, the Lord revealing things about my life and future. But now, inexplicably, I was fighting a battle against envy, rivalry, and vain imaginations.

As people streamed to the altar in response to Pastor Misael's invitation, the Holy Spirit prompted me: *Stephen, turn around and pray for him!* I wish I could tell you that my faith and obedience sprang into action, but honestly it was the last thing I wanted to do.

I weakly objected, telling the Holy Spirit I was shy, no one had formally introduced us, and he probably did not want to be bothered. But there was no reprieve. I had received a direct command!

It still took me a couple minutes to act. I grabbed Steve and we turned around to introduce ourselves. The evangelist was warm and engaging, as were the young men traveling with him. We talked casually for a minute, and when the appropriate moment arrived I asked if we could pray for them and bless their ministry.

That should have been the end of the story. I should have put my hands on them and prayed, but I didn't. I totally bailed on what the Lord told me to do. Instead I asked Steve to pray, which he did. He said amen, we all shook hands, and I turned around.

It took less than a second. The Holy Spirit firmly announced: *I did not ask Steve to pray for him. I asked you to turn around and pray.* The heat inside my chest felt like molten lava. I could either turn around (again) and pray for him right then, or face some serious consequences.

This time I humbled myself before the Lord. I asked Him to forgive me for getting competitive and worrying about how I stacked up versus another minister—when both of us served the same Master and King!

I felt a little childish and embarrassed turning around a second time and asking if I could pray for him. But he was gracious and allowed me to do so. This time I laid my hands on him and prayed from my heart. I blessed him, the team, their families, their ministry assignments—like they were dear friends or a member of my family. And when I said amen, I knew everything was much better.

I shared both of my experiences with Steve and Dennis on the way back to the hotel that night. The first one had emboldened my faith, while the second one worked on my character. We needed both moving forward, because our journey was about to take us to heights we had never seen before.

CROSSING THE POINT OF NO RETURN

From that night forward I knew we had a date with *Honduras Prays* next summer. I had no idea how it would all come together but I knew if the Holy Spirit had brought us this far, He would open the right door to meet with the right people.

We first met with the Association of Pastors for San Pedro Sula over breakfast on the outdoor terrace of our hotel. If there was going to be a citywide evangelistic event in San Pedro Sula, this group of evangelical pastors would need to say yes to the project. This is where we also met the president of the association, Pastor Raul, and talked about our dream for 2012. It was an introductory step to get further acquainted and to see if this was something that fit their calendar. We left encouraged and committed the plans into the hands of the Lord.

The next step came with them turning up at the community crusades—especially Cofradia. Seeing the huge turnout of people, the excitement of the local pastors, and the touch of God upon the services deepened the sense we were being knitted together.

We were not going to win them over because of our large ministry or well-known name—because we didn't have claim to either. Instead, it would be relationships. And the association was about to invite us to take the biggest faith step of our lives.

The meeting that officially ignited *Honduras Prays* came a couple of months later at a restaurant known as The Onion. Dennis, Steve, Pastor Raul, and I met for lunch not to discuss a project, but to informally spend some time together. Conversation drifted to our kids and how much fun it was being dads. I asked Pastor Raul to share some of the things he had learned about parenting, since his kids were grown. We never finished the conversation..

Pastor Raul stopped mid-sentence and looked directly at us. After a short pause, he said the Lord had just spoken to his heart. The Association of Pastors for San Pedro Sula, the second largest city in the nation, was supposed to open the door for *Honduras Prays* to move forward.

It was more than a partnership with the association; it meant we had just crossed the point of no return. *Honduras Prays* was now on the calendar, and our journey was about to become even more surprising!

ELISHA'S PURSUIT OF DESTINY

There are many examples in Scripture where men and women trusted the Lord with the direction of their life and it turned out beyond what they could have ever hoped or dreamed. Elisha is one such example—someone who had a divine destiny hanging over him. He reached for it and ended up impacting his generation and nation.

This remarkable destiny stretched him, challenged him, and in the end separated him from anything he could ever have imagined or accomplished on his own.

The same is true for us. You will never regret selling out for Jesus, for believing He can use you to do something enormous in the kingdom, for relentlessly pursuing the call and destiny of God hanging over you. So let's look at three things Elisha did that unleashed in him a destiny that marked him with significance (2 Kings 2).

Do Not Settle for What Everyone Else Is Settling For

Elisha knew there was a call of God upon his life. The Lord had sent the prophet Elijah, who had placed the mantle upon Elisha. At that moment, Elisha had a decision to make: to receive it or to run from it. He responded in faith and obedience! Elisha may not have understood all that lay in front of him, but he knew it held significance.

Elisha determined he would not settle for anything less along the way. So when the prophet Elijah asked him to stay behind with everyone else, he refused—not once, not twice, but three times. Even when his peers—sons of the prophets, no less—pressed him to join them in one of those cities (and let his master go), he would not relent.

This is what separated Elisha from his generation: He was

determined to press in to that for which he had been called! Later, Paul would write about that type of tenacity: "Not that I have already attained, or am already perfected; but I press on, that I may lay hold of that for which Christ Jesus has also laid hold of me" (Philippians 3:12).

There are supernatural promises hanging over you! If you have ever cried at an altar under the weight of His presence, or lost yourself in worship to the King, or had the pages of your Bible set your soul on fire, then you have tasted revival and sensed the call to something more. Its path does not follow the status quo; it is an unwavering and unrelenting heart of fire that yearns to seize that for which Jesus has taken hold of you.

It happened with Elisha. It happened with Paul. And the supernatural invitation is yours as well.

Know What You are Hungry For
Elisha knew what he wanted. When the prophet Elijah moved on to the Jordan River, Elisha remained by his side.

When they reached the Jordan River, something supernatural happened. Yes, it parted before them and they walked across, but there was something else. This was a place of divine separation where God sovereignly set Elisha apart from his peers. Here the prophet Elijah turned and asked, "What do you want, Elisha?"

Elisha knew exactly what he wanted. He asked for the inheritance a father would give his firstborn son. In a Hebrew context, it was the amount that totaled at least twice that received by any other son or daughter.

Elisha had come to this place because he wanted his life to stand out among his generation. He was hungry for every promise that hung over his life to be realized, and to walk in an intimate proximity with his heavenly Father. This is exactly what happened for him!

Paul again echoes this hunger: "I also count all things loss for the excellence of the knowledge of Christ Jesus my Lord, for whom I have suffered the loss of all things, and count them as rubbish, that I may gain Christ" (Philippians 3:8). There is nothing like life with Jesus! It has no equal; nothing else satisfies or even comes close.

Elisha and Paul both knew who and what they were hungry for. What about you? What do you want? Are you hungry for your life to count?

Pick Up the Mantle and Go
Elisha stepped boldly into his supernatural destiny. The prophet Elijah heard the desire of Elisha and responded: "If you see me when I go up, then God has granted your request." And when the moment came for the prophet Elijah to be received into heaven, Elisha saw it! (This ability to see beyond the natural—as demonstrated again when he saw the host of heaven surrounding the Syrian army trying to apprehend him—became a defining trait of Elisha.)

Notice Elisha saw the prophet Elijah go up, but the prophetic mantle fell down and missed him. It did not fall on him automatically. Instead, it landed by his feet.

Elisha could have walked away, swam back across the river, and left behind what he came for—but he didn't. Instead, he tore his clothes, picked up the mantle, and boldly returned to shake a nation and generation for God.

God had answered the prayer of Elisha, but it still required action on his part. It's God's intention for you to receive power. But even as Elisha picked up the mantle and headed back toward the Jordan River, so we must take up the Great Commission and go into the world.

When Elisha struck the waters and crossed over, everyone knew he was different. He was the same person, but the authority factor had radically changed. The anointing and favor of God rested on him, and everyone recognized that Elisha had been marked for destiny, significance, and supernatural power!

Is there a mantle of promise and supernatural power lying at your feet? Humble yourself before the Lord, pick it up, and go!

Jesus said we would receive power—a fiery power—to serve as His Gospel agents. Ask the Holy Spirit to open your eyes to see the supernatural, to fill your heart with boldness and purpose. Then pick up the mantle and go into the world.

A Warning About the Supernatural

There is a warning about the supernatural in this story about Elisha. It is evident in the attitude and response of his peers. These sons of the prophets who had urged Elisha to settle seemingly knew so much. Yet they experienced so little. This is a big caution for us!

They had not seen the prophet Elijah go up to heaven, only Elisha coming back. They recognized the divine authority given to him, but it didn't stop them from functioning in disbelief. They begged him to go looking for the prophet Elijah, to the point that it shamed Elisha.

The same men who had previously been unwilling to cross over the Jordan River with the prophet Elijah were now ready to swim over it in hopes of finding him. And this is the warning: Unbelief leads to functioning in the flesh, especially after failing to move forward in faith.

Seeing the favor and power Elisha now walked in got their attention and triggered a search-and-rescue mission. But it was too late; the prophet Elijah was long gone, and they had missed out on the supernatural.

There is so much to taste and see in our walk with God! But the key is faith and a sharp focus on the Master. You, too, have a divine destiny hanging over your life. Do not settle and leave the supernatural promises and purposes of God for someone else! You have been called to experience a life full of faith—one that others notice and leaves a mark for the kingdom of God.

KICKOFF BREAKFAST

The kickoff breakfast to publicly announce *Honduras Prays* was held seven months in advance of the target date: July 20–21, 2012. Things were already expanding in scope, but not until I walked into the Copantl Hotel in downtown San Pedro Sula and saw the banners, the media, registration tables, and a banquet hall full of pastors and community leaders did it really hit me. *Wow, this is actually happening!*

As people ate breakfast and interacted in the banquet hall, we went table to table shaking hands and hugging necks. Nineteen communities in and around San Pedro Sula had come to show their support. Many of the guests were leaders we knew from community events done over the past two years. Such warmth and enthusiasm made the morning feel more like a large family reunion rather than the official kickoff breakfast for our first national mass crusade.

After a quick interview with a television station, Dennis and I headed to our table. Pastor Raul, Steve, and the vice-president of the National Evangelical Association joined us. Nearly 300 pastors, political contacts, and media grew quiet as Pastor Raul walked toward the podium.

He led off by asking the people of each community to identify themselves as he read aloud their name. On paper it should have taken only two or three minutes—a quick way of recognizing the areas represented. But the people here were excited and ready to voice their support. So when one group responded enthusiastically, it ignited a pep-rally chain reaction, with each community of pastors and representatives trying to yell louder and more demonstratively than the ones before.

It amazed me to see such exuberance and good-natured rivalry as pastors leapt to their feet and cheered at the announcement of their area. I doubt this was how most kickoff breakfasts typically went, but by the smile on Dennis's face, he was very pleased and getting caught up in the fun of the moment.

Things had calmed down by the time Steve made his way to the podium. He gave a short overview of our four ministry accents: evangelism, compassion, transformation, and destiny. Then he invited me to come share the vision for *Honduras Prays*.

AN UNEXPECTED HUG

I pushed back my chair from the table, stood up, and headed toward the podium. That short walk from my seat to the podium, the Holy Spirit starting nudging me to be vulnerable before this gathering of leaders—to open my heart and share with them why the nation of Honduras meant so much to me. By the time I reached the microphone, something unexpected was beginning to take shape.

I shared my recent life experiences in San Pedro Sula—my seizure in Villanueva and how that intensified my desire to preach the Gospel here in Honduras. Then for the first time, I spoke of the funeral I attended the month before in Chamelecon, where one of my Honduran friends lost a brother in a gang assassination. The murder had been all over the news and everyone in the room knew the details. Both Dennis and Steve had shared words of comfort at the funeral. I did not know what to do except wrap my arms around Hector and cry with him over such a devastating loss.

I had not seen him since. But as I shared the memories of that event, I looked to my right—and there he sat listening at one of the tables. The timing was uncanny. We locked eyes and instinctively I paused.

My heart just exploded inside and I cried out, "Hector!" I set the microphone on the podium and ran to hug him. He stood up and moved toward me. In the center of the banquet hall, right in the middle of my remarks, we embraced.

It is probably not what you're supposed to do when casting vision for an event, but this was the Lord's doing. He had redirected my thoughts walking up to the podium and He had brought us to this moment.

Looking back, that hug may have carried more weight or impact than any speech. It vividly demonstrated our love for the Honduran people and only intensified the need and urgency to move ahead together.

As I sat down, one of the pastors next to Pastor Raul and Dennis whispered, "I don't know about their logistics and finances, but they definitely have the people!" That love and connection was mutual; we felt the same about them.

Honduras Prays was on the calendar and now in the hearts of these pastors and leaders. It was only the beginning.

DIVINE SPARK OF DESTINY

Our lives are marked for action. Each of us has a divine destiny, one reserved and created for us by God. It is one full of unlimited potential. It has nothing to do with our resources, abilities, or status—but His!

This divine spark of destiny has the power to be a game changer. We can live life to the fullest because of Jesus! There is a lot to say about destiny—and you have one. Let's start with these three observations.

Destiny Is Activated by Embracing Jesus

Without Jesus we are lost, empty, and upside down. You can achieve greatness on your own, but in the end life is hollow and does not satisfy. This is the lesson of King Solomon in Ecclesiastes: You cannot be happy without God! He alone is the One who gives purpose and significance to our lives.

God created us to dream big. But His intentions have never been for us to go it alone. Do you want your life to count, to make an eternal difference? Start at the cross! This is where the divine spark of destiny is activated.

The moment you say yes to Jesus, eternity breaks in: forgiveness, everlasting life, and the wondrous sense of the love and pleasure of our Lord and Savior. In the same moment, supernatural gifts and callings are divinely released—destinies with unlimited potential to change the world.

We see this in the life of the apostle Paul. He listed all his worldly achievements and ambitions: a life of privilege, education, and opportunity, but counted them rubbish in comparison to his supernatural life with Jesus (Philippians 3:4–11).

How could Paul make such a statement? Because he experienced this truth: There is nothing like life with Jesus! Only Jesus satisfies, and the destiny He wants to reveal in and through us can only be discovered at the cross.

Destiny Is Shaped Through Humility and a Fear of the Lord

The reason we can dream big is because we serve an even bigger God. He is the all-powerful and reigning King; nothing is too big for Him! But there are definitely things that are too big for us, which is why the shaping of our character and passion is so important.

The Bible teaches us that God gives grace to the humble and lifts them up in due time (James 4). Wow, there is a time when our divinely shaped character not only puts us in the middle of supernatural opportunities, but it enables us to shine and succeed in those God-ordained moments! Yes, the One who raises or lowers kings and kingdoms can do the same for you.

The life and dreams of Joseph illustrate this clearly. He was a

Hebrew dreamer who ended up as the prime minister of Egypt, the most powerful position in the world except for Pharaoh. Joseph was young and brash when he started dreaming and sharing his dreams with his brothers. And while his dreams infuriated those around him, it did not threaten or intimidate God. He remained committed to Joseph and his dreams—even through family betrayal, slavery, false accusations, and imprisonment.

God used all of it to build character and holy fear into the life of Joseph. So when the divinely orchestrated moment arrived and Joseph stood before Pharaoh, he was not only ready, he had every assurance it was the invisible hand of God that had led him to that moment. Or as he twice explained to his brothers: It was God—not them—who had sent him to Egypt for the divine purpose of saving many lives (Genesis 45:5; 50:20).

Joseph saw the fruit of a life shaped by brokenness and a fear of the Lord. It resulted in something that exceeded even what he had dreamed.

What is the dream in your heart? Present it to the Lord and invite Him to shape your life and dreams with His character and nature. You have a destiny with God! He is just as interested in you as the realization of your dream. You could even turn out to be the Joseph of this generation.

Destiny Is Sustained by the Promises of God

We do not have to make it happen. This runs counter to conventional wisdom to do something. But the destiny God wants to break you into cannot be reached by your own designs and devices. Instead, it is okay to wait, seek the face of Jesus, and stand firmly upon the promises of God's Word.

A favorite verse of my dad's is Philippians 1:6. "He who has begun a good work in you will complete it until the day of Jesus Christ."

It is a reminder that God has a major stake in our lives and dreams too. He is with us and for us, and the promises of God are yes and amen in Christ Jesus!

The key is not to measure ourselves against others. The measuring stick is Jesus. As soon as we start comparing ourselves with those around us, discontentment sets in and we get distracted. Our job is to gaze at Jesus and trust in His holy promises.

You have a destiny. It starts at the cross, is shaped through godly character, and is blessed by the promises of God. You have been created for such a time as now. It is time to dream; it is time to live; it is time to believe!

PRE-CRUSADE INTERCESSORS CONFERENCE

As we pushed into the New Year, the word growing in my heart was *Stand still and watch*. It reminded me of the charge given in the Old Testament to stand still and see the salvation of the Lord. Both heightened my awareness that something larger was at work. And over the next six months, we watched miracle after miracle unfold as the Holy Spirit paved the way for a nation to unite and pray.

It started with the Association of Pastors suggesting a series of conferences to lead up to July. It would build notoriety toward the crusade and encourage those who attended. We decided to lead with an intercessors conference in February, and it took off!

Pastor Misael Argeñal hosted it at his church, La Cosecha. To have the support of the largest church in the country gave the conference and *Honduras Prays* credibility. It went even bigger when Pastor Misael invited Enlace TV into his church to broadcast the intercessors conference live across Honduras.

The main focus of the conference was the spirit of fear and death prevalent in the city. San Pedro Sula now held the distinction as one of the most dangerous cities in the Western Hemisphere. Almost every church leader there had been personally impacted or threatened by gang violence.

Our guest speaker that evening was Pastor Andrew McMillan from Colombia. He had witnessed firsthand the power of God bring transformation to Medellin after years of violence and torment. Transformation and revival had broken through their darkness and filled the people with hope and joy. This was our prayer for Honduras!

That night was remarkable. More than the huge turnout or the Enlace broadcast, there was such a sweet presence of the Lord Jesus Christ as He loved on the people of San Pedro Sula. It was confirmation. We were moving in the right direction.

LUNCH WITH THE GOVERNOR

The next day, things only got more remarkable. We were to have lunch with the state governor! Dennis, Steve, Pastor Andrew McMillan, Pastor Raul, William, and I were excited to meet him and soon began talking about the previous night's conference and *Honduras Prays*. In the middle of our conversation, the governor abruptly stopped us, pulled out a phone, and made a call. It took less than fifteen minutes to understand what was going on—as a television crew promptly arrived at the restaurant to do an exclusive interview!

I left marveling: a massive conference then lunch with the governor. What could be next? Well, thirty-six hours later we had shared a heartfelt meeting with the vice-president of the National Evangelical Association, had tea with a representative from the Honduras Board of Tourism, visited with several more pastors, and even accidentally bumped into the minister of agriculture at the airport! Seriously, when the minister of agriculture sat down next to Steve across the aisle on our flight to Miami, we knew this assignment had the supernatural favor of God resting on it.

INSPIRATIONAL PASTORS

By March, it was very clear Someone greater than ourselves was heading up the preparations. Every time LOLI needed funds, the money was there. Every time I looked at the team roster, it had expanded. Every time Dennis and I met or talked, it was more good news.

That is when it hit me: *This is the favor of God!* I had no other explanation. We were watching something supernatural unfold before our eyes, something beyond what we could ever do on our own.

Our next visit to San Pedro Sula continued to surprise. Steve and I sat with one of the pastors from Cofradia. He spoke passionately and powerfully about the Church in San Pedro Sula: "If you removed the Church from Honduras, the entire country would implode. Now more than ever we need a strong and fervent Church in the midst of the violence, fear, and darkness." By the time he finished, he had us in tears because of his strong view of the Church and his love for the community.

I loved hearing from the pastors. The call to humble ourselves and unite as one before the Lord on behalf of their city and country resonated deeply with many of them. Now was the time to pray and seek His face for transformation!

But it was not just the pastors who sensed something at work. Doors to powerful political leaders and the media were cracking open—ones that would launch *Honduras Prays* onto a national platform.

THE MAYOR AND THE OLYMPIC STADIUM

That same week we received an invitation to meet with the mayor of San Pedro Sula. How exciting to have a chance to sit down and share our heart with the leader of the city! But those plans were quickly dashed upon arrival.

A massive riot had broken out at a nearby prison. Several people were already reported dead and the mayor had left immediately. Just another reminder of the city's thirst for blood and violence!

I expected the meeting to end right there. But instead of dismissing us, his staff led us into a private room and asked what we wanted to drink. They told us it would be a couple of minutes, as the mayor was sending his most trusted advisor to sit in on his behalf. A few minutes later, we stood as the mayor's closest ally walked into the room—his wife!

We settled onto the couches and she opened with: "I had an encounter with Jesus Christ!" Such an introduction certainly fast-tracked us into the heart of the matter. She shared her testimony and love for the city, and we talked about our dream for *Honduras Prays*.

If that was where the conversation had ended, it would have been enough to label the meeting as supernatural. But just before it wrapped up, she dropped an enormous bombshell: "You should do it in the Olympic Stadium!"

From the moment I had seen the stadium years ago and heard about the couple of Christian events that had occurred inside, I had quietly dreamed of one day preaching the Gospel there. So when she came out and proposed we use the stadium, fire surged up and down my spine. The dream was starting to come true. If there was ever a time to believe for it, this was the moment!

A NATION'S HOPE

The March visit ended with Pastor Misael's city crusade. This time there were no revelations or character modifications, only a curious coincidence.

A political appointee shaking hands with the people in our section greeted us too. I don't know if he knew Dennis, but when he heard about *Honduras Prays*, he stopped and came back to me and Steve. The first words out of his mouth: "I had an encounter with Jesus!"

I was blown away. In the course of a couple days, two different officials had told me their lives had been changed because of an encounter with Jesus. This was their country's only hope!

It was confirmation. The Holy Spirit was bringing together all the components for July: political leaders, spiritual leaders, and media. Yet, inexplicably, the biggest door of them all was about to swing wide open.

A CUP OF TEA WITH MOM AND DAD

In the midst of this divine activity, I found myself retreating back to one of the things I loved most about my Welsh upbringing: hot tea and long talks with Mom and Dad. It was an oasis, a place where I could bare my soul, marvel at the direction this path had taken, and find strength in their prayers for the days ahead.

One afternoon, after another round of tea and biscuits, Mom walked me out to the car. She looked at me and said, "Do you know what the Lord said to me about you and *Honduras Prays*?"

I had no idea, but I learned a long time ago when my mom asked me a question like that, it was not really a question. It was a prelude to a heavenly download. The Lord had spoken to her as a mother: *Stephen is walking on water—pray he keeps his eyes on Jesus!*

It was a gentle but firm reminder that success would ultimately be determined by our focus, not our efforts. It did not matter the size of our ministry, Jesus was the One who was sustaining and supporting us.

With so many supernatural things breaking out all around, now was not the time to get distracted. Absolutely! The most important thing was to keep our eyes fixed on Jesus.

CHAPTER 17

BEFORE GREAT MEN, DON'T BE GREAT

"**COULD THIS REALLY** be happening?" I leaned over and asked Steve. We were both on the edge of our seats, flying into the capital city of Tegucigalpa.

It had nothing to do with landing at one of the most dangerous runways in the world. One that sits inside a volcanic rim, requiring a fast, circular descent and giving you the impression that you could literally reach out the window and touch the cars and rooftops zipping by. Instead, if all went as hoped, our April meetings would take us to a place we had never before imagined.

ENLACE HONDURAS

The largest and most influential television network in Latin America is Enlace. Prior to this day, Dennis and I had interviewed with them at a couple of our Honduras events. But this was a different opportunity entirely. Today we were meeting with them at their national headquarters to ask about partnering in *Honduras Prays*.

I walked into the conference room and took a seat on the opposite side, directly in front of the flow of cold air coming out of the air conditioning units. I was already nervous, so the last thing I wanted to do in such an important meeting was start sweating.

Steve and Dennis flanked me to my right and left. The rest of the room filled out with Pastor Raul, the Enlace station president, and one of the most influential pastors in Tegucigalpa.

I sat at the conference table wondering how many other ministries had sat in this same room petitioning the participation of Enlace. What had they said? Did they impress them? Had they been successful?

I determined right then if this was a God connection, I could share the dream of *Honduras Prays* straight from my heart. No flash, no hype, nothing polished—just raw and real. I would not try to impress them; rather, if the Lord was in it, He would speak to their hearts and unite us.

Something connected between us that day. I could never have imagined how big their contribution would be toward *Honduras Prays*, but their kindness and generosity started immediately.

We barely had time to catch our breath. We suddenly found ourselves sitting in front of cameras doing a one-hour live TV program broadcast to all of Honduras. And in case we had any doubts that this was the leading of the Lord, the name of the TV program was called *Enlace Honduras Prays*!

We left the studio rejoicing and headed for lunch. A brief call from the studio only heightened our mood. They liked the television interview and decided to rebroadcast it that night in prime time!

The trip to Tegucigalpa had started with a home run, but the wow factor was just getting started.

AT HOME WITH A CONGRESSMAN

Lunch was just winding down when Dennis's cell phone chirped. He flashed a big smile and asked if we would accept an invitation from a congressman to join him at his house that night. Such a request had never been made of us before. Yes, we would be absolutely delighted!

The drive up to the top of the volcanic rim consisted of a series of sharp curves and an ever-widening view of the city lights below. We reached the gate that wrapped around the property and waited for the guard to open it. We drove inside, greeted one of the dogs, and moved quickly to the front door.

We had arrived ahead of the congressman, who had been tied up in a meeting. But his wife introduced us to the family and other pets before we settled outside on a side porch. With her serving us hot tea, I felt right at home.

The congressman arrived and treated us to an insider look at the challenges he and his colleagues faced in enhancing security in Honduras. He highlighted drug traffic coming up from South America and finished by requesting prayer for wisdom in dealing with such difficult issues.

This was more than a private audience with a congressman. He was opening his heart about his family and his country. And he was asking for divine intervention!

Dennis, Steve, William, and I gathered around him and his family and laid hands on them. My heart burned as we prayed for them and Honduras. It was another indication the Lord was interested in both the people and the nation itself.

ABRAHAM'S FAVOR WITH KINGS AND PRIESTS

The favor of God enriches our lives and purpose. Reading through Genesis, for example, it amazes me how many times Abram (later called Abraham) encountered kings or priests.

The Bible describes him as a man of faith, a man of favor, and a person blessed of God (Hebrews 11 and Romans 4). But more that just the number of occurrences, his encounters with these leaders shaped global affairs.

Chapter 12

Here his faith is exhibited in obeying the word of the Lord: He pitched his tent but built an altar. The willingness to pitch a tent indicated a determination to move with God throughout the land. His building of altars served as markers/reminders of encountering the divine favor of God.

Abram leaves Bethel and moves southward. The land had experienced famine, forcing him into Egypt. But the favor of God extended there, too, as Abram meets with Pharaoh, and his family is preserved.

Chapter 14

Abram hears how an alliance of four powerful kings had invaded and defeated the southern kingdoms of Sodom, Gomorrah, Admah, Bela, and Zeboiim. The invading armies had taken Lot captive (Abram's nephew), along with plunder from the cities, and retreated northward.

In faith, Abram gathers his 318 trained servants and his three neighboring allies and pursues the armies of the four kings. Coming upon them, he divides his forces and attacks at night. The kings who had earlier defeated five united armies flee before this man of favor!

Returning from victory with all the plunder and people previously taken, Abram is met by two kings: the ruler of Sodom (one of those previously defeated) and the king-priest of Salem. Melchizedek, the priest of the Most High God, blesses Abram and declares: "Blessed be Abram of God Most High, possessor of heaven and earth; and blessed be God Most High, who has delivered your enemies into your hand" (vv. 19–20). Abram responds by giving the king-priest of Salem a tithe of everything.

To the king of Sodom, Abram returns the captives and their possessions. The Bible notes he kept nothing for himself, even though he had a right to the spoils as the victor. By doing this, Abram indicated God had won the victory, and it was not the result of his own ingenuity and strength.

Chapter 20

After the destruction of Sodom and Gomorrah, Abraham migrates in a southwest direction and settles in a place called Gerar. Here he meets Abimelech, the king of that city-state.

Again, Abraham experiences the favor of God. The Lord dramatically intervenes to protect both Abraham's family and the promise of an offspring.

The taking of Sarah would have ruined Abraham's family and the Messianic line of descent. But God was watching over His promises! Or as Psalm 105 recorded: "Yes, He rebuked kings for their sakes, saying, 'Do not touch My anointed ones, and do My prophets no harm'" (vv. 14–15).

Abraham certainly walked in incredible favor. It is interesting to note following the incident in Genesis 20, the next chapter opens with the Lord ministering to Sarah: "Sarah conceived and bore Abraham a son."

The King of Kings

More than the earthly kings and priests he met throughout his life, Abraham kept encountering the King of kings! From counting the stars in the sky, to negotiating the number of righteous people needed to spare the city of Sodom, to offering Isaac on an altar, to leaving his country to go after the promises hanging over him, Abraham had an intimate relationship with God.

This was the key to finding favor. Abraham walked out the call not just to meet with the kings of the earth, but with the King of Eternity.

PRESIDENT LOBO OF HONDURAS

The call of a lifetime had come the night before. The office of the president of Honduras had confirmed our appointment for Friday, April 27, at his office at 8:30 a.m. It seemed too incredible to believe that the next morning we would actually get dressed and head over to meet with President Lobo. But it was actually happening!

The next morning, I sat in back on the passenger side, staring out the window of a quiet car. All of us—Dennis, Steve, William, and I—were lost in thought about what this day would mean. The car in front of us had several national leading evangelical leaders, and when we reached the main gate the guards spoke primarily to them. We sat there for several minutes but it felt like hours, as the absolute last thing any of us wanted was to arrive late for our meeting with the president.

Finally the gate opened and we passed through. In surprisingly short order, we went from parking, walking through the Casa Presidencial Arch, up the grand staircase, and to a small gate on the left-hand side. With one turn of the key, we stepped into the second floor of the inner courtyard and were escorted to a small reception room.

One of the aides came into the room and asked if any of us had cell phones. The obvious answer brought us out of the reception room and into a hallway. There lined up on the opposite wall were several personal mailboxes, each having its own key.

I placed my cell phone inside and locked the box. Suddenly, the two towering doors on my left burst open. There standing in the entrance was the president of Honduras!

Instinctively everyone fell into a single-file line. President Lobo warmly shook our hands and welcomed us into his massive office.

I walked into the room and noticed first his desk at the far end with the Honduran flag beside it. To our immediate left, two beautiful chairs lined the wall with a small table between them. It looked like something

I had seen on television where heads of state sat and faced each other to talk while cameras flashed.

In front of those two chairs were couches and more chairs. No one had mentioned a seating chart, so I found one of the couches and sat down. That is when I heard my name.

I looked up to see President Lobo Sosa inviting me to sit in one of the two chairs against the wall. I could hardly believe it. Here in the office of the president, I was now sitting next to the most powerful man in the country.

The meeting was extraordinary. We had been advised fifteen minutes to brief the president, then take a couple of pictures. But something connected between us and the brief window stretched into a forty-five-minute conversation!

Dennis and Pastor Raul shared the heart for *Honduras Prays*, and President Lobo spoke of challenges facing Honduras. The final minutes were reserved for me.

I had sought the Lord beforehand for a word of direction or a Scripture for such a moment. He had answered my prayer with a verse out of the book of Proverbs: *Before great men, don't be great!*

It was not what I had expected, but now it was burning inside my heart like fire! This was not the moment to try to impress anyone—especially the president.

I humbled myself, making a point to say we were servants in his country, honored to have a role in calling the nation to pray for God's intervention and blessing.

The moment those words came out of my mouth a holy boldness fell upon me. I mentioned the culture of fear and death in San Pedro Sula. There were some very real political and economic challenges confronting the nation. But this was not a political or economic crisis only; this was a spiritual war.

It continued to pour out. As ambassadors of the Lord Jesus Christ, we carried a power inside us that could break the darkness warring against the soul of Honduras. It was not a confidence in ourselves but in a God who loved the people of this nation. If we could call the country to unite and humble itself before God—underneath the banner of 2 Chronicles 7:14—the promise of Scripture was He would hear us and heal the land.

VIDEO PROMO WITH THE PRESIDENT

In the aftermath of our meeting, we took turns having pictures taken with the president in front of the Honduras flag guarding his desk. He surprised me by agreeing to shoot an official invitation for *Honduras Prays*. The idea: shake hands, invite people of Honduras to join us this summer, and have him bless the event. No problem, right?

Standing next to the president, with the national flag framing out the shot, the camera began to roll. I focused on shaking his hand firmly and looking him in the eyes as I spoke. That is when he smiled knowingly and offered me a piece of advice: "Talk to the camera!"

I had tried so hard to focus on him—the handshake, the eye contact—that I forgot this was an invitation to the Honduran people. It was one of those funny moments everyone in the room could appreciate. Obviously, I wasn't used to shaking hands with heads of states in public service announcements.

So if you ever see the short video, you will notice we both have huge smiles on our faces, because it is the retake!

SQUEEZING THE VICE-PRESIDENT

If I thought the video would be the most embarrassing moment of the day, then I was shortsighted. As we walked out of his office, a lady appeared in the hallway where we had stored our phones. She greeted us warmly, and William whispered, "Quick, go get your picture taken with her!"

So I did what any Texan gentleman would do in such a situation: I walked over, put my arm around her, leaned in, and smiled big for the camera. This informality must have taken her by surprise, because she had a quizzical look. Only after a couple of others stood by her for more formal shots did someone tell me I had just squeezed the vice-president of Honduras.

I could not believe it. The last thing you do with royalty or someone of her status is touch them uninvited—let alone put your arm around them. Outside in the parking lot everyone found it hilarious, and I deserved every bit of. But I also made a mental note that I could not let that happen again.

As we drove off, something of a holy awe settled into the car. The pieces for July were more than just falling into place; this was a divine orchestration!

GROWING IN THE FAVOR OF GOD

There is nothing like walking in the favor of God. It is more valuable than rubies or gold—nothing compares to it! It cannot be bought or manipulated.

Favor comes from a place of surrender and a desperate hunger for His presence. It is connecting with the Holy Spirit, inviting Him to shape our character and choices. It is the awe-filled awareness that the direction and details of our lives are being prepared by the invisible hand of God.

Seeing so many miraculous doors open, it was clear what He was establishing dwarfed any amount of financing, networking, or human strategizing. Those who knew us best just shook their heads, threw their hands up in the air, and said, "This has to be God!" How else could you explain what was happening other than divine favor?

For several years, two passages regarding the favor of God burned in my heart. The first is 1 Samuel 2:26: "The child Samuel grew in stature, and in favor both with the Lord and men."

What a testimony—as he matured in age and in his walk before the Lord, Samuel experienced favor! He grew in influence and insight as a priest, a prophet, and ultimately a kingmaker. His legacy: The child grew up to become a nation shaker and history maker!

This same plan applies to our lives: to hear and discern the voice of the Lord, to develop godly character, to recognize the favor of God working in our lives, and to follow it wherever it leads.

Luke 2:52 echoes the process of the first passage. It reads: "And Jesus grew in wisdom and stature, and in favor with God and men."

With Samuel and in the life of Jesus, the Bible says they increased in stature and favor. How can we not prayerfully seek out these same characteristics for our lives? To grow in character and favor not only shapes us, it directs us.

Are you hungry to look like Jesus and give your life to His calling and purposes? Ask for favor, wisdom to recognize it, and to be full of the Holy Spirit. Every time you see the favor of God, follow it!

It will make your relationship with the Lord stronger. And the character and nature He develops in you will influence and impact others.

SECOND AND THIRD MEETINGS WITH THE PRESIDENT

Five days after meeting with the president of Honduras, the phone rang. President Lobo Sosa wanted us to come back and present *Honduras Prays* to his cabinet!

At that meeting, he revealed his intentions. He would join us Friday,

July 20, at the Olympic Stadium in San Pedro Sula for the opening night of a national call to prayer.

But there was more. Two days later, my phone rang again. "You ready for some really good news?" Dennis asked. It was better than good; it was incredible news.

The president had called again. He was more than committed to coming in the summer. Now he wanted us to organize a luncheon of the most influential pastors and Christian leaders in the San Pedro Sula area so he could personally advise them about *Honduras Prays*.

I was stunned. It had been an honor of the highest order to meet President Lobo Sosa in his private office. It had been remarkable to receive an invitation to return and address his cabinet. But this new wrinkle left me dumbfounded.

It was one thing for *us* to *fly* to Tegucigalpa to meet with him. But it was a totally different matter for the president to get on a plane and fly across the country to have lunch with us.

But that is exactly what happened. At the Hilton Princess in San Pedro Sula, the president publicly endorsed *Honduras Prays* for the first time. Not only did he come, he also paid for the lunch!

It was as if the president of Honduras had become one of our crusade directors. We could not have received any larger endorsement than the executive of the nation to give us his stamp of approval. That these developments had happened in just a couple of weeks left us breathless at the favor and intent of God.

BLESSING OF MIKE EVANS

The day before the luncheon with President Lobo, we held our annual fund-raising golf tournament in Texas. At the awards ceremony, I told the players about the buildup to our first national event. My heart was overflowing with emotion, as there was no other explanation about this sudden rise other than the hand of God sovereignly maneuvering pieces on a chessboard to bring about His divine purposes for *Honduras Prays*. I asked the players to join me in praying for Honduras, and all the thoughts and feelings that had been mounting up inside my heart for weeks flooded out.

Yes, I knew this was a golf tournament and not a prayer meeting, but I could not stop what poured out of me. I prayed for God's favor and blessing on the preparations, on the missions week, and on the team coming to serve. I petitioned God to personally reveal Himself to the president of Honduras and his team of advisors. I cried out for the nation of Honduras. Then I sat down.

One of the players in the room that day was New York Times Best Selling Author and Middle East Correspondent Dr. Mike Evans. He raised his hand and asked if he could say a few words. We were way beyond the status quo of a golf fund-raiser. It now had a prophetic edge to it. What he said over the next few minutes impacted me powerfully.

He noted most of the men and women in the room had known me since I was a kid and watched me grow up. But now they had a responsibility to recognize what was going on. Having met with many world leaders, Mike Evans emphasized you do not just meet with a head of state, or have a follow-up meeting, or a third meeting where he flies across the county. This was the favor of God, and it was the players' opportunity to get behind what God was doing.

At that moment, something happened to me. A vivid picture popped into my head: one of Samuel pulling out a flask and pouring oil over the head of a shepherd boy, David, before the men who knew him best. I'm not comparing myself to David, but that public affirmation—in front of many whom I consider fathers, mentors, and friends—was like an official pronouncement of the stamp of God on my life and calling.

BLESSING OF REINHARD BONNKE

Three days later, I walked into the green room at the Daystar studio. Reinhard was there and we had a thirty-minute window before the taping to meet privately. Again, it was one of those divinely orchestrated moments.

We quickly stepped away from the others and sat down at a table for a chat. We talked about family and personal notes of interest before moving to what was burning in my heart.

I wanted to thank him for his investment in my life, and affirm that even though he had people continuing his legacy in Africa, he also had lasting fruit in Latin America. I shared about *Honduras Prays*, the scope of what was happening, and how much of it could be attributed to him challenging me to see my destiny several years ago. It visibly moved him, and I was grateful for the chance to express my heartfelt gratitude.

I put my hands on the table and asked Reinhard to pray for me and the upcoming crusade. With a heart full of fire, he interceded for Honduras and its president. He prayed for a mighty harvest of souls, miracles, and an outpouring of the Holy Spirit. And when Reinhard Bonnke said amen, there was zero doubt in my mind: Heaven was about to invade Honduras in a powerful way!

His blessing was also one of those last details—a final touch on top of everything the Holy Spirit had been masterfully crafting for nearly eight years. From the fields of Africa to *Honduras Prays*, He had been directing all of this and it was awesome to behold!

SLEEPLESS NIGHTS AND DEUTERONOMY

With so many supernatural things taking place, it occurred to me that faith may have initiated the journey, but the favor of the Lord was driving us forward.

My objective was to stay as close to Jesus as possible. The weeks counting down to the crusade resembled being on call twenty-four hours a day—to pray, to wait on Him, to humble ourselves before Him.

The Holy Spirit started calling me out of bed in the middle of the night. In the living room, He would examine, refine, and challenge me. It seemed like the more His favor evidenced itself, the more He wanted to work on my character.

It was during this time I rediscovered the three books referenced most by the New Testament writers: Deuteronomy, Psalms, and Isaiah. The last two encouraged me during this time of preparation, but Deuteronomy lit my soul on fire and caused my faith to soar!

So many things leapt off the page: from reminders that God is the One who fights our battles and goes before us, to the promptings not to forget what He has done and to remain strong for what lies ahead. Deuteronomy not only sharpened my resolve, it deepened an intimacy in my own heart.

TENACIOUS FOR HUMILITY

During our last preparation trip to San Pedro Sula, one month before the crusade, the Holy Spirit had a final nugget of information to reveal. As Steve and I climbed into our hotel beds, conversation drifted toward the Argentina revival and revivalists. The uncanny thing was the more we talked about the presence and power of God, the more the Holy Spirit burned in our hearts. It finally reached the point where we got out of our beds, fell to our knees, and started crying for revival.

As we prayed, a phrase dropped into my heart: *You must be tenacious for humility!* Steve had referred to a conference he attended years ago, where a group of Argentinian preachers had started the service by kneeling down and asking the audience to pray for them. It was an act of humility and surrender—publicly acknowledging they needed the Spirit of God to do what they could not.

Steve sharing that example had awakened something deep within me while we prayed. It was a strong reminder we were called to walk lowly. No matter how big the event became, there was a fiery call to action burning inside my soul—one outlined by these four fiery words: *Be tenacious for humility!*

I stopped praying and told Steve I sensed the Holy Spirit calling us to the same thing. We needed to publicly humble and surrender ourselves. Like the revivalists, the very first thing we needed to do on the platform at *Honduras Prays* was to be in total submission before the Lord Jesus Christ.

The crusade was not about us. It was about Him—a holy assembly between the Lord of heaven and earth and the citizens of Honduras. If we were going to participate in calling a nation to humble itself before God, how could we not humble ourselves before them and ask for their prayers?

Kneeling by the bed, I knew something was happening in us and with *Honduras Prays*. The Holy Spirit had done something unexpected and wonderful. He had fanned the flame for evangelism and given a directive about our posture on a national platform. *Honduras Prays* would be here soon, and His heart and strategy were shining through.

ENLACE INTERNATIONAL

I had barely returned home when the phone rang. A friend wanted to connect me to someone heavily involved in Latin America. That meeting boiled down to one question: "Have you connected with Enlace?"

I misunderstood the question. Assuming he meant Enlace Honduras, I said yes, we had met in Tegucigalpa. He graciously listened, then reloaded the question.

"Have you connected with Enlace International? Have you spoken with its global director?"

The answer was no, but now I understood. It was good to have met with one of the country directors, but would I be open to meet the founder and global director of Enlace.

"Yes, absolutely," I replied. "I would love to meet the president of the largest and most influential Christian TV network in Latin America!"

My friend Shawn and I walked into TBN Enlace headquarters on Tuesday, June 25. The director of US operations received us warmly into his office. He was energetic, funny, and easy to talk with. He was also hungry!

At lunch we met Jonas Gonzalez Jr., global director of Enlace. Warm, full of faith and encouragement, he shared the remarkable story of how his father founded Enlace. Two hours flew by.

Back at the Enlace offices, Shawn and I toured the studio. On one of the sets we met Juanita, the wife of Jonas. Elegant and gracious, she talked about Honduras, Latin America, Enlace, family, and a lot about Jesus! If it was not for the fact they had a show to tape, we might have been there for the rest of the afternoon.

She asked if I would bring Alisa next time I came to the studio. She wanted to do a full taping on *Honduras Prays* and share it with her global audience. While we were in Honduras, the nations would be interceding for Honduras, for souls, and for transformation!

It had happened so fast; an introduction led to lunch. Lunch paved the way for a private tour. The tour resulted in an unexpected meeting. And the meeting opened the door for an interview seen across Latin America.

God was at work! He had brought us this far. Now it was time to board a plane and see what He had prepared for *Honduras Prays*!

CHAPTER 18

A Historic Gathering

THE IMPROBABLE HAD sprung to life. How could a part-time ministry, based out of the front room of our home, have such a platform? After twenty crusade and compassion weeks across five nations, our path had reached San Pedro Sula—to call the nation to turn its heart toward Jesus!

Simply stated, the Lord had opened impossible doors, captured and united hearts, and provided in ways we could never have imagined. There was no other explanation; it was the work of the Lord and it was marvelous in our sight!

PSALM 138

On the plane I opened my Bible and started reading Psalm 138. "In the day when I cried out, You answered me, and made me bold with strength in my soul" (v. 3). It was exactly what we needed: to call on Him and receive supernatural power.

The next verse intensified my heartbeat. "The kings of the earth shall praise You, O Lord, when they hear the words of Your mouth" (v. 4).

To read that verse just before landing in San Pedro Sula struck me as more than coincidence. Soon we would join with the political and Christian leaders to look into the Scriptures and humble ourselves collectively before the Lord.

The sixth verse brought the tears. "Though the Lord is on high, yet He regards the lowly." It held a double meaning. Yes, He regards the state of the humble and the broken. But to read the word *lowly* in my Bible at that very moment also held a larger and much more direct meaning: God regarded the call and ministry of LOLI!

After eight years of pioneering and dreaming, eight years after Reinhard Bonnke, eight years of desperately clinging to His promises for our lives, it was overwhelming to see the desires of our hearts transforming into precious reality.

I closed my eyes. Over and over again I started whispering, "Thank you, Jesus. I love you, Jesus!"

LIKE HOSTING A CONVENTION

Our very first crusade week in Tela, we had rejoiced over eleven people coming to launch the dream of crusade ministry. But now with over 150 short-term missionaries pouring in, and sixty-plus hotel rooms needed to host them, it was like organizing an international convention.

Everyone was bounding with energy and excitement. If you ran into someone at the hotel you didn't know or recognize, no problem. There was a very good chance you had just connected with someone else on the *Honduras Prays* team.

Morning devotions focused on a deeper prayer life, with a three-hour window during the afternoons designed for the team to pray for Honduras and seek the Lord. Different worship leaders rotated hourly to keep the atmosphere of praise and intercession fresh and unbroken. Many people spent the entire three hours soaking in His presence, with testimonies surfacing of calls to ministry, inner healing, and cries for more of God. Yes, it was *Honduras Prays* week, but He was calling our names too.

AIM FOR THE SUN/SON!

The sense that we are living in supernatural and prophetic days is energizing! There is an upward call to dream big for the King, a longing to leave an eternal footprint in our generation, community, or family. The time to do something significant for God is now!

Everyone has a Gospel-empowered destiny. Activate yours in kingdom ministry by serving in a local church, participating in missions, investing in prayer with a team of intercessors, or walking beside people full of faith and vision.

It is time to start dreaming the impossible and moving ahead in faith. It is time to do something great for God!

The Lord has never once rebuked me for dreaming big, especially if it concerns souls. But having said that, He has and does examine the motivations of my heart. Am I dreaming big for personal promotion and selfish gains? Or are those dreams kingdom minded? The immensity and outworking of kingdom dreams will lead people to marvel: *Look what the Lord has done!*

One of the sayings my dad drilled into me growing up was: *"Aim for the sun! Even if you miss and land on the moon, you have still gone further than you ever imagined."* His challenge: "Dream big, impossible dreams!"

Refuse to settle for that which you know you can do on your own. If you do not need God to break you through the impossible, then you are dreaming the wrong kind of dreams.

Now is the time to dream big things for God. It is not too late! Ask the Holy Spirit for kingdom dreams and to forge the character and faith to walk out that divine destiny for His name's sake.

DREAM BECOMING REALITY

The dream had been to do a large event one day in San Pedro Sula. But as it actually began to materialize, the dream became bigger than just a city.

It was about bringing people together from all kinds of demographics across the country to pray for Honduras. It involved political leaders from the red and blue parties, churches and organizations across denominational lines, and Christian and secular media. It reached out to city dwellers and farmers, rich and poor, educated and uneducated—people everywhere who made up the heart and fabric of Honduras.

It was a holy convocation, a national assembly. Underneath 2 Chronicles 7:14, it was a moment for the nation to pause and present itself before God.

It also had been raining. The forecast for Friday and Saturday night: more heavy outbreaks of stormy weather.

It didn't matter. If necessary we would pray and preach in the rain! What did matter was the people were of one heart and one mind, and that would make Friday night historic and supernatural.

A REMARKABLE GATHERING

On July 20–21, 2012, a nation paused to unite and humble itself before the Lord. The Friday night gathering began with declarations and prayers from many of the evangelical pastors: cries for intervention, transformation, healing, and revival. Their unity and shared hope for Honduras was the first miracle of the evening.

Psalm 133 reveals how pleasing it is to the Lord for people to gather together in unity, despite their differences. "How good and how pleasant it is for brethren to dwell together in unity! . . . For there the Lord commanded the blessing—life forevermore." To witness the Christian leaders of a nation uniting and humbling themselves in prayer for their nation set the stage for what came next.

The mayor of San Pedro Sula and the president of Honduras—members of the two rival parties—stood together on the platform. After what had taken place only a couple of years earlier, this too was a miracle. The preceding president had been ousted and kicked out of the country, followed by international sanctions and a time of tremendous civil stress. For the two of them to be standing in agreement on the same platform, at a national evangelical prayer rally, had never happened before in the history of the country!

The president's cabinet officials, members of Congress, governors, and other city mayors joined us that night to pray for social justice, transformation of the city from a culture of fear and death, and to prophetically declare the best days of the country were in front of it and not behind it.

Pastor Misael Argeñal, Pastor Raul, the pastor's association of San Pedro Sula, and members of the National Evangelical Association gathered next to the president and prayed for him and the nation. They prayed for the mayor, the city and national leaders, and for the future of Honduras.

Pastors Misael and the vice-president of the National Evangelical Association let me know afterward that for twenty years they had invited political leadership to their rallies and crusades. Tonight marked the first time either the mayor or president had attended, and both had come!

It was a miraculous, groundbreaking gathering of political leaders.

To look upon the excitement and emotion of the pastors only underscored how precious this moment was to them and to Honduras.

PRESIDENTIAL FAITH

The afternoon of that historic day, a light rain started to fall around four p.m. The rain was not isolated to San Pedro Sula; it stretched out across much of the northern section of the country.

What I did not know was back in the capital of Tegucigalpa, the president and his advisors were having a serious conversation. Some of his advisors urged him to cancel his trip to San Pedro Sula, as surely the initial night of *Honduras Prays* would be rained out.

That night in the Olympic Stadium, President Lobo Sosa addressed the citizens in attendance and to the nation via live TV and radio. He noted the recommendation of some of his staff to remain in the capital. But he had come anyway. Why? Because he informed *them* Christians would be praying for it not to rain *in the stadium*. So if they were praying, that was enough for him to fly across the country to be part of *Honduras Prays*!

President Porfirio Lobo Sosa then made this declaration: "I am here as president of the nation to ratify my subordination to the power of God, because I am president because God so desired it through His people. . . . How important this crusade is. I want to congratulate all the churches and mayor of San Pedro Sula, Juan Carlos Zuniga, who is present, and I want to tell everyone that there may be great power in tribunals and in public power, but the only thing that can change Honduras is prayer. God can change the minds and hearts of many who are on the wrong path. . . . As leader, I know that the only thing that can give total peace to the nation is the changed hearts of those who do not want peace. All is going to improve. . . . I know that God will open the hearts of those who can help their fellowman, that they will understand that we ought to extend a hand of solidarity because only social justice brings peace to a nation.... By God's delegation, I am here reiterating my subordination to Him and asking together with you that He enlighten the hearts and minds of all Honduran people and bring us peace, tranquility, prosperity, and the best for the nation."

PEEKABOO WITH PRESIDENT LOBO SOSA

When the president had finished, there was a crush of people around him as he exited the platform. Security, photographers, pastors, and others pressed in as he made his way graciously over to our tent.

For the second time that evening, he greeted my parents. The president paused and invited Dennis's six-year-old son over for a picture. After greeting a few more people, he spied Anna, our recently turned two-year-old daughter.

He motioned to her to come. But instead of stepping forward, Anna covered her eyes with both hands. The president of Honduras smiled broadly, then remarkably for the next few seconds humored Anna in a game of international peekaboo! I'm sure she has probably forgotten the exchange with the leader of Honduras, but I will let her know when she gets older.

A MODERN CRY FROM 2 CHRONICLES 7:14

Seeing all the pastors, watching the president address the nation, and hearing Pastor Misael pray for him went beyond anything we had dreamed of. To describe the walk toward the platform—to preach the Gospel and call a nation to its knees—is beyond words! How else could you sum up what was going on except to acknowledge this was the outlandish grace and favor of God!

It did feel a little anticlimactic climbing the steps attached to the platform. After all, how do you follow a speech by the president of

Honduras? Still, when I reached the top, Holy Spirit fire was burning inside my soul. I stepped forward toward the podium.

I asked Alisa and a few others to join Dennis and me on the platform. I knew this moment was coming since the night Steve and I crawled out of our beds a month ago in our hotel room to pray. But this was not our room and we were not alone; this was the largest stadium in Honduras.

We knelt down before the people and humbled ourselves. I asked them to pray—for me, Dennis, our team, and for the message—that what would flow out of our hearts tonight and tomorrow night would be pure Jesus.

In the moments afterward, the platform cleared and I opened my Bible to one of its most familiar passages: 2 Chronicles 7:14. "If My people who are called by My name will humble themselves, and pray and seek My face, and turn from their wicked ways, then I will hear from heaven, and will forgive their sin and heal their land."

I shared my dream for Honduras: a gathering of the nation and a response from Almighty God. A gathering where political leaders joined evangelical leaders, its wealthy stood beside the poor, factory workers hand in hand with farmers. And with the nation gathered in one place, I dreamed about what would happen if the assembly turned their eyes toward heaven.

I knew this was a prophetic moment; the president had just acknowledged God as the hope for their nation. This meant a huge spiritual door had just opened because of the authority he carried. The pastors had united across denominational lines to pray and this, too, held significance. It paved the way for something supernatural to happen. And if there was ever a moment for the nation of Honduras to ask for transformation in the name of Jesus, now was that time!

This was the cry from the Messianic second Psalm: "Ask of Me, and I will give You the nations for Your inheritance." That was why we were assembled: to ask the Lord Jesus for Honduras, to revive it with power and purpose.

This was the cry of the prophet Joel, who urged the ministers—the governmental and religious leaders of the nation—to weep between the porch and the altar. It was a heart cry for revival and national restoration. That was what this first night was about.

This was the message of 2 Chronicles 7:14 and what burned so passionately in my heart for Honduras. Israel had gathered to dedicate its Temple. King Solomon had cried out to God, essentially asking, if the nation would turn back to God, would He heal it, forgive it, bless it? The initial response was fire fell from heaven and His glory filled the Temple! Then a few nights later, the Lord appeared to the king in a dream and said: "I have heard your prayer and the answer is Yes!"

This is Good News for a nation. Yes, it is a promise for Israel, but the Lord will deal mercifully with all nations if its people humble themselves, pray, and seek the face of God, turn from all wickedness, corruption, and perversion. If a nation would do that, the heavenly promise is God would hear their prayers, He would forgive their sins, and God would heal their land! It is not only a promise to the individuals, it is a promise to the land itself.

I stepped to the side of the pulpit and asked the people in the stadium and on TV, radio, and the Internet to join together as one voice in presenting Honduras before the Lord. Across the stadium pastors, leaders, and people from every walk of life knelt and prayed for national transformation and spiritual awakening.

This time I not only went to my knees, I fell on my face. Pouring out from my soul that which He had deposited and cultivated within me for several years, I cried to God to do what He alone could do: change a nation.

MEETING THE MINISTER OF THE INTERIOR

The next morning, it felt wonderful to put on shorts, a shirt, and flip-flops. It was a welcomed contrast to the formal and historical weight of the night before. I was excited to join our team near the pool for devotions and hear their stories and perspectives from last night.

I was just about to step into the elevator, when I heard, "Mr. Evans, Mr. Evans, a word, please." I turned around to see the Honduran minister of the interior!

He was, of course, immaculately dressed. Shaking hands he said, "The president wants you to know he was pleased with last night and thanks you and your congregation for blessing our nation and calling us to pray!"

I could hardly believe what was happening. What were the chances of our team staying in the same hotel as the Honduran minister of the interior? Or that I would end up on the same floor as him? Or that morning we would meet at the elevator so he could relay a presidential word of encouragement? And then this quick thought: *What in the world am I wearing?*

I was processing this when he caught me off guard by asking if he and his wife could have a picture taken with me. What? I should be the one asking him for a photo. And I was supposed to be on my way to a meeting near the pool, not a photo op with one of the members of the president's cabinet!

Dressed in shorts, a team T-shirt, and flip-flops, I followed him into the executive lounge. Things quickly went from embarrassing to downright humiliating, when I noticed the only other people in the room were my mom and dad!

The look of concern on my mom's face said it all. It only took her a nanosecond to catch the distinct difference in attire, followed by a million unspoken questions of why her son had just walked into the room with a dignitary dressed like *that*.

We managed to make it through introductions and the pictures, but for months to come, Mom loved to recount this story. Forget the miracle of the meeting itself; the real news had been the vivid contrast of wardrobes.

Looking back, it was a funny encounter. But it would soon fade in comparison to what was brewing for the Saturday night service. It was something just as astonishing and memorable as the night before, and this time it would be full of fire.

THIRTY THOUSAND POUNDS OF FOOD

The team also found the surprising encounter hilarious, especially the reference to them being my congregation. As a collection of believers and churches, these short-term missionaries were to be commended for working hard as a team all week.

It had started several days before the group at large arrived. An advance team had come to organize and package our largest effort yet: 30,000 pounds of beans, rice, flour, oil, and sugar. Stuffed into 6,000 bags, the food was sent to six distribution centers in and around the San Pedro Sula area. And when the teams arrived, they delivered it throughout the surrounding communities.

It took three and a half days. But when the last team returned Friday, every bag of food had been given out—in addition to hundreds of stuffed animals, ice cream, Bibles, and lots of hugs. Working with the local pastors, the teams had conducted elementary school assemblies, made Gospel presentations in parks, and walked house to house in many of the poorest neighborhoods in northwest Honduras.

The pastors were happy and grateful, but the impact on those who went might have been even more profound. Most of the teenagers and University students had not encountered such poverty. So to spend a few days meeting people who lived in trash collection sites, along muddy riverbanks, or in squatter communities with shacks made of tin, wood, and wire shook their senses and touched their hearts.

These were beautiful people they were meeting. Despite the conditions, they had a hard time saying good-bye. This is why Proverbs says: "The righteous considers the cause of the poor" (29:7). It is not just for their good; it affects everyone involved!

SATURDAY NIGHT RAIN BLOCKAGE

Saturday night the weather was better—at least initially. More buses and more people buzzing around outside the stadium amped up the excitement. Inside the parking lot we unloaded and walked through the glass doors that led underneath the stadium. There were a couple of moments alone with our family and friends before stepping out on the other side to the sideline in the middle of the field. The place was full of anticipation.

The weather began to turn. And when my six-year-old daughter saw lightning in the distance, she grabbed my mom's hand and retreated back underneath the stadium. We were receiving reports of rain across San Pedro Sula, which led dad to pray: "Lord, what we need tonight is fire, not rain; help us!"

Just like that it stopped. It may have kept raining everywhere else in the city, but for the rest of the night, not a single drop fell inside the stadium. A few minutes later, the time to speak had arrived.

WHAT IF WE LIVED WITH HOLY SPIRIT FIRE?

Elijah was not intimidated by the Baal priests on top of Mt. Carmel. He knew that God was a consuming fire. When he cried out to heaven, fire fell and everyone present knew it was God. This is one of the characteristics of fire: it comes from heaven!

Likewise Daniel had a burning and bold witness. He wrote: "The people who know their God shall be strong, and carry out great exploits" (Daniel 11:32). This is a second characteristic of fire: it burns!

The 120 people in the upper room were on fire for Jesus and His Gospel. Their witness spread like wildfire throughout Jerusalem and to the world. This is a third characteristic of fire: it spreads!

If God could challenge a nation through the fiery witness of one man (Elijah), and if He could set ablaze the first-century world starting with 120 spirit-filled men and women, then what could He do with a large stadium gathering? What if we, too, lived with such Holy Spirit fire?

Cities, nations, geographic regions, even continents could encounter this mighty salvation and radical transformation. Friends, family, neighbors, even strangers would be set on fire for Jesus and His Gospel.

These are three of the characteristics of the fire of the Holy Spirit: it comes from heaven, it burns, and it spreads. Loaded with the firepower of the Holy Spirit, every one of us can boldly go as a witness to His resurrection love and power!

Yes, Honduras can be saved. Yes, Central America can be saved. Yes, North and South America can be saved. The nations of the world can be saved if we will live with Holy Spirit fire.

RESPONSE TO SALVATION INVITATION

Something amazing was waiting to happen. In the twenty previous campaigns, I had never seen what happened on Saturday night during the salvation appeal. Thousands of people started pouring out of the stands and made their way to the altar.

From the other end of the stadium, I watched young men run at top speed down the track as if they were trying to win a gold medal at the Olympics. But they were coming for something much more precious: eternal life!

By the time people had responded, the entire section of the curved track was at maximum capacity. It was almost like one of our crowds at an earlier crusade—people in need of Jesus.

After Dennis prayed for salvation, the fire of the Holy Spirit fell on the people with enormous power. People speaking in new tongues, miracles, freedom from demonic power, and cries of deep hunger for more of the Lord. I fell to my knees and cried, "Oh God, ignite revival. Bring national transformation. Let it fall like a blanket on this nation from the Mosquito Coast to the capital, from border to border."

This is why we had come to San Pedro Sula for *Honduras Prays*. Call the people to pray and encounter the life-transforming presence of the Lord Jesus Christ!

As worship rose from the altar, the stands, and around the stadium, the glory of the Lord kept washing over us. It was a night, a weekend, a journey I will never forget.

CELEBRATION DINNER

The teams left the next day. It had been a life-impacting week, and a part of me was sad to see it end. After everyone had left, Dennis and I, along with our wives and families, joined together for a special dinner.

As we ate, the heavens opened and down came the heaviest rainfall of the week. Surely, the Lord had shielded us from a washout.

It had been an amazing journey and we had much to give thanks for. But sitting there at dinner, it was not the end—only the beginning. We had walked into something deeper and more challenging than anything we had faced before. And we would realize it almost as soon as we got home.

CHAPTER 19

More than Another Mountain

THE MIRACLE OF *Honduras Prays* was that the entire journey happened on a part-time schedule, operating out of the front room of our house! Alisa had been teaching, and I continued to serve on Dad's pastoral team. In such a nurturing environment, the Lord had slowly but surely grown and established Light of Life International.

But with *Honduras Prays* behind us, there was a knowing inside us that it was time to spread our wings and move to full time with LOLI. I had served Dad until he retired and the eighteen months through the transition period. It had been the right decision.

But there was no denying the Lord had carved out a place for us in evangelism, intercession, and mission outreach in Latin America. We had the blessing of our families and senior pastor, but walking away from two guaranteed incomes was a big first step.

I thought about a principle shared once by Reinhard: our lives often go around the same mountain over and over again. The test of faith is when the Holy Spirit calls you to break out of that rut: one of security, familiarity, and routine. It is a moment He calls you to leap with everything you have toward that supernatural destiny.

We had felt that initially when we moved to Orlando. Now it felt even stronger to jump forward and trust God.

It was an urgent call to step out in faith and obedience. The Lord spoke to me in prayer: *If you do not leap, then I will give LOLI to someone else who will!*

Less than a month later, we jumped and never looked back.

MOUNTAIN RANGES

The whole thing was a divine setup. Everything that had happened—the seven community crusades around San Pedro Sula, a lunch with Pastor Raul where the Lord spoke to his heart, launching a national campaign, and the remarkable meetings leading up to July—seemed to point to one big summit: *Honduras Prays*.

It was recognizing that Someone far greater was at work throughout the entire climb that had so emboldened us to leave our comfort zones and trust Him with the rest of our lives! And while all of that was good and true, it had only set the foundation for a divinely surprising twist.

We had been so close to the mountain of *Honduras Prays* and fixated on it for so long, we had been blocked from seeing what lay on the other side. That was the wrinkle; this was not about one mountain. He had recruited us for an entire mountain range, and *Honduras Prays* was only the first climb!

It is often like that with God. You step out in faith and believe for what is directly in front of you. But God, who sees the end from the beginning, knows the larger picture. Yes, He sees you overcoming the mountain in front of you, but sometimes it is there to propel you to greater heights!

He is often calling us to more than what we could ever imagine or achieve on our own. But He does it step by step. To show His intentions all at once would easily crush and overwhelm us. This is the nature of faith: You intended to climb a mountain, only to discover it was a mountain range!

TWO CRUSADE STRATEGIES

We had no idea what to do next. The magnitude of the summer campaign had consumed all of our time, finances, and energy and left us in unfamiliar territory. Where do we go now?

The answer turned out to be Nicaragua. In my mind if things went well, we would invest the next couple of years and follow a similar strategy as the one revealed for *Honduras Prays*. We would do several area crusades, build relationships, then see if a door opened to the capital city of Managua.

The problem was the more I prayed over our initial scouting trip, the more I had a gnawing sense Nicaragua would not follow the same script as Honduras. By the time it reached the forty-eight-hour mark until we left for Managua, it was more than a sense; it was a mandate.

I picked up the phone and dialed Dennis. I blurted out, "What if the Lord wanted to do a national crusade and call to prayer in Managua, Nicaragua—right now!"

I knew it was way out of reach. San Pedro Sula had stretched us. So to believe for a city easily twice its size—not to mention it was the capital of Nicaragua—qualified as outlandish. But the more it poured out, the stronger it burned inside.

I believed the Lord had given us two strategies over the past twenty-one crusades. The first twenty had taught us how to impact villages and communities. But *Honduras Prays* had ushered us onto a national platform.

Both were vitally important. Looking at Nicaragua, I did not sense He was calling us to the first strategy. Instead faith was rising for the impossible again. If this was the leading of the Holy Spirit, then He would confirm it over the next few days.

SLEEVES AND BILLBOARDS

We arrived in Managua on Thursday for three nights of seeking the direction of the Holy Spirit. From the moment we checked into our hotel room, we started noticing things—things that normally would be dismissed as coincidence.

When we walked into our room, for example, Steve noticed the words on the sleeve for our hotel key. It read: "Open Doors You Never Knew Existed." An hour later we headed out to see the city. We had just settled in when out of my right-hand window a billboard read: Think Big!

We had not been in the country three hours, and hints about open doors and big dreams were popping up everywhere! No, it was not enough confirmation to launch a national campaign, but it did leave us curious.

NICARAGUA GENERALS

Dennis had identified seven of the spiritual generals in Nicaragua. Denomination heads, pastors of the largest churches, presidents of evangelical alliances and apostolic lines—they were all leaders with a knowledge of the nation's pulse.

We had appointments set with none of them. In Managua, I knew meeting with one of them would be a miracle.

It turned out the Lord gave us several miracles. We not only found an audience with one of the generals, we met with all of them, and some of them multiple times! To happen in such a small window with no advance appointments only added to an awareness we were being positioned for another remarkable climb.

The very first meeting set the tone for the three days. What was supposed to be an informal meeting at the hotel with a denomination leader grew into something more when Steve and I walked into a room of nearly a dozen pastors. Our hearts connected immediately. These men were hungry! When Dennis showed a clip with the president addressing the nation, it was too much for one pastor to contain. He looked at us with pleading eyes and cried, *"Nicaragua Prays* too!"

Meeting after meeting, leaders affirmed now was the time—for unity, prayer, and humility. Our hearts were on fire. But the moment that sealed *Nicaragua Prays* for me came on the last night with Pastor Marenco and his wife.

One of the significant pastors in the nation, he greeted us warmly and we talked easily. Soon our conversation became intimate, and we asked them to pray for us and our families.

When Pastor Marenco's wife started to pray for our wives and children, the Holy Spirit touched her—and me. In tears, she blessed us, then started to pray in her prayer language. Fire streaked through my body and I knew right then the Holy Spirit had just commissioned us to another national assembly.

Dennis escorted Pastor Marenco and his wife down to the lobby. My spirit was burning. All we had seen and experienced that night and throughout the duration of our stay had only stoked the flame for revival, intercession, evangelism, and a deeper desire to live for King Jesus!

I had no idea how He was going to do it, but I knew *Nicaragua Prays* was going to be remarkable.

NO GIBEONITE RELATIONSHIPS

Trying to organize in nine months what previously had taken a few years, and doing it on a larger scale, in a capital city, at the exact moment Alisa and I were stepping out on our own was a daunting task, one more complicated by the fact we hardly knew anyone in Nicaragua.

Many times I pleaded with the Lord to guard us from the wrong people and grant discernment in whom to trust. It was during such a time, at a Thursday night gathering of intercessors, that the Lord spoke directly to my heart. It was advice not just for *Nicaragua Prays* but also our ministry calling and future development. It was three simple phrases: No Gibeonite relationships, no Ishmaels, and no Achans.

No Gibeonite Relationships

The children of Israel had crossed the Jordan River and entered the Promised Land. They had seen God's favor and power, bringing down the walls of Jericho and giving them a mighty victory.

The report of this victory plus all that the Lord had done in the desert in providing and protecting them had reached the ears of their enemies. The Gibeonites knew the children of Israel would soon be attacking them, so they set out to deceive them into making an unholy alliance.

Based on their appearance and story of coming from a far land, Joshua and the leaders believed them. Without consulting the Lord, they entered into an agreement. When it was discovered three days later that the Gibeonites lived in towns nearby, the Lord ratified the agreement of peace and protection!

This is typical of the enemy. He seeks to entangle us with unholy alliances, ones that block, hinder and negate our destiny. If Joshua and the leaders had sought the Lord on this matter, He would have revealed to them the deceptive spirit. The Gibeonites were not allies—they were enemies!

The warning was to be careful with whom we built relationships and agreements. We did not want to make the same mistake Joshua made. So in praying for the Lord to guard us from those who would try to take advantage of, harm, or hinder us, we started to declare: "No Gibeonite relationships in the name of Jesus!"

Do Not Create Any Ishmaels

It was an amazing and supernatural journey Abram (later called Abraham) had experienced. He had encountered the Lord as a guide, a deliverer, a protector, and a supplier. He had made a covenant with God, been promised generations, and met face-to-face with angels.

Despite these encounters and experiences, the ongoing delay of the promise of a son only frustrated him. So they devised a human solution to a spiritual promise. It only created pain and heartache.

In Nicaragua, we could see the hand of God at work. It was His work! And it was to be performed His way, for His glory. We were not to meddle with His plan.

But the temptation to give God a helping hand is always real. Human ingenuity or intervention always risk marring the work and purposes of God. So in seeking the Lord to help us walk humbly and do things His way, in His time, our heart-cry became: No Ishmaels in Jesus' name!

No Achans

The children of Israel had an amazing victory in Jericho. The Lord required them to dedicate all the plunder of their first victory to Him. It was to be His; it was to be holy.

Achan, however, wanted some of the spoils for himself and hid it in his tent. The disobedience of one man triggered national consequences, as the armies of Israel were defeated in the next battle.

A distraught Joshua sought the Lord, and He revealed: "Sin is in the camp!" Achan and his entire family were eventually discovered and suffered the deadly consequences.

In Nicaragua, the call was to stay pure and transparent before the Lord. It was a reminder that He is holy. So as we asked the Holy Spirit to help us walk holy and uprightly, we came together in unity: No Achans in the camp!

KICKOFF LUNCHEON

The official announcement for *Nicaragua Prays* came in December 2012. If the reception we received at the airport was any kind of indication of the next several days, we were in for quite a week.

As we walked up the jetway, a man stood holding a dry-erase board with our names on it. He welcomed us, then escorted us past the entrance to customs and immigration, past a group of security officers, and down a long hallway. At the end of the hallway, we turned left and walked into a private airport lounge. There waiting for us was one of the pastors and Dennis!

They offered us sodas, and a couple of minutes later we were cleared to go. We headed down some stairs, out the back door, and into the parking lot, where our bags were waiting for us on the curb! Newcomers to Nicaragua, they had certainly rolled out the red carpet.

A couple of days later came another wonderful surprise. A pastor had warned us not to hope for a large turnout at the kickoff for *Nicaragua Prays*. Historically, events like these garnered minimal interest. But when we arrived at the Holiday Inn banquet room, it was packed with people.

The seats for 360 plates were filled. The hotel brought more chairs but ran out of food. By the time Dennis stood up to share the vision, it was standing room only.

But it was more than presenting a vision and telling the story of our journey. The people were hungry for the Lord! Dennis and I had barely sat down when the call went out for political representatives to come to the front of the platform.

We were asked to pray for them. After we said amen, leaders and pastors began hugging us. This was more than just getting acquainted; the people of Nicaragua had stolen our hearts!

MINISTER OF GOVERNMENT

By February, we were again watching the invisible hand of God at work, opening doors with key leaders. Dennis told me we had been invited to meet with the minister of government. It was more than a meeting; she had invited us to be the keynote speaker at the first private gathering of evangelical and political leaders—in the auditorium of the government building!

Sitting in an assigned seat on the elevated stage, I watched her walk in. It was a small auditorium with fold-down individual seats. I stood as Minister of Government Ana Izabel Morales Mazum came up on the platform. She took a moment to warmly greet the guests and dignitaries on the platform, and then to my complete surprise, she sat down next to me.

After the national anthem, some preliminary introductions, and a couple of songs, Dennis went to the podium to introduce *Nicaragua Prays*. I was just getting comfortable with the idea of sitting next to someone of such importance and power, when suddenly all the dignitaries stood up and headed off the platform to relocate to the front row.

Alone now on the platform, I was staring directly at those who had been beside me one minute ago. I tried not to feel conspicuous, but it was not working as I felt the historic weight of the moment. I was about to address the minister of government and other leaders inside the government auditorium.

I spoke about the blessing on Joseph given in Genesis 49:22–26.

Despite many challenges, the Lord had blessed him and so, too, had his father, Jacob.

I was in the middle of my remarks when something unintended happened. It had not occurred often in the past—especially not in moments like this. But as I spoke I saw a picture, and it had to do with the church of Nicaragua.

The picture was a person fully dressed underneath the covers of a bed. And this was the idea: The church of Nicaragua was fully dressed, alert, and ready. No one knew yet how alive and dynamic they were, because they were covered. But this was part of the purpose for *Nicaragua Prays*. The covers would be pulled off, and nations would see and hear: The church of Nicaragua is alive and growing!

Dennis and I exited the platform and found a couple seats on the second row. A number of pastors followed with prayers for the government, then the meeting finished—or so I thought. The emcee had a final request: Could Dennis and I come to the front for a private moment of prayer with the minister of government?

I flashed back to meeting the vice-president of Honduras ten months earlier. I did not want to embarrass myself again, especially in front of the right-hand person to the president of Nicaragua.

But as I walked up to her, she warmly reached out her arm toward me. So I put my arm around her and opened my heart. Speaking quietly enough so only Dennis and she could hear, I told her Jesus loved her, cared about her, and cared about her nation. Then I prayed over her, her upcoming trip to Europe, and the prosperity of Nicaragua.

ENLACE NICARAGUA

The next morning we arrived at Enlace Nicaragua. I had been interviewed before in the Enlace studios of Texas, Costa Rica, and Honduras, but this was the first time for me to preach before a live studio audience.

We arrived to a room full of people crying out to the Lord. Something was stirring. This was not just a television audience; these people were hungry for Jesus!

The hour assigned to preach on prayer and fasting flew by. I was grateful to have the people praying and talking back to me in the studio. Their passion to hear the Word of God made it easier to pour out our hearts.

Afterward, Pastor Guillermo and Mirtha Osorno treated us to lunch. From the very beginning, their family received us with open arms. At the end of the meal, Mirtha reached across the table, took my hands, and prayed the Lord to reward us for serving Him. It did not take long; it was only twenty-four hours away.

CHURCH OF GOD NATIONAL CONVENTION

Things were moving quickly: the minister of government, then Enlace, and now lunch with national and international leaders of the Church of God. Their national convention was that night. They had three speakers: the director for Central America, the director for all of Latin America ... and me.

The speaking lineup almost sounded comical. Two international leaders within the Church of God and someone who had never preached at a national denomination convention before. It was a huge honor and proved to be very rewarding.

When we left the hotel that night, the intel said be ready to speak to 700 national pastors. We decided to go early so we could get a feel for the meeting. The first phone pinged before we had even escaped the parking lot: the speaker in front of us had just finished. They had three songs prepared, then the mic would come to us. So much for getting there early!

Halfway through we received another call: they were starting the second song. We drove through a poor neighborhood, and I wondered where we were headed. We had left the city buildings behind. What type of place would fit 700 pastors here—a church?

The third ping told us the band had started the final song. But that did not matter anymore, as we had arrived. It was a campground, and we were not just speaking to several hundred pastors. The place was crammed with cars with thousands of people everywhere.

I scrambled out of the car, walked onto the outdoor platform (underneath a huge structure), and said hello to several thousand people. It was a wonderful surprise and a big honor to stand before such a group of people.

I spoke on the fire of the Holy Spirit. The power of God fell on the campground meeting as the people pressed in, hungry for Jesus.

I knew that night the Lord had connected us with them, like He had with Enlace and the minister of government. Something was stirring in this country—and our hearts as well!

Once again we found ourselves with a national assignment, something that was beyond what we could do or carry out on our own. But without a doubt we were not alone.

HE ENJOYS OUR COMPANY

A couple weeks later I went to listen to a well-known author and pastor. He shared a story about an evangelist who received a powerful word from a local intercessor. She had listed multiple things about him that no one outside his immediate family knew. So when he asked if that was it, she said there was one more thing: "God enjoys your company—add two more hours a day to your prayer life!"

It might as well have been me talking to that intercessor, because those words hit my heart. What more could a believer want to hear than "Well done!"? The idea that God enjoys our time together and would kindly request more of it—how could we not say yes to that! I did not feel conviction as much as desire to increase the time spent alone with Jesus.

Alisa and I agreed it had been a gentle invitation to linger longer at the feet of our Savior. So I set my alarm two hours earlier than usual and decided to lovingly implement the discipline for the days leading up to the next planning trip to Nicaragua.

Those mornings began to transform my life. The sweetness of His presence and the power of His word fueled my hunger and passion. I loved being alone with the Lord in the stillness of our living room!

And as if the Lord wanted me to know just how much He enjoyed those times, He provided me an example. My daughter Anna (a natural morning person) soon realized she could find me in the living room when she woke up. So armed with her blankets and stuffed animals, my three-year-old baby would come racing to the couch, snuggle up next to me, and start the day just her and Daddy. Every morning was different: Sometimes we read a book, sometimes we played with the stuffed animals, and always we had a good snuggle.

I loved those moments! And I caught the double meaning: As much as I looked forward to seeing Anna come around the corner, the Lord enjoyed my company too. It was always fresh: sometimes rejoicing, many times in tears, and always enough for the day ahead.

SHILOH AND THE TEMPLE

The coming of Jesus into the Temple (as recorded in Mark 11) was a prophetic event. When Nehemiah rebuilt the Temple after the people returned from Babylon, the prophet had a message for those old enough to remember the glory of the original one. He urged them not to weep over the second Temple's lack of elegance in comparison to the first, because *the glory of this latter house would be greater than the former one.*

This is what happened when Jesus (who is the radiance of the Father's glory—Hebrews 1:3) walked into the Temple. The fulfillment of what Nehemiah had promised was not the shell or design of the building, but the presence and substance of the Godhead bodily, the only Begotten of the Father, the great I AM, the Lord Jesus Christ!

Everyone knew this rebuilt Temple had never been sealed by the Shekinah of God—His manifest presence. But here is Jesus, the substance and presence of God, not only fulfilling the prophetic word by standing in the Temple, but delivering a message that astonished them all.

Having driven out the moneychangers, His words shocked the people to the point the chief priests and scribes were *afraid of Jesus*. So what did Jesus say that impacted them so profoundly? The answer is the same challenge the Holy Spirit lays before us.

Jesus said: "Is it not written, 'My house shall be called a house of prayer for all nations'"? But you have made it a 'den of thieves'" (Mark 11:17). This is a reference to Jeremiah 7, a passage the religious leaders would have been familiar with: "Has this house, which is called by My name, become a den of thieves in your eyes? Behold, I, even I, have seen it, says the Lord. But go now to My place which was in Shiloh, where I set My name at the first, and see what I did to it because of the wickedness of My people Israel" (vv. 11–12).

What Happened to Shiloh?

Shiloh was the original spiritual capital of Israel. After they took possession of the Promised Land, they set up the Tabernacle in Shiloh with the Ark of the Covenant inside it (Joshua 18:1). And for over 300 years (from Joshua to Samuel), the spiritual capital of Israel remained in Shiloh.

Then something awful happened. Years of people doing what was right in their own eyes resulted in the righteousness on which the nation had been established to be largely forgotten. The priests and leaders were corrupt, and Israel hardly looked anything at all like those who had fought to take possession of the Promised Land three hundred years earlier.

So what happened? In 1 Samuel 4, Israel warred against the Philistines. It went very badly for Israel. As a last resort, the carnal priests brought the Ark of the Covenant to the battle. The result was devastating: 30,000 men slaughtered, including the priests, and the Ark was captured.

The lament is picked up in Psalm 78: "[God] forsook the tabernacle of Shiloh, the tent He had placed among men" (v. 60). In a swift and dramatic moment in Israel's history, the spiritual center was no more. The tabernacle was gone.

What Happened to the Temple?

So when Jesus quoted the passage about His house being a place of prayer, not a den of thieves, He was linking *them* to the time of Shiloh. Not only had they become corrupt and self-centered, they had failed to recognize the prophetic revelation of Jesus as Messiah!

No wonder the chief priests and scribes feared Him and people were astonished at Him. He was not only rebuking them for their compromise, He was saying the same thing that happened to Shiloh could happen to them too. And remarkably, less than forty years later, Jerusalem was invaded, the Temple was destroyed, and the nation of Israel disappeared out of history for nearly 1,900 years.

It would not have brought joy to Jesus to say this. On the Mount of Olives, Jesus had cried out, "Jerusalem, how I wanted to gather you to myself, like a mother hen does her chicks, but you were not willing!"

What About the Houses of Prayer?

Yes, these words of Jesus ring a strong national tone. But they have a deeply personal application as well.

Even as there was a transfer from Shiloh to Zion (from a tabernacle to a Temple), there has been a transfer from a place to people. On the day of Pentecost, there came a mighty rushing wind, and glory filled the house where 120 believers had joined to pray, and they all spoke in tongues.

At the commencement of the Tabernacle and the first Temple, fire fell from heaven on both occasions. This was the intention of a house of prayer: to be filled with fire, His presence, holy substance, and to serve as a sign to the nations that God dwelt inside.

That is what we are today! We are the Temple of God. Our lives are meant to be filled with a holy flame, to be a prayerful place and a sign to people and generations that God is real and resides inside us.

The words of Jesus that brought astonishment that day also examine our hearts now. We are called to humility, holiness, honesty, and undefiled worship. We are His houses of prayer!

STREET PREACHING AND HAT VENDORS

The more I visited, the more I fell in love with the people of Nicaragua. We were coming often now and staying longer. I started speaking in dozens of venues, meeting more pastors and interacting with people everywhere.

We spoke in large city churches and smaller rural churches. We preached in the rain to less than a hundred underneath a small tent, and after midnight to over 30,000 people at an all-night meeting of prayer and celebration.

One of the pastors asked if we would preach in the street—literally! He planted a small stage in an alleyway one evening, blocking two-way traffic and opening a gathering place for the neighborhood to assemble. He even found a screen to go with a portable sound system so Dennis and I could preach beyond those in attendance. Such was the passion of the pastors and the hunger of the precious Nicaraguan people.

Sometimes it was multiple venues in the same night. We would run into the start of one service to share, then drive across town to speak at the close of another meeting. Many of these services experienced glorious touches of the presence of God.

A man stood outside one church on a Wednesday night selling hats to the people coming and going. We had raced by him on the way in, because the service was nearly over and the pastor wanted to give us the final minutes. We shared so fast, we turned it back to the pastor without making an invitation. But the Lord corrected us, because one person came to the front anyway without an invitation. It was the hat vendor! He had come inside, walked to the front, and asked if he could give his life to Jesus.

SURVIVING A GUNSHOT WOUND

Years earlier, the first time I visited Managua, I had the privilege of speaking to a group of people underneath a large tent. At the end of the service a man came forward, lifted up his shirt, and revealed a nasty gunshot wound.

The man frequented bars and often got into fights. When one particular person turned up at the same place, it was only a matter of time. The two would begin arguing, then punches would start flying.

One night, like many times before, the two men ended up at the same bar. Things quickly turned nasty and a fight broke out. But this time was not like brawls of the past. In the middle of it, the other guy pulled out a gun and shot him in the stomach, leaving him to die.

The man at the altar said one thought had consumed him after surviving the gunshot. He was hunting for that person and would not stop until he put a gun to his head and pulled the trigger.

The man who had shot him in the stomach would die. At least that was the plan until he stepped underneath the tent that night.

The message on the power of forgiveness had penetrated his soul. He listened closely to how Jesus had suffered violence, yet cried out, "Father, forgive them!" Revenge and evil intentions began to wash away as he found himself responding to the love of God and the call of repentance. He had come forward to ask forgiveness and invite Jesus into his life.

Now he really needed to find the person who shot him. No longer to harm or kill, but to testify how Jesus had preserved and transformed his life. He wanted his enemy to know Jesus could do the same for him!

SIXTEEN MAYORS

As we got closer to the summer, God's favor continued to present remarkable opportunities. The plan was to drive to another one of the large cities in Nicaragua to meet with the pastors and the mayor. The first half went according to plan, but word soon reached us the mayor was at a meeting in another town.

What seemed like disappointing news turned into a blessing, with an invitation to join him at the meeting. What originally was hoped to be a brief introduction to a mayor suddenly expanded to a platform of sixteen mayors from across the country!

We arrived to the mayors discussing tourism. Laptops, papers, and drinks lined the tables as the meeting was in full swing.

The one mayor we had hoped to meet stepped out, and the pastor introduced us. Dennis shared about the compassion aspects of *Nicaragua Prays*. He not only loved it, he interrupted the meeting and handed us the microphone!

We certainly were not part of the original agenda, but we jumped right in. Most of them liked how we were buying large quantities of food items in Nicaragua to give out to the poor in and outside the capital. Dennis whispered to me that we should pray for them. So before we handed the microphone back, we prayed for them, their families, growth in tourism, and a special blessing upon *Nicaragua Prays*.

THREE SIMPLE WORDS

Summer quickly descended on us. With so many wonderful relationships having developed over the past several months, a genuine sense of family had heightened the hopes and expectation for *Nicaragua Prays*.

In Managua that was fantastic news, but at home it meant increased logistics and financial challenges. Even before we started seeing pastors joining together or hearing people talking about it, *Nicaragua Prays* was stretching our faith. But now with so much momentum, we were being pushed to our breaking point.

At a Thursday night gathering of intercessors, I poured out my heart to the Lord. He had been the One who called Alisa and me to leap out of our comfort zone. He was the One who had prospered our relationships and labor in Nicaragua to the point it was now moving beyond what we could handle. It was a miracle to see the invisible hand of God at work again, but it had taken us to the edge of what was humanly possible for a ministry still operating out of a home office.

That night the Holy Spirit strengthened my heart with three simple words. He told me: 1) *Do not be afraid;* 2) *you do not need to know how; and* 3) *stay very close to me.*

The first dealt with my emotions, not to let fear or doubt creep into my heart. The second dealt with my mind. If the answers would be supernatural, then I did not need to find a human solution or even understand how He would do it. I needed to trust Him!

The third dealt with my focus and proximity to Jesus. The prompting was not to be around Him or even near Him; the remaining path to *Nicaragua Prays* required us to stay very close to Him.

It was as if we needed to cross a canyon gorge and only had a balance beam to get to the other side. Because the strip to cross over was so narrow, there was every likelihood we would fall. But the whisper of the Holy Spirit that night served as a faithful reminder: Do not be afraid; you do not need to know how; just stay very close to Me. If we kept our hearts, minds, and eyes locked on Jesus—not on the beam or the gorge—He would bring us to the other side.

These three words sunk deep into my heart. No matter what type of challenges we faced in the capital or at home, we could trust Jesus! It also reminded me of one of my dad's favorite verses: "He who has begun a good work in you will complete it until the day of Jesus Christ" (Philippians 1:6).

The same is true today. No matter where you are at this moment, hear the word of the Lord: *Do not be afraid! You do not need to know how it's going to work out! Stay very close to Jesus!*

CHAPTER 20

Nicaragua Prays

IT WAS THE LAST TRIP before *Nicaragua Prays*, less than three weeks away. Dennis and I had returned to Managua to join with scores of pastors and leaders to pray and cast a tone of unity for the coming crusade week.

PASTORS PRAYER SUMMIT

The date of the pastors prayer summit fell on a national holiday. This made travel in Managua impossible due to street closures, parades, and festivals. But the hunger and determination of pastors to gather across denominational lines to pray for the country was unwavering. Hundreds of pastors, from the largest churches in the city to the smallest churches in outlaying villages, joined us at Hosanna Church.

I stood next to Pastor David Spencer, the senior pastor of Hosanna for many years and a spiritual father to the nation of Nicaragua. Together we watched one pastor after another step up to the platform. Each prayed passionately for the challenges and needs in the capital and nation. Denominational leaders, executives from Christian TV and radio, heads of evangelical alliances all praying, all declaring, all uniting for revival and transformation.

Tears started streaming down my cheeks as the onslaught of prayer by leaders and alliances continued. It was not just because renowned men were praying from the platform, it was also due to the hundreds of pastors on the main floor praying strongly in agreement. I put my face in my hands and started crying over and over, "Your generals are praying, Lord, your generals are praying!"

Part of the dream for *Nicaragua Prays* was happening: the uniting, humbling, and crying out of the evangelical church before the Lord Jesus Christ. This was something beautiful and supernatural: as the Holy Spirit ignited and fanned the passion for prayer, unity, and holiness.

Dennis and I stepped up to give a final word about *Nicaragua Prays*. But it was more of a request. I asked, "Could we kneel as an army of one before God and ask Him to seal all that has been accomplished in our midst today?"

I knelt beside the podium with Dennis and started pouring out my heart in prayer and intercession. All over the sanctuary pastors knelt, linking hearts for their nation. I left encouraged, but much more was coming soon.

EARLY MOMENTS OF NICARAGUA PRAYS WEEK

Alisa, Riley, Anna, and I flew into Managua a couple days early. My first surprise of the week came as we left customs. There waiting to greet us was Dennis, William, and Pastor Marenco with his team!

That the senior pastor of one of the largest and most influential churches would be at the airport to welcome my family, and roll our bags to the car, was unbelievable! We are talking about a very busy and important person taking valuable time to welcome us to his country.

His kindness and hospitality meant so much.

The next morning we bumped into Pastor Danillo from the National Evangelical Association of Pastors. For months he had traveled with us in and around Managua, introducing us to pastors and serving us tirelessly. His joy, passion, and sense of humor had made him more than a friend; it felt like family! So I could not help but smile when I saw him and heard the first words out of his mouth: "I thought you loved me, then you send me out with the advance team!"

I guess no one told him how hard the guys worked to organize the food and have it set up in five base areas for next week's distribution. But he said it with a huge smile on his face. Like the rest of us, he was fully anticipating the *Nicaragua Prays* week.

NATIONAL PRESS CONFERENCE

I woke up Monday morning expecting to wear a brand-new blazer for the national press conference—one purchased for such a moment. It had been tailored to fit, but the alterations took longer than expected.

It barely made it to Nicaragua. Mom and Dad had picked it up and rushed it over to our house just as we were leaving for the airport. Now moments before the national press conference, I was slipping into the blazer for the first time.

Imagine the horror when I pulled my arms through and instantly realized it was a size too small. I could get into it, but it was tight under the armpits and would not button without squeezing me tightly.

I was also out of time. I would have to go to the press conference in what felt like a good-looking straightjacket.

The media, dignitaries, and some members of our team gathered in the ballroom of the hotel on Monday morning. Seated behind the rectangular tables were leaders of two denominations, president of the National Evangelical Association, Pastor Marenco, Pastor Omar

Duarte, Dennis, and me. It was a picture of unity and excitement, with secular and government TV channels 2, 4, 6, 8, and 12 there to record it.

The press conference didn't take long. I made a short statement about *Nicaragua Prays*, and each of the pastors added their comments. But as soon as it was over and Dennis and I stepped around the tables, we were cornered by microphones, recorders, cameras, and bright lights.

It took about fifteen minutes to answer questions and a few more to shake hands with everyone. But once the room cleared, it took less than five seconds for me to take off the blazer. I was drenched in sweat but happy to have seen the word go forth regarding unity and prayer, evangelism and compassion, and transformation and destiny. It was a good start to the week.

CONTAGIOUS ICE CREAMS

As ninety-one short-term missionaries from the United States and Canada poured into the large meeting hall for devotions, the energy and excitement gave it the feel of something like a family reunion. People were busy reconnecting from previous trips and making new friends. (This is part of the blessing of coming on these trips!)

Our distribution had a surprise. Once again we were going to give out ice cream. But this year the biggest ice cream company with the best treats was doing something we had never seen before. More than provide treats, they were sending trucks and staff to make sure it was the best ice cream experience ever!

The Lord had given us favor with them from the beginning. It was assumed that we would buy their cheapest ice cream. But Bruce, who was leading our distribution efforts for the *Nicaragua Prays* week, would not accept the deal, insisting LOLI wanted to put their best and most popular ice cream in the hands of the Nicaragua children.

The decision made an impression on the government official who had set up the meeting. It also excited me about the possibility of offering children who had never had ice cream on a stick before the very best taste in town.

Seeing a company get on board with the daily distribution to pass out thousands of their most popular ice creams only widened the smiles of the team. Their excitement must have been contagious, because by the end of the second day, managers from our hotel had taken a day off to join the effort! Not only had the compassion work touched the kids in some of the most impoverished neighborhoods, it now impacted the lives of people working at the hotel.

GOVERNMENT RADIO PRAYERS

The day after the press conference, Dennis and I found ourselves sitting behind another set of microphones. We had received a surprise invitation for an interview on government radio, and we jumped at the opportunity.

Everything about the interview seemed normal. Questions and dialogue flowed naturally. But halfway through the program, we suddenly went to break.

I had no idea what happened. Had we said something wrong? The answer was not what I expected.

The interview had been interrupted by a call from the house of the president. That call had brought with it a specific request. The man asking questions now nodded his head as if he was verifying an order relayed into his earpiece. He then turned and looked at Dennis and me.

He asked, "Would you pray for the president? Would you pray for the people of Nicaragua listening in on government radio right now?"

I have no idea who was on the other end of the call coming out of the house of the president or who suddenly authorized us to pray on government radio, but what an opportunity! In that radio station, it was my honor to lift before King Jesus the leader of the country and the beautiful people of Nicaragua.

Several hours later, a similar scenario would again present itself. The Lord was orchestrating the final touches for *Nicaragua Prays* and beyond!

SECULAR TELEVISION PRAYERS

The invitation that night was to appear on the Managua evening news. Four of us sat down behind the large desk. The news anchor said the interview would span fifteen minutes—much longer than I had expected.

After footage from *Honduras Prays* and brief comments from the panel, our TV segment was over. All that remained was for the anchor to sign off—or so I thought! With cameras zooming in for a closeup, he turned to me and asked, "Would you mind praying for the viewers?"

This request caught me completely off guard. Here in the capital city of Managua on the nightly news I had just been asked to pray for the viewers! Can you imagine the news in the United States making this type of request?

For a moment, my pulse quickened and I got nervous. But this was another amazing opportunity. I closed my eyes and in the name of Jesus asked God's blessing to rest on this nation and those watching on television.

MIRACLE OF MANAGUA

It had been a special week—open doors in the media, hotel managers joining the team on distribution, political guests dropping by to welcome the team during devotions, and lots of excitement among the pastors. So much had already happened, but now it was time to gather ourselves before the feet of Jesus.

As I was getting ready in our hotel room, I glanced out the window.

What I saw brought joy to my heart. Bus after bus after bus passed by below, all headed toward the plaza. Many of them were decorated with streamers or posters, all of them jammed with people. Even a few floors above the street, I could hear some of the music coming out of the buses, and their excitement only added to my own.

The Plaza of the Bible was packed. Churches, denominations, and people from all types of backgrounds covered the grounds.

As I looked out on the Plaza, people were waving flags, young men at the back had climbed trees to see, and Enlace Nicaragua and Maranatha had set up to capture all of it live on TV and radio for the rest of the country. There was a massive screen at the back of the platform. Bright lights, big sound, huge crowd—the place was electric!

One of the executives of the National Evangelical Association walked over and declared, "This is the Miracle of Managua!" He said that not because of the response of the numbers of people—surely there had been larger meetings—but because of the unity and cooperation of so many prominent leaders, churches, and organizations.

All of it made a beautiful statement: Something was stirring inside the hearts of people. Now was the time to unite, to humble ourselves, and to call on the Lord Jesus on behalf of Nicaragua.

POWER IN THE NAME OF JESUS!

The word burning in my heart Friday night dealt with power—His power! There is power in the name of Jesus, there is power in the blood of Jesus, and there is power in the united body of Jesus.

That night, under the biblical banners such as 2 Chronicles 7:14 and Psalm 133, the multitude and pastors gathered to pray. With Alisa kneeling beside me on the platform, we humbled ourselves before the people and cried out for His kingdom to come and His will to be done in Nicaragua even as it is in heaven.

When I stood up, it was time to deliver a message for the lost and hurting, those bound and blinded by demonic and wicked forces. It was a message burning in my heart—one resonating that there is great power in the name of Jesus the Christ!

The Resurrected and Glorified Jesus

There is an awesome picture of Jesus in Revelation 1. John, arguably the best friend of Jesus during His earthly life and ministry, was on the island of Patmos. While praying in the Spirit, he heard a loud voice, like a trumpet. He turned around and saw Jesus.

Who John sees is nothing like to the One he knew on earth. Jesus is now clothed in glory and splendor. When John sees Him, he falls as a dead man at His feet. The one who knew him best on earth is totally overwhelmed by His majesty and power.

This resurrected and glorified Jesus is the same One we serve today! There is unfathomable strength and authority in His name. In boldness and confidence we can declare right now: There is power in the name of Jesus!

The Power of the Name of Jesus

The resurrection power attached to the name of Jesus is documented in Acts 3–4. Peter and John are walking to the Temple, when they encounter a lame man. The man begs for alms, but Peter looks at him and commands, "In the name of Jesus Christ of Nazareth, rise up and walk." The man is healed instantly.

The crowd quickly began to gather to see what happened. How could this be? Peter speaks again—not to the man healed but to the crowd. He challenges them with the death and resurrection of Jesus, then answers their question: "His name, through faith in His name, has made this man strong" (v. 16).

Word of this dramatic miracle spreads like wildfire. It quickly reaches the ears of the Jewish leaders and they arrest Peter and John.

The next morning the disciples are brought before the Sanhedrin. They have one question they need answering: "By what power or by what name have you done this?" (Acts 4:7).

Peter, full of boldness and Holy Spirit fire, responds: "Let it be known to you all, and to all the people of Israel, that by the name of Jesus Christ of Nazareth . . . this man stands here before you whole" (v. 10).

Over and over again, Peter and John sound forth this message: There is power in the name of JESUS! This is an eternal reality; it has not changed. There is still power in the name of Jesus for salvation, for healing, for deliverance, for transformation!

The Bible says: "God also has highly exalted Him and given Him the name which is above every name, that at the name of Jesus every knee should bow, of those in heaven, and of those on earth, and of those under the earth, and that every tongue should confess that Jesus Christ is Lord" (Philippians 2:9–11).

The Bible also says: "Nor is there salvation in any other, for there is no other name under heaven given among men by which we must be saved" (Acts 4:12).

We have this promise in the resurrected and glorified person of Jesus Christ: There is power in the name of Jesus!

NEW GUINEA WITCH DOCTOR

One of the most vivid demonstrations of this power comes from a testimony out of the jungles of New Guinea. With my dad in attendance on Friday night, I shared one of his stories at *Nicaragua Prays*.

The missionaries had received a challenge. Their presence in the village and the stories about Jesus did not sit well with everyone in the tribe. It had especially angered the local witch doctor. He had issued a warning.

That night Dad shared the Gospel. In the middle of his message the witch doctor arrived and positioned himself directly in front of Dad and his translator. Then the witch doctor started to levitate.

It was clear what was going on. This demonic agent had come to stir fear in the hearts of the people and distract them from the Gospel. His actions instantly terrified the translator and threatened to shut down the meeting. But there was something even more radical coming: a Holy Spirit counterattack.

Dad said to his translator, "Say the name!" The man must not have heard him, as he did not reply at first. Dad said again, "Say the name!" The translator looked at him, and this time Dad commanded, "Say His Name!"

The translator opened his mouth and cried out, "JESUS!" And the instant the name of Jesus came forth, the demonic power was broken, and the witch doctor crashed to the ground.

Reinhard Bonnke often used this analogy of the devil as a lion. Today, if you are in the mouth of the lion and only have one hand to raise, raise it to Jesus. If you are in the mouth of the lion and only have one knee to bow, bow it before King Jesus. If you are in the mouth of the lion and only have one breath to breathe, breathe out the name of Jesus.

There is a name greater than all black magic and demonic power combined. It is the name of Jesus. If you are in bondage, in darkness, without hope and dying today, call on the name of Jesus. He will save you! There is power in the name of JESUS!

MINISTER OF GOVERNMENT ARRIVAL

The vehicle came with an armed escort. Moving slowly down the closed-off road behind the stage, it was unmistakable. The minister of government had arrived for the Friday service. But something was wrong.

Though the SUV had come to a stop, she remained inside the vehicle. It seemed like it would only be a matter of time before she would step out and make her way to the platform. It never happened.

Just as smoothly as it arrived, the vehicle now moved off with its escort. She was gone. The reason came later: security. There were too many people.

The next morning the military turned up at the Plaza. From one side to the other they swept the field, roads, and platform for explosives or anything suspicious. They stationed nearly one hundred police officers on and around the Plaza to secure the venue.

I appreciated them searching and securing the premises, because it meant she would be there Saturday night. I also realized there might not be a more secure place in Latin America to preach the Gospel. And that was exactly what I intended to do.

SATURDAY NIGHT DECLARATIONS

Saturday night was even more lively, if that was possible. As Dennis and I went toward the platform, a television reporter stepped in front of us with a microphone and the camera rolling. We answered a couple questions then moved up the steps.

The minister of government greeted us warmly. I was happy to see her, along with many other pastors and dignitaries. I sat down briefly and readied myself to preach before calling for the fire of the Holy Spirit to fall.

The Scripture burning inside my heart for months as we moved around Managua ministering in the churches was 1 Thessalonians 1:5. "Our gospel did not come to you in word only, but also in power, and in the Holy Spirit and in much assurance, as you know what kind of men we were among you for your sake."

We had seen so many people saved and healed during the services as the Lord responded to the hunger of the people. Tonight I would make three declarations over the beautiful people of Nicaragua: "The Gospel is powerful, Jesus loves you, and the best days of your life are not behind you, but in Jesus' name they are in front of you!"

These three declarations would lead to a call for people to respond to a love that demonstrated itself vividly through the death and resurrection of Jesus Christ. Then the fire of the Holy Spirit would fall on the crowd.

Indeed there is power in the mighty name of Jesus. The best days of our lives, our families, our churches, even the nation lie in front of those who put their total trust in Him. This promise is true not just for today but also for eternity! You have a glorious future in Jesus.

A SUICIDE NOTE

In the middle of the message, I shared something that had taken place a couple days earlier. This is what happened.

No one knew the lady when she walked into the church service on Thursday night. Nor did anyone know the dark secret she carried.

Only one hour earlier she had written a note to her family. It was not a birthday card or get-well-soon note. This one was left on the table for someone to find later.

She walked out of the house with no intention of ever seeing it again. By the time someone found the suicide note, it would be too late.

Tragedy was looming when she saw the church. Most churches in Nicaragua are not big air-conditioned complexes but small neighborly spaces. Here fans are attached to the walls to spread the breeze filtering through open windows and doors. She did not intend to visit a service that night, but something drew her.

One of the LOLI teams presented the Gospel that night. The message: There is nothing like life with Jesus. It is one of hope, power, and eternal life.

The lady was listening. In fact, the more she heard about the Gospel and Jesus, the more her outlook began to change. The shadow of death was retreating as the Light of heaven began to fill her heart. She found the pastor, told him everything, and gave her heart to Jesus!

This is the power of the Gospel and the amazing love of Jesus. But what I did not know as I was sharing this testimony of redemption on Saturday night was that in the crowd another lady stood listening intently. She, too, was carrying a dark secret—a plan that would not end one life but three.

As people came forward to testify Saturday night, many were stories of salvation and healing. But something was also happening in the heart of this woman.

The story of the suicide note had resonated with her. She had resolved to kill her two sisters then take her own life. But the grace of God that reached the lady with the suicide note on Thursday now penetrated the darkness of this girl standing in the crowd two nights later. In such a short period of time the Holy Spirit had rescued four lives and countless heartbreaks among family and friends.

Jesus says in John 10:10, "The thief does not come except to steal, and to kill, and to destroy. I have come that they may have life, and that they may have it more abundantly." Suicide is a demonic lie. It is a permanent solution to a temporary situation. Our lives have value, purpose, and power in Jesus. The Enemy of our soul knows this and craves any opportunity to crush it.

This is why we preach: because the Gospel is powerful, Jesus loves you, and in Him the best days of your life are not behind you; they are in front of you!

MIRACLE MANIFESTATIONS

The fire of God fell Saturday night with tremendous power. It was like a heavenly explosion hit the crusade grounds as people lifted their hands and cried out to the Lord.

I handed the microphone to Pastor Danillo. As our teams made their way into the crowd to pray, he passionately took up the cry for fire, miracles, and revival.

I heard the Holy Spirit speak to my heart: *Sit down and pray!* My part was done. I found a seat on the second row, left the service in the hands of Dennis and the pastors, and started praying for Nicaragua.

Meanwhile people started streaming to the platform. Jesus had done so many wonderful things! A lady who had remained on her bus for the duration of the service because of the extreme pain in her back testified to the healing grace of God. Previously she had trouble standing up, which is why she never left her seat, even after everyone exited the bus. But with the cry for fire, she felt power rush through her body. She stood up pain free. A lady who had earlier refused to exit the bus because of back pain not only got up and exited, she made her way through a multitude of people and climbed up the platform stairs!

Before we left the Plaza, a key pastor who had become dear to us came over. He had a small problem. He did not teach on miracles in his church or believe in the supernatural. But that night four members of his congregation had testified to healing! By the broad smile on his face, it was obviously not a real problem, just pure joy and gratitude for what the Lord had done.

TIRED ON THE OUTSIDE, ON FIRE ON THE INSIDE

As in Honduras, the Lord had opened the doors in Nicaragua to meet with local and national leaders in government and evangelical circles. This invisible hand of God had stirred hearts and brought the people together to pray for their nation, their leaders, and their future.

In both cases, Christian and non-Christian media received us warmly and readily gave us local and national exposure. It was more than we could have ever hoped for or imagined. Thinking back to the beginning of the journey and the number of blunders we made along the way, it was overwhelming to see where the Lord Jesus had brought us and what He had commissioned us to do.

I knew there were more mountains ahead to climb, but Honduras and Nicaragua had stolen our hearts. Both had pushed our faith and abilities to the limit, but the Lord had seen us through to the end. Yes, we were tired on the outside, but on the inside we were absolutely on fire!

CHAPTER 21

You Are an Overcomer

THE ROAD FROM NICARAGUA would only continue to climb. In Panama City, I found myself standing on the shoulders of my dad, who had ministered powerfully there twenty years ago. In Panama, the door would open to Mexico City, one of the largest cities in the world.

The Holy Spirit continued to forge our character and stretch our faith. It seemed like the higher we climbed the more impossible the assignment. We could never have imagined or even chosen this path, but one thing He was teaching us: With the Lord, nothing is impossible. You are an overcomer in Christ Jesus!

THE VOICE OF TRUTH

That first trip to Panama challenged me. We had seen God do amazing things in Honduras and now in Nicaragua, but we were still adapting to doing more prominent and national venues. In so many ways it still seemed like a beautiful dream.

Looking out the window of the aircraft as we crossed from the Atlantic to the Pacific side, I was in for a shock. The plane banked one last time to line up its run parallel to the coastline and into the airport. Dozens of tankers and merchant vessels were parked below at sea, waiting for their turn to pass through the Panama Canal. I had expected to see that.

What I had not anticipated was the towering skyline along the coast. Skyscrapers reached for the sky filled by banks, luxury apartments, and multinational corporations. It painted a dramatic picture. Panama City was unlike any place in Central America I had ever seen. It more resembled the coastline of Miami or one of the big cities in Asia!

My heart jumped in my throat. *What are we doing flying in here?* said my brain in bold capital letters. The more I stared at the skyline, the more I felt we might as well get on the next plane and go home. This was way too big and expensive for us.

It was one thing to spend several years in Honduras and then Nicaragua and see the Lord promote us onto a national stage. We had expended everything we had to be faithful stewards—our time, our hearts, our finances.

This was an entirely new level. To think we were ready to make a quantum leap into a place of such wealth and development overwhelmed me. It was an impression I had not anticipated or readied myself for. I was already defeated.

We touched down a few minutes later and pulled up to the gate. While we waited for the doors to open and passengers to file out, the plane filled with quiet music. I was still staring out my window when something unusual happened.

The Asain-type music suddenly resembled a Casting Crowns song. Stranger still, the same verse kept pulsating through the speakers over and over, as if it was somehow stuck on repeat. I suddenly recognized the lyric coming at me in waves. I was hearing: *"The voice of truth says, 'Do not be afraid!' . . . The voice of truth says, 'Do not be afraid!' . . . The voice of truth says, 'Do not be afraid!'"*

In a matter of ten minutes I had gone from disqualifying us from doing anything in Panama City because of the overpowering first impression, to hearing this lyric over and over again on the airplane! I received it as divine encouragement. I asked the Lord for a favor as we disembarked: Give me eyes to see what He sees, ears to hear what He hears, and a willingness to do what He wants done.

We were not fifteen minutes away from the airport when confirmation arrived in a most unexpected manner. Riding in the back of an SUV on the way to the hotel, I sat next to the young man traveling with me from the United States. I told him my initial impressions of Panama City and asked if he noticed anything different about the music on the plane.

He barely noticed the music. So I shared my experience—how it seemed like the music had morphed into one line from a Casting Crowns song. This caught his attention and he asked, "Which song?" I told him all I heard was this phrase repeatedly: *"The voice of truth says do not be afraid."* He was stunned.

Something was going on. He finally explained a few days ago that he had attended a weekend conference. On the last day he was asked to sing a song as a testimony of what the Lord had done. The song he chose was "The Voice of Truth."

What were the chances that within a few days of each other, I would hear a song on the overhead speakers that matched exactly what my friend had sang at a weekend conference? I was still trying to process the possibilities when he asked, "Do you know the next line in the chorus?"

The answer was no. My brain was still stuck on not being afraid of skyscrapers! He smiled and said, *"The voice of truth says, 'Do not be* afraid!' AND the voice of truth says, 'This is for My glory!'"

I had been on the ground in Panama for one hour, and the Lord had given me two affirmations: *Stephen, do not be afraid, and this is for my glory!* More than confirmation, it was another indicator we were being led by the invisible hand of God.

PANAMA PRAYS

There is a lot that could be written about *Panama Prays*. It was another leap of faith to believe for a crusade in Panama City. But the assignment was much larger than that.

The Holy Spirit had brought us here to believe for something beyond anything we had seen in nine years of crusade ministry. He was not calling for one crusade, but two!

Instead of focusing solely on the capital, the dream growing in our hearts was to plant our feet on both sides of the Panama Canal. It meant working the two main cities (Panama City on the Pacific and Colon on the Atlantic) at the same time.

Both Panama City and Colon served as the gateways for the Panama Canal. By working both coasts and cities, *Panama Prays* would ultimately culminate in a crusade in Colon on Friday night, then Panama City on the Saturday night.

I loved the idea. But working two cities *at the same time* to do two crusades filled my stomach with the same butterflies I felt flying in. If it was scary to dream about doing something in such an expensive capital, then how outrageous was the thought of adding Colon to the mix? It was impossible in the natural to consider such an undertaking, but inside my heart it was burning like wildfire.

So to make sure *Panama Prays* was definitely His doing, the dates were not set for the summer of 2014, which would have been our preference. Instead, it was pushed forward several months into the spring to prayerfully target the national elections in May!

The timing turned out to be perfect, not only because of what would take place in Panama, but ultimately it would unlock the door to preach the Gospel in Mexico City in November and launch a new vision to build an army of one million Latin intercessors.

MEETING ALBERTO MOTESSI

Supernatural doors continued to open at home too. During the preparation for *Panama Prays*, my phone rang. The head of our intercessors network, Alvaro had received an invitation for the two of us to attend a local Hispanic service.

It was no ordinary service. Evangelist Alberto Motessi, one of the revivalists out of Argentina, was the weekend speaker. His mark across Latin America and around the world was sizable, and I jumped at the opportunity.

The news only got better. Alvaro knew the senior pastor, who also had followed our progress in Honduras and Nicaragua. He asked if Alvaro and I would be available to join him and Evangelist Motessi for lunch on Sunday.

Sitting at the table with one of God's generals was remarkable. His passion for souls and revival, the testimonies from his encounters with national heads of state, and the breakthroughs in the mass crusades all stirred up fire in my soul!

I shared the vision in my heart for Central America and talked about the work we were involved with in Panama. I asked him to pray for me and Light of Life International. I laid my hands on the table in front of him, and he covered them with his. In the middle of his prayer, he declared a word over my life and the ministry.

He said, "The Lord is going to give you a heart to understand the Latin people—to have the same feelings they have. It will not be the same way as Reinhard, but I will show you what to do." It was a validation of the first ten years of ministry and a real sense that we still had more to do for the kingdom.

WHAT IS THE VALUE OF A SOUL?

You could not spend a few minutes around someone like Evangelist Motessi and not feel his passion for Jesus and for lost souls. And it begs the question: What is the value of one soul?

It was a question the Lord put to me in Tela, our first crusade, to search my heart and to learn more about His. The Bible points out: "God . . . desires all men to be saved and to come to the knowledge of the truth. . . . Jesus . . . gave Himself [as] a ransom for all" (1 Timothy 2:4, 6).

The Gospel message applies to everyone, because each person is precious and deeply loved by King Jesus. A soul is much more costly than rubies or anything else in this world. There is nothing more valuable than a soul!

What Is the Value of a Soul to God?

The Bible says: "For God so loved the world that He gave His only begotten Son, that whoever believes in Him should not perish but have everlasting life" (John 3:16).

The Bible further says: "For God did not send His Son into the world to condemn the world, but that the world through Him might be saved" (John 3:17).

What is the value of a soul to God? God so loved US that He GAVE!

The question that must be addressed is, what is the rationale for such a gift? The answer is found in His nature and disposition. Ephesians 2 tells us that God is rich in mercy and grace.

Mercy simply indicates we do not receive what we deserve: punishment for sin and rejection by God.

Grace, on the other hand, indicates we receive what we do not deserve: pardon for sin and a new relationship with God.

This is the value of a soul to God. He gave because of His extravagant love for you and me.

What Is the Value of a Soul to Jesus?

Jesus had many things to say about souls: "I have come to seek and to save the lost. . . . I have come that they might have life, and that they may have it more abundantly. . . . What would it profit a man if he gained the whole world but lost his soul?"

Nothing in this world compares to the value of one's soul. The value is set by the purchasing price. You cannot buy redemption with silver or gold. You cannot buy it with good works or merit. Even nobility or status by birth lacks the value to redeem a single soul.

The price for a soul was too high for any of us! But the Bible reveals: "You were not redeemed with . . . silver or gold . . . but with the precious blood of Christ" (1 Peter 1:18–19).

The blood of Jesus alone has the power to redeem someone. There is power in the blood of Jesus to save. There is power to heal. There is power to transform your life! It is the shed blood of King Jesus that makes you more valuable than anything else.

This is the value of a soul to Jesus. He loved us so much, He laid down His life to pay the full price for our redemption!

What Is the Value of a Soul to the Holy Spirit?

Jesus said to His followers: "It is to your advantage that I go away; [so that you might receive the Holy Spirit.] And when He has come, He will convict the world of sin, and of righteousness, and of judgment" (John 16:7–8).

Note the Holy Spirit came to convict, not to condemn. Condemnation pushes us further away from God. Conviction draws us closer to God.

The Holy Spirit has come to expressly draw all eyes and hearts toward Jesus!

The Holy Spirit also begins the process of revolution and transformation. Jesus said: "You shall receive power when the Holy Spirit has come upon you; and you shall be witnesses to Me" (Acts 1:8).

This is where value comes in. When the Holy Spirit and fire settles on you, it will remain there forever to transform your life and ministry. The Bible says in 1 John 2 that we have an anointing that abides!

We see this with Moses. When he encountered the burning bush, his entire life changed. The point of the meeting was for the fire in the bush to become the fire in his heart. The fire of God empowered Moses to not only confront Pharaoh but to lead a nation out of bondage.

You are valuable to the Holy Spirit! When you encounter His fire, it will ignite you to a supernatural destiny for the glory of God.

What Is the Value of a Soul to You?

Father God loves you. Jesus came and died for you. The Holy Spirit is calling you. Hear that again: The Father sent, Jesus came, and the Holy Spirit invites you to be transformed and entrusted with the power of the Gospel.

The Bible says: "As many as received Him, to them He gave the right to become children of God, to those who believe in His name" (John 1:12).

You are valuable! In Christ Jesus, you are a child of God. You have been bought with an enormous price and you are deeply loved.

Each and every person is precious to God. Proverbs 11:30 says, "He who wins souls is wise." And James 5:20 says, "Let him know that he who turns a sinner from the error of his way will save a soul from death and cover a multitude of sins." In a world that places so much value on beautiful things like diamonds, the highest value is a soul.

TAKING IT TO THE STREETS

The Friday night crusade in Colon was amazing! Leading up to it we planned on using the baseball stadium, until the local team surged toward the playoffs. It resulted in a switch that was better suited to reach souls. When the governor and congressman signed off to shut down the main boulevard that weekend, it was as if the invisible hand of God had dropped us right into the central gathering point of the city!

We had never had anyone shut down the main boulevard for us to preach Jesus in the heart of a city before . . . until Colon, Panama. Thousands of people packed the two sidewalks, the dual-lane highways, and the park in between. People were everywhere, including the balconies of the apartment buildings. With these buildings, McDonald's, and grocery stores all framing the main boulevard, there was nowhere for the sound to escape. So it carried the Gospel even blocks beyond the lights and festive crowd!

We came to build an altar in Colon, a place where Jesus would be celebrated as Lord of the city. We were not there to celebrate a canal waterway; we had come to rejoice over the highway that ran from the throne of God to this city! Even as we were calling the country to pray, we were asking the Lord Jesus to make Colon a citadel of His presence.

There on 8th Street, in the heart of Colon, I spoke on the divine instructions for transformation out of 2 Chronicles 7—from darkness to light, from bondage to freedom, and from defeat to success. The solution found in verse 14 was not Solomon's idea. It was not man's idea. It was the direct words spoken by the Lord to Israel.

The same solution can be applied today in cities and nations as Father God is inviting the Church to humble itself in prayer and seek His favor in order to receive His blessing.

The most exciting part came when the fire call went forth and one of the teenagers on our team cried out, "Did you see the blind man get unblinded?" But seeing so many pastors in tears over their city and nation, people responding for salvation, the mighty manifestations of God's power, and all of it happening in the downtown streets of Colon made it a night that will stand out for a long time.

YOU ARE AN OVERCOMER!

There were more than a few times I was overwhelmed by the task assigned us in Panama. As I was reading Revelation chapters 2–3, the Lord dropped a significant word into my heart. It was a word to encourage all who believe and desire to press forward to do something significant for God. The word is this: *You are an Overcomer!*

I've read through these two chapters many times before, and I know they contain sober warnings to the seven churches. But that night as I read through them in my Panama hotel room, something happened to me.

The Lord gave me a new focus. My heart was encouraged, and the more I read the concluding verses of each section about the churches, the more the Holy Spirit emphasized to me the words *overcomer, overcomer, overcomer*!

Here is a sampling of some of those of verses:

> Revelation 3:21 says, "To him who overcomes, I will grant to sit with Me on My throne as I also overcame and sat down with My Father on His throne."

> Revelation 2:26 says, "He who overcomes, and keeps My works until the end, to him I will give power over the nations."

> Revelation 3:5 says, "He who overcomes shall be clothed

in white garments, and I will not blot out his name from the Book of Life; but I will confess his name before My Father and before His angels."

Revelation 3:12 says: "He who overcomes, I will make him a pillar in the temple of My God, and he shall go out no more. I will write on him the name of My God and the name of the city of My God, the New Jerusalem, which comes down out of heaven from My God. And I will write on him My new name."

Wow, by the time I had finished reading, I was on fire! It was time to shake off discouragement, rise, and move forward.

This is likely what John was going through. Banished to the island of Patmos for his testimony, he was isolated and alone. Moreover, John would have been carrying the burden for these seven churches—many of whom were struggling.

But Jesus comes to John and changes everything. It is as though Jesus says to John: "I know who you are, I know where you are, and I know what you are facing. I also know the condition of the churches. And despite their present predicaments, I have a plan and purpose for them."

The same is true with us. Jesus knows who we are and where we are. If you are in a place of discouragement, weighed down by the burdens of ministry, struggling in the assignment entrusted to you, I have good news!

The good news is found in the word *overcomer*. What Jesus says about those who overcome in the midst of some of the most difficult situations is astonishing. It is a powerful reminder and tremendous motivator. You have been created in Him to be an overcomer!

We Overcome Because of Jesus!

Overcoming is not the result of self-effort, human ability, or achievement; rather, it is the outworking of the life and ministry of the Lord Jesus Christ.

The Bible does not say you would never have troubles or challenges. But Jesus did say: "In the world you will have tribulation; but be of good cheer, I have overcome the world" (John 16:33).

The Bible doesn't say there would never be demonic assaults or spiritual battles. But it does say "they overcame him by the blood of the Lamb and by the word of their testimony" (Revelation 12:11).

In other words, we overcome because the God of the Bible is awesome! Jesus is our Lord and King and the ultimate answer to all of our challenges!

You can overcome the temptation of letting your fire diminish and your love grow cold. You can overcome the intimidation and pressures of the world. You can overcome sexual temptation and all forms of perversion. And you can overcome the tendencies to waver in your faith and compromise your values. You can overcome all of this because of the power of Jesus!

This is the encouraging word from Revelation 2–3. You are an overcomer! The Bible also says that greater is He that is in you than he who is in the world . . . that you will overcome him by the blood of the Lamb and the word of your testimony . . . that if God is for you who can be against you? You are ordained to be an overcomer!

If you are tempted by wickedness, pressured by stress, or challenged to adopt a form of godliness that denies the manifestation of His power, please remember Jesus provides an alternative. In Jesus, you can conquer. You can overcome.

We Overcome Because of the Power of the Holy Spirit

The life of Jesus is not just a philosophy—something you think about or discuss. The life of Jesus is a reality—something you live! This is why Jesus says in Revelation 2-3 over and over again: It is critical to have *ears to hear what the Holy Spirit is saying.*

Jesus told the disciples it was for their benefit for Him to go away. The Helper would come and teach them all things. He did not just come to enlighten them with truth; He also came to embolden them with power.

Jesus said we will receive power when the Holy Spirit comes upon us, that we might be His witnesses. A witness is an overcomer!

Tremendous Blessings for the Overcomer

The privileges afforded and blessings provided to an overcomer are astonishing. Note some of the things documented by the Lord Jesus in this book.

As an overcomer, you receive eternal life. Your name is written in the Book of Life! You are also given a redeemed name. Your old reputation has been cancelled.

As an overcomer, you are given the authority to influence nations. This is what the Great Commission is all about!

As an overcomer, you are deemed worthy to walk with Jesus in glory. You will be clothed in white robes of righteousness.

As an overcomer, your name will be declared before Father God and the angels. The name that is heralded throughout eternity in heaven is the name of Jesus. But He will take a moment to call your name out! This is beyond comprehension!

Consider the paradox: In Isaiah 6 the prophet hears the voice of the Lord cry out: "Whom shall I send, and who will go for Us?" But in Revelation 3:5 Jesus says He will declare your name to the Father!

Jesus has also promised: Overcomers will be given the privilege and right to sit with Him on His throne (Revelation 3:21). The magnitude of these blessings is far too glorious to fully grasp. Yet they are given to those who overcome!

Seven times Jesus challenges His people to overcome. Each time it is attached to the prophetic admonition: "He who has ears to hear, let him hear [what the Spirit is saying to the churches.]"

To you overcomer, it is time to do something significant for God. You can rise above your fears and your failings; you can go from success to significance. This is your calling; this is your destiny; this is the blessing: You are an Overcomer!

THE INVISIBLE HAND OF GOD

The anthropomorphic term "the hand of God" while invisible is nevertheless discernible. His seal and signature is seen in creation, it is seen in the Church, and it has been evidenced in our lives.

There really is nothing like life with Jesus. The Bible says: "Taste and see that the Lord is good." And He is very good, especially to those who love Him and walk in His ways.

We did not choose this path. It chose us. What started with a heartfelt desire to make a difference (for our lives to count for Him!) has transformed into something beyond what we could ever have orchestrated or imagined.

If you are dreaming and believing about doing something significant for God with your life, wonderful! There is no greater purpose in this life than to serve King Jesus in His kingdom work. Ask Him to expand your dreams, your purpose, and your calling beyond the natural—beyond anything you could ever do on your own. Invite the Holy Spirit to lead you, empower you, and reveal through you His glory and presence.

Dream big dreams and cast huge vision, but ask the Lord to forge character into the DNA of your life and calling. It is not enough just to reach your goals. It is crucial to arrive with the character and nature of God entrenched within you, so you not only get there but you thrive!

Jesus is the prize. You will have times of discouragement, even failure. But He has created you to be an overcomer, a witness to His faithfulness and power, and in the end a shining example of someone who walks with God through the impossible.

Walking with your hand placed squarely in the invisible hand of God leads down a path beyond what you can see or do. It requires His strength, His favor, His guidance, and His power. It is a road full of challenges—many impossible. But remember nothing is too difficult for God! This is the life and destiny you dream about: one of faith, one of wonder, one of character, one of challenges, and one of breakthrough and triumph!

You can be the next game changer, nation shaker, and history maker. It is not about who you know, what you have, or how qualified you are. It is a simple passion for Jesus and an unquenchable fire for your life to count. Hear again the words of Jesus: "You shall receive power when the Holy Spirit has come upon you; and you shall be witnesses to Me."

You have a story to write and a life to live. There is a giant to slay, a mountain to climb, a Pharaoh to confront, and a world that desperately needs Jesus. The invisible hand of God is reaching out to you right now. Take it and never look back.

EVANGELIST STEPHEN EVANS is the founder and president of Light of Life International, an international evangelistic ministry. For over ten years, he and his LOLI team have conducted Gospel campaigns throughout Latin America and the Caribbean. Thousands of people have poured into soccer stadiums, city boulevards, and castle grounds to hear the good news that Jesus saves souls and transforms cities/nations.

Stephen has addressed audiences all over the world—most notably President Porfirio Lobo Sosa of Honduras. His support and participation culminated in the 2012 *Honduras Prays*—LOLI's first national call to prayer and evangelistic crusade in San Pedro Sula, Honduras.

Stepping into the next ten years, LOLI is casting the net for 40 million souls in Central and South America. As he learned firsthand from serving Evangelist Reinhard Bonnke in Africa in 2004, today Stephen and his LOLI team are believing: *Latin America shall be saved!*

Stephen Evans is available to speak or for interview. He and his wife, Alisa, live in Fort Worth with their two children. **Contact: info@loli.org.**